I nodded at the RTO and had begun calling basecamp when the first rounds banged into the longhouse.

We rolled over on our bellies and watched the river. Captain Y Lull and his alpine troops literally flew down the bamboo ladder and joined us. But before they could get comfortable, five or six more rounds sought out our small group.

For the moment, the Rhade captain was frozen. "Open the net, dumbass!" I shouted at his RTO. "Get your head off the ground, Doctor. Try and see where those rounds are coming from!"

I changed tactics and spoke kindly to Captain Y Lull. "Order that roving squad that's across the river to get those bastards, sir."

Also by William T. Craig
Published by Ivy Books:

SCARE TIME

LIFER!

From Infantry to Special Forces

William T. Craig

IVY BOOKS • NEW YORK

Ivy Books
Published by Ballantine Books
Copyright © 1994 by William T. Craig

Library of Congress Catalog Card Number: 94-94042

ISBN 0-8041-0688-6

Manufactured in the United States of America

First Edition: July 1994

10 9 8 7 6 5 4 3 2 1

This book is humbly dedicated to:

My wife, Hatsuko, for staying with me and making me a better person.

My children, Kathy and Jim, who taught me more than I taught them.

My parents, brothers, and sisters.

All the officers and enlisted personnel who paid the ultimate price in the wars that have preserved our entity and self-respect. Especially the following, mentioned in this text, who paid that ultimate price for you and me.

Biber, Gerald M.	Laos
Bischoff, SFC	Laos
Card, Willie	Thailand
Gabriel, James Jr.	Vietnam
Luttrell, Bruce I.	Vietnam
Marchand, Wayne	Vietnam
Moon, Walter H.	Laos
Patience, Bill	Vietnam
Payne, Eldon	Vietnam
Stark, Willie E.	Vietnam (MIA)
Wofford, Craig	Vietnam

PREFACE

      BETWEEN US, my father and I served over fifty-two years in the United States Army—five decades that covered World War I, World War II, Korea, and Vietnam—the entire time served in the enlisted ranks.

The following narrative was gleaned from many sources besides my own observations: letters my mother preserved, many of which came from distant places; interviews of my family and friends; our U.S. Army discharges and service records.

The book is as accurate as I could make it, but allowance should be made for the passage of time and the fading memories of those interviewed. The dialogue is, therefore, not accurate word for word.

The book is not intended to be a putdown of the officer corps. Certainly this segment of the armed forces has its problems, but I will leave it to its members to relate their side.

It is not my character or intention to gloss over the problems that my family and I encountered during this long period of enlisted service—if mistakes are not revealed, solutions will not be forthcoming. Besides, many of the institutional injustices noted in Chapter 1 of *Snake Eaters!* have been corrected by the armed forces, which only serves to prove my point.

Finally, I have added and subtracted the debt this country owes me and it comes to $0.00—zilch. I was paid, as was my father, for every day served. And besides, I had a ball.

CHINA

Yalu River

Ch'onglin

NORTH KOREA

Antung

Hamhung

Hungnam

East Korean Bay

West Korean Bay

P'YONGYANG

Namp'o

Wonsan

Imjin River

P'Yonggang

DMZ

Haeju

Kaesong

Chorwon

Yangyang

38th Parallel

P'anmunjom

SEOUL

Inchon

Yellow Sea

Ch'ongju

SOUTH
KOREA

Taejon

Kunsan

Taegu

Kwangju

Pusan

Korea Strait

Izuhara

Tsushima Strait

Cheju Strait

Sasebo

JAPAN

Cheju

Korean
Peninsula

CHAPTER 1

THE COLD November wind swept down the great plains, over the Wichita mountains, and buffeted the wooden rectangle that was the Fort Sill Station Hospital, where my mother, Mrs. Katherine Brusenhan Craig, lay in a spotless Army hospital bed and sobbed softly. "Why me, Lord? What have I done to offend You? Help him, Lord, please help him. They say he's lost two pounds in only three days. He can't eat with that harelip and cleft palate. I can't feed my own baby. He has to be fed with an eye-dropper. Be kind, Lord, and help us!"

Mrs. Cheryl Johnson left the latrine, walked to her bed, and seated herself. Before opening her bedside-table drawer and taking out her hairbrush, she watched my mom stare at the peeling paint of the ceiling. "The enlisted are certainly lazy this morning. I'll have them up and about in no time. Believe it! Katie!"

My mother turned her head to face the officer's wife. "Yes, Mrs. Johnson? And how are you feeling this morning?"

"Katie, let's dispense with the niceties. The major will be here shortly, and my hair is a sight. Please brush it as quickly as possible."

"Really, Mrs. Johnson, I just don't feel up to that sort of thing just now."

"Katie," Cheryl said sternly. "Here's the brush, get on with it!"

Given no choice, my mother, the wife of Corporal Roamey T. Craig, sobbed softly as she followed the move-

1

ment of the brush through the well-kept hair of her "superior." In 1926 the Army caste system was very distinct and harsh, enforced downward and affecting every individual that was associated with it. My mom recalled the Mexican laborers who'd toiled in her father's Texas cotton fields. She thought they had had it better than she did.

The next afternoon two stern-looking Army physicians walked down the aisle of the maternity ward and stopped at Mom's bedside. The doctors looked at each other, shrugged their shoulders and woke the patient.

"Sorry," said one doctor, "but it's very important, Mrs. Craig."

Mom's heart leaped, but the doctors were quick to read her.

"No, no, Mrs. Craig, the baby is alive and eating that eyedropper out of house and home. We talked to a doctor in St. Louis today who says he can fix your boy's mouth, inside and out. Doctor Brown is a plastic surgeon who learned his trade working on the faces of World War I vets. He's the best there is in the whole U.S.A., Mrs. Craig."

Mom looked upward and said aloud, "Thank you, Lord, for not abandoning us."

"There are some drawbacks, but we think they're minor. Doctor Brown has done a lot of work for the Army, and the Army will foot the bill for the boy. However, there are no provisions for you," said the doctor kindly.

"You mean I can't go with my baby? That can't happen!"

The other dependent wives in the ward were becoming aroused at the conversation as well.

"No, Mrs. Craig, it simply means that the Army can't pay your bills for the trip. If you go, you will have to foot your expenses. We must have you and your husband's permission to ship the boy to Barnes Hospital in St. Louis—the sooner the better. We're looking at nearly two years of hospital time and God-only-knows how many operations. We'll be back Monday with the paperwork for both of you to sign. If you want this for your son, have Corporal Craig here at 1300 hours on that day. We think it's the only chance your son has to live a normal life, but it's up to you." The two departed the ward.

"Not much choice," Mom said aloud. Two enlisted wives at her side agreed as Mrs. Toy Shanahan spoke for the pair.

"Don't worry, Katie, we'll come up with the money for your trip. What are you going to live on while you're up there?"

Mom's thoughts went to Dad's $44-a-month paycheck and the $17 subsistence allowance before she replied. "I've been a waitress for these many years. I'll survive. My daughter Pauline will stay with my sister Mary until I get back. Just pray for the baby. I love all of you for your help. Thanks, ladies."

The entire Army post chipped in for our train ride to the big city. Doctor Brown had lined up a waitressing job for Mother even before she arrived. Visiting me while living on her wages would see her through my first eighteen months. When the folks at Fort Sill finally saw me again, on my second birthday, they knew that the effort had been worthwhile.

In those eighteen months, my mother proved to the world what a mother's love was all about. She worked at a café for a dollar a day, food, and tips, then visited me every day six blocks away in Barnes Hospital.

Finally, after a dozen or so operations, Dr. Brown told my mother the ordeal was over. We bundled up against the Missouri cold and rode the train 650 miles to my new home in Lawton, Oklahoma. At two years of age, I entered the life of an Army brat. I'd already been indelibly stamped with one handicap; I was about to acquire another, a life of near-poverty and the prejudices experienced only by dependents of enlisted swine in the small, bumbling pre–World War II United States Army.

CHAPTER 2

MY FATHER, Roamey Thomas Craig, of Scotch-Irish descent, was born into the poverty of his time in an East Texas cotton patch near Mount Pleasant in 1897. World War I came along and the good-looking fourth-grade dropout went to war. The war, Europe, and the Army were quickly forgotten after he received his first honorable discharge in 1919. A year of toil in the cotton fields back home nudged his memory of the good things the Army had provided during his first hitch. He had come out of the Army a horseshoer by trade. The heat of the Texas sun and constant bending that picking and planting cotton required provided him with an excuse to reenlist a year later. He would not leave the Army for another twenty-seven years.

My father left the cotton fields forever and was shipped to Fort Sam Houston, Texas. There, he was assigned to the Recruit Depot Post. While working as a recruiter for the Army, he met and married my mother. Miss Katie Brusenhan, from Colorado City, Texas, was eighteen years old. Corporal Craig's recruiting assignment moved him and his bride from Texas to the Army town of Lawton, Oklahoma. In 1923, he was transferred to the horse-drawn artillery at Fort Sill.

Corporal Roamey Thomas Craig's family reached its height of ordinance around the year 1939. By then, Dad was a range NCO for the School of Fire at Fort Sill. Now known as the Field Artillery School, the unit was respectively composed of the white detachment and the colored detachment. This arrangement was the nation's answer to

4

the Civil War and Jim Crow. The separate-but-equal unit system was strictly adhered to and hardly altered until the Korean conflict in 1950.

Due to the officer preference system then in effect, only a small percentage of NCO personnel were allowed to live on post. My father's low rank forced our family into a rented house at 908 South Ninth in Lawton.

Lawton, in 1939, had a population of ten thousand souls, mainly farmers, cowboys, ranchers, businessmen, camp followers, and the hated GIs. Of course, the despised soldiers were the only real reason for the town's existence. Located south of Fort Sill by six long miles of dirt road, the city was compact and little else. From Ferris Avenue on the north to Lee Boulevard on the south, it ran for eighteen blocks. Stretching east to west from 1st Street to 23rd Street, the city was just about square.

The small, square residence at 9th Street and 1st Avenue was composed of four rooms, two of them small bedrooms. The toilet was a shack joined to the house by a plank boardwalk. Adjoining the back of the house was the cement storm cellar that was standard protection for homes in "tornado alley." A large cottonwood tree shaded a backyard, which was anchored by a sewage canal that meandered out of town and emptied into Cache Creek. Our small rented palace was home to a family of five children and three adults.

My grandmother, Lizzie, had a bedroom to herself that no one dared enter. Mom and Dad slept in the adjoining bedroom. The kitchen was next to their bedroom and led outdoors to the privy. It also served as a sleeping facility for the three boys—myself, Buzz, and Joe Bob. The folding bed—when deployed—allowed very little room for eating, much less cooking.

In the front room, a large bed served as sleeping quarters for my two sisters, Jean and Pauline. Crowded? Certainly, but not uncommonly so for the time and the economic conditions of Oklahoma and the nation.

Lights were extinguished between nine and ten o'clock

on weeknights and no later than midnight on weekends. In 1939 we three sons were thirteen, eight, and four, and waited patiently in our unfolded bed for the other members to doze off. When the magic moment arrived, I would begin the storytelling. Often, the tales would elicit giggling that disturbed other members of the household and brought retribution. Discipline, in that day and age, came in the form of the GI garrison belt, a thick, two-inch-wide leather strap otherwise used by soldiers to round out their Class A, Olive Drab, uniforms. Being the oldest, I received the majority of the blows, but no one got off scot-free.

Grandma Craig, eighty years if she was a day, rose at 0430 for the ritual coffee making then practiced by most families. The water would be hot in a short time and, more often than not, the light and conversation between her and Dad awoke three boarders who had been disciplined the night before for the same offense. That was one of the first lessons of the old adage that still lingers today in the Army. Rank—indeed—does have its privileges.

After the head of the household had ridden off on his bicycle for the seven-and-a-half-mile jaunt to Fort Sill, the banging of pots and pans signaled that it was time for pillows to be redeployed, among other things. Even so, a fretful two hours passed before we rose for our meager breakfast and preparation for school. Washing hands would signal the serving of cornmeal mush that had been simmering for thirty minutes or more. If bread was available, we would be given a sandwich in a brown bag; if not, the supper meal would be available at five. Joe Bob would be left at home to fend with his mother for noontime nourishment.

My mother, who had waited tables the previous night in the café, would not rise until ten. She would be back at work by the time we were home from school. Her income meant the difference between surviving and not surviving.

Saint Mary's Academy, located at 7th Avenue and Gore, taught grades one through twelve to the Catholic children of the Lawton–Fort Sill area. The minority Catholic school in a hard-shell Baptist community was an even mile from us South Side kids. Because we had no overcoats, in the winter we ran the distance in order to stay warm. After going to the heated rooms, we awaited the arrival of the officer brats from Fort Sill, who were delivered by a luxurious Army bus at precisely 0750 while we poor folks watched in anger. While the sisters watched a GI driver unload the vehicle, they would make comments such as:

"Such nice children and so well-mannered and well-dressed. Why can't these other bums emulate them?"

"No training at home, Sister! Their mothers had rather work than to stay home and raise their children. At least we put a stop to some of their mischief last week."

"We did right! Can you imagine an enlisted man's son mooning over an officer's daughter? What will they think of next?"

To help defray the two-dollar monthly tuition, I stayed after school every afternoon and cleaned the classroom. The sisters were determined to get their money's worth out of my hide. I was just as determined to transfer to a public school if ever given the chance. When my parents divorced in 1942, I had that opportunity and took advantage of it. I never entered the Catholic school again and vowed that no children of mine would ever have to endure slave labor for two dollars a month.

Our parents' divorce changed many things forever. My youngest sister married a GI and moved to Fort Bragg, North Carolina. Pauline, my older sister, finished nurse training in Arkansas, and married a second lieutenant of all things, and also moved away. Joe Bob, my youngest brother, moved to Louisiana with my mother. Buzz, like many Okies, went to California to make his fortune in the entertainment field. I stayed with my father and new stepmother, but I didn't stay much. I had not only become bitter at the world, I had in fact become a child of the streets.

Playing high school sports became my preoccupation and school work was all but forgotten. The two years before graduation were an academic disaster. I did just enough academically to be eligible to play sports; nothing more.

After the Japanese Empire made its horrendous mistake on December 7, 1941, everyone's lives changed. My father welcomed the June 1, 1942, Pay Bill, under which privates were paid an unheard of $50 a month. Sergeant Roamey T. Craig's pay shot up as well. From the pittance of $54 plus $20 specialist's pay, his base pay went to $105 or $3.50 a day plus specialist pay of $20 a month and subsistence. The $135 paycheck enabled him to pay our grocery bill in full for the first time in the family's existence. Sasser's Grocery Store had supported the South Side poor folks, black and white alike, for years. The boom enabled them to pay their debts for a change as well. Because of the enormous pay boost, other things also changed.

Front yard signs such as SOLDIERS AND DOGS STAY OFF THE GRASS were eradicated. Residences on the North Side could now visualize the pain and destruction a mobilized Army might wreak if the signs were allowed to remain. The 45th Division of the Oklahoma National Guard was mobilized and the "I'll be back in a year lil' darling" draftees were in for the duration and six months. Other changes much closer to home were notable as well.

My father and his new wife, Ann, purchased a house on D Avenue near the only white public high school in town. Soon, along with my grandmother and stepmother, I found myself living in a house with my own room and a better physical environment than I had ever dreamed possible. I was sixteen and for the first time had a bathtub in which to bathe. On the other hand, my father departed his cushy job as range NCO for the Far East battleground.

Harry Shanahan, the son of my father's first sergeant, and I had spent many years at St. Mary's Academy before transferring to Lawton High School. We banded together to fight the life we had been born into. The fight would be long and would prove that we faced more enemies than just the GI caste system. Despite the horrendous scar on my upper lip and a speech defect that by then was almost nonexistent, we managed to stop the taunting of the more obnoxious students. The teenagers—and a few adults—who stubbornly continued to point out others' blemishes did so at the risk of bodily harm or in private.

We quit our newspaper routes and went to work in the Post Exchange system at Fort Sill. Here, during the summer months, our paychecks were $10 a week, enormous money for sixteen-year-olds of that period. Working nights in the Post Exchange annex that sold the GIs' favorite liquid was an education in itself. The Regular Army enlisted men had tricks that we were unaware of, tricks that were obviously condoned by a well-educated officer corps.

Over a few beers, the now-rich NCOs told us about loopholes in the system that would be closed before Harry and I had our bout with the U.S. Army. Gaining rank through normal promotions was very difficult in the thirties so if an EM was about to retire (at the time, after twenty-five years "good" service) as a corporal for instance, his sergeant would voluntarily be reduced and the corporal would be promoted to sergeant, a rank he would maintain until his imminent retirement, when the former sergeant would resume his earlier rank. All for a small consideration, of course.

Many NCOs had been reduced at least a dozen times. Many of them also had "bad" time—time lost through periods in jail or absent without leave (AWOL) time, which did not count toward retirement and had to be made up before they could retire. To my personal knowledge, many of them made up at least five years of this type of duty before retirement. My father was an exception—he had no bad time that I was aware of.

Another unique enlisted situation in the Army of that period also stood out, at least in my mind. After World War II I began to pay particular attention to retirement. Enlisted personnel retiring with thirty years' service at the rank of private first class or corporal were common. Why? Certainly, the size of the Army had something to do with this phenomenon but other factors prevailed as well. Personnel who fell into this category were not motivated to self-improvement, to say the least. To them the Army was a means of survival and survival only. This reality was reflected in the civilian attitudes and conclusions regarding the professional Army. "If you don't want to work or can't succeed in civilian life, you can always make it in the Army." (This attitude still exists in many civilian communities throughout the land. Of course, where it does, just once I would ask those civilians to run five miles a day and jump from an airplane. Once they managed to loaf through those events I would credit their remarks, but not before.)

In the fall of 1944, my senior year at Lawton High School, I became eighteen and eligible for the draft. I was examined at Oklahoma City and placed in category 1-A—eligible. I would remain in that category until hell froze over in Korea, but many of my classmates volunteered to enter the armed forces at midterm. Their reasons were varied. The flag, Mom, and apple pie may have had something to do with it, but I could not discount the obvious. Upon their return they would have a free high school diploma, an exact duplicate of the one I was presented the last day of May 1945.

My mother and father, who had rotated back from the Philippines, came to the graduation. It was a happy yet sad occasion for me. I spent the summer months working at Fort Sill in preparation for college.

My father was skeptical of my college ambitions, and for good reason. My grades since transferring from St. Mary's were, to be kind, an unmitigated disaster. Many of my high school coaches thought the same as my father and one, who will go unnamed, said so. "Hell, you couldn't hardly pass here at LHS. Why waste your time and Oklahoma A&M's?"

My answer was always the same to the doubting Thomases: "I can pass at Harvard if I have a mind to, but thanks for the encouragement anyway."

My father eventually relented and even promised me spending money while I was attending the aggie college at

Stillwater, Oklahoma. Serving as the batting-practice catcher saw me through the room-and-board financial overload. And, to everyone's surprise but mine, I not only passed my courses, I excelled—at least in comparison to the other freshman jocks. My new friends were very numerous so I'll try on just a few for size. Clarence Tully, a freshman from Shawnee, and a lineman on the Sugar Bowl champions of 1946, had a sense of humor that was very different. John Carey, the second-string quarterback, was a state high school golf champion in 1945. Carey taught me the gentleman's sport, but couldn't swing me over to the gentleman's viewpoint. Bob Fenimore, the three-time All-American tailback, taught me modesty at its best, and Neil Armstrong, the senior class president and an All-American end, was a training aid in using popularity to build egos in lesser humans. Neil eventually became the head coach of the NFL's Chicago Bears. Bob "Pee Wee" Williams was a senior who hailed from Lawton and an Army brat as well. Mr. Williams, at five feet, was instrumental in pointing out that personality and a sincere, caring attitude could win more friends than a bucket full of bees, handicaps be damned.

It was through and because of people such as these that I enjoyed the happiest year of my life. Professor Bounds, my journalism teacher, helped make my year complete. "Admittedly, you're one of my best students. However, I wish you wouldn't allow the whole damn athletic department to copy from your work." After that I couldn't wait to run into some of my misguided high school coaches.

My grades zoomed before I reported to my summer job with Frank Spruiell, also a substitute halfback on the Oklahoma A&M Cowboys Sugar Bowl champions. During the summer his father employed both of us at his gasoline station in downtown Lawton. A year away from the Army environment had changed my outlook on life, and more important, on myself. I flaunted—somewhat—my 2.5 (C+) grade-point average when presented an opportunity.

The war that would start two more was over by then, and

my hometown had changed very little. That the local populace was regressing to its prewar opinions of the Army did not go unnoticed by most of the Army brats. At the local pool hall and meeting place, I finally enjoyed the upper hand over my old high school coach. He started it all. "Well, I heard you passed, but damned if I know how," he conceded.

"Because, Coach, I had some good professors and enough people I cared for to want to stick around. I'll be a three-point-oh student next year."

Unfortunately, that did not happen after all. My pal Harry Shanahan came back from the Army and he wasn't mentally ready for college and, apparently, I wasn't ready for my sophomore year. Like the Okies we were, off we hitchhiked to California to see the country.

Between the Sierra Madre Mountains and Reno, Nevada, lies the Herlong Naval Ammunition Depot. Because many discharged veterans drew their 52/20* unemployment rather than work, we were hired there as ammunition handlers. After nine months of work and dropping our earnings in the slots and card games of Reno, we returned home the way we had departed—B-R-O-K-E and hitchhiking.

Before we could do more than get reacquainted with our families, we were offered athletic scholarships at Eastern Junior College, a two-year institution located 185 miles east of Lawton near the Cookson Hills. Coach Bob Williams, the former trainer at Oklahoma A&M, was Eastern's assistant football coach and the head basketball coach for the Mountaineers. We were given room, board, books, and fees and we snapped at the chance.

Harry did well on the up-and-coming football team and I made the basketball and baseball teams, but the college town of fifteen hundred had little or nothing to offer the students. So we stayed on campus and studied. As promised, my grades did climb to 3.0—or B—level.

I did not miss the pressure of the Army-town environ-

---

*Fifty-two dollars for twenty weeks after discharge from the service.

ment and apparently neither did Harry; we went home only at Christmas time. Our fathers had retired by the summer of 1949, and we stayed home and worked during the off season. Only a torn cartilage in my left knee spoiled my vacation at home.

Doctor Grable, a local orthopedic surgeon who was a specialist in this type of corrective surgery, performed two of the knee jobs in the same twenty-four-hour period, Clarence Avery, a redheaded LHS quarterback, being his other victim. While I rotated between living with my dad and living with my mother, my father and I had the longest conversations we had ever had. I was jarred by Technician 4th Grade (Ret.) Roamey T. Craig's complete lack of activity. He admitted that he wished he was back in the Army and that he had no civilian ambitions at all. This did not surprise me, but another observation of his did.

"I see no reason why a ceiling on the amount of years served by enlisted men exists at all. If I want to serve until I become too feeble to perform, who would be hurt by that? A general can stay forever. Why can't I? Retirement life to me is a waste of time. I ain't gonna hit a lick at a snake even if it bites me."

Unfortunately, I had no answer for him. And my father and Shanahan's father did very little more until their dying days.

After the operations, I worked hard on conditioning because my old basketball coach at Eastern had interceded on my behalf with Eastern New Mexico University at Portales, New Mexico. Besides myself, Bill Fife, Fred Banks, and Dave King, all athletes from Lawton, were offered scholarships. However, my knee just did not respond, and at midterm, I was cut.

With no money to support my degree ambitions, I was once again adrift in Lawton. I was also adrift with a new philosophy about college in particular, and education as a whole, and questions now formed in my mind. Could I become a coach at a four-year college and cut a kid from his bread and butter because he had injured himself? Worse yet, could I use and misuse forty young people to further my ambitions, then forsake them when they were in need?

My father and mother had preached to all of us children that an education was the cure-all of life. But was it true? Hell, I could read and write the English language. What else did I need? Should I have studied and worked for four or five years to become like my old LHS coach, who was dumber than a brick wall and respected neither by his charges nor by the administrators?

My thoughts turned to my second major, journalism. Work for a newspaper? I liked writing for the LHS *Tattler* and the college newspapers. It would be a great hobby, I decided. But a career? Get serious! I finally concluded that if you aspired to be a lawyer, a doctor, or a scientist, you really had no choice but to carry on with an education. A teacher? No, I believed that "those who can, do! Those who cannot, teach!" It would take me many years to change my negative observations.

Bill Fife, D'Armand Henry, and I planned our next escapade meticulously, but I found myself $300 short. I went directly to someone who cared enough to help me solve this problem, Comanche County Sheriff Ed Gartrell. My father did not have the time nor the money for a project of this magnitude.

I found Sheriff Gartrell playing dominoes in the back of the local pool hall but he had time for me, as usual. He walked the entire one hundred yards to the City National Bank of Lawton with me and drew the funds. I pledged to repay the debt ASAP. We spent the last week of March 1950 testing Bill Fife's new automobile on the Alcan Highway. (As D'Armand Henry the boxing Indian lad remarked, "A highway built by men for fools to travel on".) Fairbanks, here we come.

CHAPTER 3

ON JUNE 25, 1950, with the urging and blessing of Communist China and Mother Russia, the North Korean army took advantage of the ill-prepared leader of the free world, crossing the 38th parallel and beginning its trek south. When the United Nations condemned the invasion as aggression, the United States Armed Forces were called to war for the second time in a decade. For the second time in a decade, they were Pearl-Harbored into a situation their small, ill-trained forces were not prepared for.

The war to end all wars had only ended one era and begun another. This time the U.S. military would learn lessons that apple pie, Mom, and the flag had not taught it in World War II. Militarily, we would never be caught with our pants down again.

Northeast of South Korea—6,213 miles to be exact—lay Fairbanks, Alaska. Soon to be the forty-ninth state, Alaska was beginning to thaw out from the winter of 1950. Despite a slump in the Fairbanks economy, as a twenty-three-year-old college dropout I had managed to wrangle a job as a carpenter's helper at Ladd Air Force Base, located just outside Fairbanks proper.

Playing softball for The Talk of the Town night club was all the politics I needed to land the lucrative assignment. The carpenters I was assisting would take the entire summer to remodel the Ladd AFB Noncommissioned Officers Club. The pay was seven times the union scale in the States and about six times what I thought I was worth. But I would need every penny to pay room and board in Alaska's inflated cost of living. Long before June 25, 1950, I had my own room in a motel while the two friends who had driven the Alcan Highway with me were still living with friends and working odd jobs for life's necessities.

On July 3, 1950, a greeting from the Comanche County, Oklahoma, draft board caught my attention and requested me to report to Lawton on July 15 for a pre-induction physical. Mrs. Carla Williams, head of the board and a good friend of mine, had enclosed a hand-written note to the effect that she would, if requested, transfer my records to Fairbanks for the physical. But the unpleasant reality of possibly training in frigid Alaska was obvious. Two days later, Fife, Henry, and I were enjoying the four-day trip home.

By the middle of July, I was in charge of a busload of Comanche County's first twenty-five draftees of the Korean conflict. The group had all been classified as 1-A a minimum of five years, and no complaints were heard as the bus pulled out of Lawton for mighty-pretty Oklahoma City early in the morning. The group would be back home for the evening meal. Twenty-four lives were changed forever on that humid day in July. One Indian lad flunked the physical. How? No one could ever figure out.

"You shall make yourself available for induction within the next thirty days. You will not join any unit of the regular Armed Forces, National Guard, or Reserves." Our group read and reread our orders for clarification. We deduced that we were to stay home and check our mail for the next month for further instructions.

President Truman then chose to throw Oklahoma into shock by ordering the state's 45th (National Guard) Infantry Division to active duty effective September 1, 1950. In addition, the 40th of California, the 28th of Pennsylvania, and the 37th "Buckeye" Division of Ohio were also to be activated.

Oklahoma's own 45th Infantry Division, the Thunderbirds of World War II fame, began drills and recruiting efforts immediately after the alert. Units from the Lawton area that were affected were Headquarters Company, 2d Battalion, 179th Infantry Regiment; 700th Ordnance Company; and line companies E and F, 179th Infantry, from Walters and Frederick respectively. Recruiting of veterans and nonveterans became fierce, with most World War II vets staying away in droves. In Lawton's infamous bar section, my draft-eligible drinking pals became prime targets. Gene Gower and myself were propositioned many times. The recruiters, who will go unnamed to prevent mayhem, must have done well with their "Go with the men you know" line of malarkey. Gower made his move and I was not too far behind. Gower was my high school teammate and state tennis doubles champion so his enlistment attracted a few other jocks and friends from the local area. The next day at Fort Sill, the recruited personnel reported to the 2nd Battalion Headquarters, 179th Infantry, were given physicals, and sworn in.

I knew in my heart that I was violating the draft laws by enlisting, but the 45th Division recruiter, a silver-tongued devil, convinced me that it was completely legal; I knew that the recruiter wasn't much smarter than I was and lied a lot to compensate for his lack of knowledge.

A motorpool area near the enlisted swimming pool in the new post served as the training area for Headquarters, 2d Battalion. After being sworn in by Captain Jack Fox, we newbies were issued personal clothing and a wall locker. The rest of the day was spent with administrative chores.

When I arrived home around 1800, my dad knew something out of the ordinary had taken place. As my stepmother banged away at cooking supper, I confessed. To my surprise, my father did not appear to be too upset. "Well, you were going anyway. So I guess you did the right thing. Hope it works out for you. They won't send those weekend warriors to Korea; that's for the Regulars, son."

I was not impressed with my father's reasoning. "I don't know a helluva lot about the Thunderbirds, but they managed to make the European Theater of Operations in WW Two," I said, defensively.

"So did everyone else. It's not the same."

"I just want to get it out of the way. I don't give a damn where we go. I hate the Army and always have, especially officers' kids. Hell, you know that."

The old soldier seemed hurt by my remark but tried to laugh it off. "You kids from Lawton fought 'em all your life. Why don't you give up the ghost? Don't judge all officers by a few. There's good and bad in everything. Remember this: If a person graduates from West Point, he becomes an officer. If I had your education, I'd have been one myself."

"Dad, I never got a degree, so the education's not helping me much. Anyway, I'd feel like a traitor if I became an officer." Chow call ended one of the longer conversations I had ever had with my father.

August was spent in weapons training, physical training, proper wearing of the uniform, and dismounted drill. On the fifteenth of the month, the entire unit took a physical examination at my birthplace, the Fort Sill Station Hospital. I had as much luck there as I did at Oklahoma City—I passed.

Bidding farewell to my mother, Katie, who was by then living in Lawton again, my youngest brother, Joe Bob, and Dad, I boarded the troop train to Camp Polk, Louisiana, on September 1, 1950. It would be my first day of active federal duty. I pulled guard on the train and it served to remind me that I was "in the Army now."

In 1950, Camp Polk was a rundown, seldom-used installation that would change for the better. I was assigned to the Pioneer and Ammunition Platoon for training. Draftees—mostly from Texas and Oklahoma—began filling up the all-white and Indian units from the badlands.

Why wasn't the division from a Jim Crow state being integrated with blacks? Apparently, Oklahoma's politicians were not ready to commit political suicide in front of the predominantly white voters of the state. The T-birds would have to go to Leesville to associate with other races than white or Indian.

The unit, draftees and all, went through basic combat training (BCT) drills in good fashion. NCOs and officers with combat experience from World War II took the reins and drove on. I found that I liked dismounted drill, the M-1 rifle, and even the firing range, but when inspections got chickenshit and asinine, I rebelled somewhat. The twelve-mile marches at a pace of two and a half miles an hour were not punishing to the young soldiers, but some of the cadre had problems with them. I especially liked paydays. After taking out three bucks for laundry, an E-1 recruit actually had $72 to spend, whether he needed it or not. Not bad spending money in those days.

When the Army almost doubled in size in 1950, its logistical system could not keep up. Walking twelve miles, firing your weapon, and walking back twelve miles on an empty stomach made you wonder if your country was busted or had turned its back on you. Soldiers of the unit recall one trying day when we stood in line for twenty minutes to receive one half slice of bread. It was no wonder my friend Carl "T-bone" Brooks volunteered to be a spoon (cook)—if he prepared the meal, he might possibly get enough to eat from time to time.

Despite the diet, the National Guard and its draftees otherwise continued to march. We knew in our hearts that the officers and NCOs were not eating any better and were not complaining about it. I noticed the lack of flab on the troops, but was not too impressed because, at 150 pounds, I had none to spare to begin with.

With basic combat training and kitchen police, time passed quickly. Everyone loved KP, simply because you got something to eat. In fact 1st Sergeant Hatfield had a helluva time keeping the NCOs and officers off of his duty roster.

After qualifying with the World War II–era M-1 rifle, the unit moved into tactics. Here, Gower and most of the former athletes excelled. One hot, humid day into the third month of Camp Polk, the P&A Platoon witnessed a tank-infantry assault demonstration. The demonstration by the 45th Tank Company and an infantry rifle company was by the book and to perfection. Even the narrator made an impression on his audience.

In the late forties, Dan Blocker had been a tackle for Sul Ross University at Alpine, Texas, and was hailed as one of the largest linemen in college football. The draftee from the Lone Star State was six foot eight inches tall in his "stocking, large" feet. He weighed in at 285 pounds. Dan said that his weight varied rapidly. "In fact, Bill, I can lose five pounds just by brushing my teeth." More about Mr. Bonanza and Company F, 179th Infantry, later.

After BCT, I was rewarded for my hard work by being demoted to company clerk simply because I could use a typewriter. Despite protest that bordered on the company punishment level, the first sergeant and I endured each other.

At the end of a month, the topkick relented and I and one Clarence Avery, also of Lawton, were shipped to Fort Gordon, Georgia, for a six-week message center school. I wasn't too happy about it. "Good thinking, Top. I don't want an office job, so he sends me to school so I can work in message center."

In Georgia, Avery and I, like the good privates (E-2) that we were, lived in wooden barracks built for the soldiers of World War II. Although living conditions in the coal heated, two-story buildings were not ideal, the abundance of food made the conditions better than Camp Polk.

The school was a snap for two college dropouts. A couple of weekend trips to the 19th Hole in Augusta provided some entertainment for the pair of us. The most memorable event of the course was furnished by one of the draftees from Mississippi as the NCO instructor briefed our class on its final exam. "Remember," said the NCO, "how long a foot is. How many inches in a foot, Jones?"

"Don't rightly know, Sarge. I reckon it's according to how long your foot is," Jones answered.

The class roared. The NCO was not as amused. "You dumb son-of-a-bitch, tomorrow your goddamn foot had better be twelve inches long."

Two tired T-birds arrived back at Polk by train and the latest news was reported to us upon arrival in Headquarters Company. The only disappointing development to me was the hurry-up formation of the 10th Ranger Company. It was my first missed boat to airborne training, but there would be others. Gene Gower, Carl Brooks, and James Dunn were on board when the train pulled out for Fort Benning, Georgia, leaving myself only a few days from an unexpected visitor.

PFC Craig was giving his first class ever to the Pioneer and Ammo Platoon when told to report to the orderly room. My assistant instructor took over the class on construction of the double apron fence and I trotted off.

A large cowboy hat with the sheriff of Vernon Parish underneath was talking to Captain Fox when I knocked on the orderly room door. First Sergeant Hatfield bade me enter and stood up from behind his desk. "Were you drafted into the Army in August, Bill?"

I explained my side of the disagreement and when I finished, Captain Fox looked at me with disgust. Apparently his memory of the "go with the men you know" days was faulty.

The sheriff looked a little confused as well. "I have a federal warrant for your arrest for failure to report for induction September 15, 1950, soldier boy."

Naturally, I looked to my superiors for some help in this very peculiar predicament. All I received for my efforts was a red-faced captain who appeared near cardiac arrest and a blank stare from First Sergeant Hatfield. I slapped my ID card on the topkick's desk.

"If you arrest a soldier on active duty for ignoring a draft notice that came fifteen days after he was inducted into the Army, you're going to look like an idiot."

Captain Fox came closer to heart failure, but Hatfield looked like he had found an out for his wayward soldier.

"I believe the man is right, Sheriff. He was federalized on September 1, and reported for duty at Fort Sill. His ID will verify that. I don't believe you have a case for failure to report." Hatfield smiled.

Captain Fox's blood pressure appeared to decrease somewhat.

The sheriff of Vernon Parish looked at the warrant and back at the U.S. Army identification card. "Son, you sure caused a heap of trouble, but I have to agree with you. We don't have a case. I'm gone." And he was.

Hatfield addressed Fox after the hasty exit. "Anything else, sir?"

"Yes, get this fuck-up back to the P&A Platoon and keep him there. Any more trouble outta him and I'll jail him."

I was gone, and muttering to myself as I strolled back to the platoon training area. "Now, I'm a fuck-up. Screw you, Captain." I knew in my heart that there would be no reconciliation between myself and the commander. Growing up OD had at least taught me that much. I would be proven right.

On February 24, 1951, at a division parade, the Thunderbirds were alerted to their pending assignment to Japan. The teamwork and precision displayed at the parade opened more than a few eyes to the improvement attained in preparing civilian soldiers for war. Captain Fox, cordovan boots and all, led Headquarters Company, 2d Battalion, 179th Infantry Regiment, through its paces. From the privates to the battalion commander, Lieutenant Colonel Spears, we could not help but feel the pride of accomplishments attained in only a few short months. As I passed the reviewing stand at eyes right, my view of the brass and civilian guests reminded me of my father's remarks a few months prior. "Dad, it looks like a helluva long weekend."

With the move to Japan slated for April 1, the division gave each soldier the opportunity to take a ten-day leave. During the Korean conflict, wearing civilian clothes was a no-no, and the Lawton–Fort Sill environment was not the place to test the well-practiced preparedness of the military police. Hence, the soldiers on leave would be seen in and out of the pool halls and bars in ODs, overseas caps, and brown shoes. Most of the retired soldiers in the Army town commented favorably on our appearance, the blue braid of Infantry on the overseas caps notwithstanding.

The leaves and goodbyes were over all too quickly and the troops were back at Camp Polk packing, stacking, and loading unit supplies for the long voyage to Hokkaido, the northernmost island of Japan. Even so, the P&A Platoon found time to train.

The demolition training fascinated us combat engineers. The land mines and booby traps caused fear but fear of the unknown slowly faded as familiarity set in. We soon found out that military explosives were safe, or at least as safe as the handler permitted. A rifle bullet will not detonate TNT, C-3 plastic explosives, or military dynamite. The demolition manual, *FM 5-25*, became my Bible and I appropriated one for my own and began memorizing it. Though I didn't know it at the time, the knowledge I picked up from it would stand me in good stead in the coming years.

Weapons training was an everyday affair. For the most part, the platoon carried the semiautomatic M-1 carbine of World War II fame. I managed to appropriate an M-2 that would set me apart from my platoon. Identical to the M-1, it had a selector switch that enabled the soldier to fire the gas-operated weapon on automatic. An enlarged thirty-round box-type magazine came with the improved weapon.

Cross-training consisted of our learning to use other World War II weapons such as the Browning Automatic Rifle, M-1 Garand rifle, and the 60-millimeter mortar. If the 45th Infantry division was preparing to fight the last war again, so was the U.S. Army as a whole. The evolution to modern weaponry and equipment would take some time and some doing.

One weekend before departure I and my young sidekick, Johnny Hill, decided to end the boredom of garrison confinement. Loaded down with $72 monthly pay, Saturday afternoon found us in our olive drab uniforms walking the streets of Leesville. It was the first trip to the quaint Louisiana town for either of us.

After five or six beers in three different slop joints, we became separated. In addition, because of the long layoff, I had become somewhat inebriated. For some reason, the blue braid on my overseas cap became an irritation to some of the artillery personnel of the 158th Field Artillery.

The fight started inside the bar. Several cannon cockers and I were still getting it on outside when the military police did their thing. I was the only one who received a pink "Delinquent Report" card. "I thought it took two to tango," were my parting words to the large 45th Division MPs. "So much for military justice." I continued to march. Staggering on up the streets of Leesville, I stopped in another large establishment. This time it was the scarlet-and-white braid of the Corps of Engineers that upset the harmonious atmosphere. When I couldn't get them to pay attention to my slurs, I became incensed and managed to dump all their beers on the floor.

I exited the bar with half of the 45th's engineers in hot pursuit. Halfway down the block I turned to make a stand—I wasn't standing long. In defense of my poor performance, I did manage to take one engineer with me. We were both being stomped to death when the 45th Military Police, for the second time, rescued a battered private of Infantry.

After hearing the story, the cops handed me my second citation of the day. In addition, they hailed the post bus and placed a battered troop on it, giving specific instructions to the driver. For my part, the fun and games of a boring Saturday afternoon were over. Now the ball was in the corner of Captain Fox and the first sergeant. They proved they could perform.

The not-so-amused topkick did not even offer me a seat when I reported to the orderly room on Monday. I was not offended by the oversight because I was too busy wondering what the former 82nd Airborne captain was going to do.

Escorted into the lion's den by Hatfield, I faced an old airborne soldier who was seated on his throne. I came to attention and reported to the commander and was not given "at ease."

"Well, Fuck-up, you really did it this time. I'm giving you a break by just giving you an Article 104—company punishment. I should jail your ugly ass. What do you have to say for yourself, soldier?"

Amazed that I was permitted to speak, I thought a minute before replying. "I'm twenty-four years old and kinda high spirited, sir. Guess I was acting like those paratroopers I've heard so much about. Wouldn't mind being one." Hell, it was worth a try.

The captain flushed. "You wouldn't make a pimple on the ass of an airborne soldier."

Now it was my turn to blush.

"I do not detect any guilt associated with your answer. You are hereby restricted to the battalion area until we depart for our overseas assignment. First Sergeant, get this dud outta my sight. Dismissed!"

I saluted, did an about face and walked out of the cubicle with Hatfield. I signed the company punishment book, and went back to the training in progress, mumbling as usual. "Friggin' Army. I thought that's what we were in here for, I fought the best I could. Screw you, Captain, you ugly bastard."

The 179th Regimental Combat Team (RCT), 3,200 strong, sailed down the Mississippi into the Gulf of Mexico and on to Panama. All the troops knew about their ship was that it was a three-stacker, it was crowded, and it was uncomfortable. Much to the disgust of Hatfield and Fox, Johnny Hill, Clarence Avery, and I somehow survived a seven-hour liberty in the Canal Zone and Panama City.

The ship docked in San Francisco but no one was allowed liberty. We got to watch as some AWOL soldiers were brought aboard. To our amazement, some of those who missed shipment in New Orleans were noncommissioned officers. "Very sad. But at least they made an effort to join the people who count, their friends," I remarked.

The ship was back at sea by nightfall. Thirty-two hundred National Guard and draftees resumed our trying eighteen-day trip to the land of the rising sun.

In the holds—"holes" would be a better word to describe them—bunks were five high, aisles were small, and schedules for chow and physical training were strictly adhered to. Sleep came only when the body said so and not before.

Physical training—by battalion—proved to be the brightest part of the day for us seaborne GIs. Me and my shipmates knew we were in deep kimchi when we cheered just because PT hour was announced. In spite of our having to stand up to eat, another bright spot of each day was chow time. The food was plentiful.

Bull sessions were the only shipbound entertainment available. When "Land ho, land ho," was heard over the intercom, the troops joyfully secured web gear, packs, and weapons. P&A Platoon Sergeant Van Dyke remarked, "Fastest I've seen you people move since you last went on leave."

To the officers and men of the 179th, me not excluded, "If you have to join, stay outta the damn Navy," turned out to be a much better slogan than "go with the men you know." We strolled down the gangplank and two and a half miles farther down a dirt road to our train transportation to Chitose Air Force Base. We enjoyed every minute of it.

Curious Japanese lined parts of the roadway to catch a glimpse of the first combat troops on Hokkaido since the 1st Cavalry Division had departed for Korea. The much more curious soldiers stared back at the first Orientals most of us had ever seen. It was love at first sight.

Chitose was an abandoned airfield that had been used in World War II by the Japanese to train kamikaze pilots. In the winter of 1950 it was surrounded by woods and covered by twenty feet of snow. It was home to a tent city for the 179th. Other camps utilized by the division were Camp Monte Strong, Camp Crawford, and Camp Enniwa. The 179th Regimental Combat Team would not stay at Chitose very long before moving to Enniwa.

CHAPTER 4

WHETHER THE Japanese were ready for the T-birds the 179th Regimental Combat Team never found out, but the Russians were another matter—broadcasts from Sakhalin Island routinely berated us weekend warriors. "These wretches were released from prison in America in order to make life miserable for the people of northern Japan. They are nothing more than ex-convicts and thugs who will ravish your land."

The troops who owned radios heard remarks of this nature every day. I heard one young soldier exclaim, "I don't know how they found out but I wish they wouldn't spread it all over the goddamn island, the assholes."

For the P&A Platoon, training continued. The combat engineers helped construct the new tent city at Enniwa while some of us gave classes on barbed-wire construction, demolitions, and mines and booby traps. The spring thaw caused the terrain to become muddy and wet but we did not mind. The logistical system of the U.S. Army had finally caught up with its adopted sons, and the supplies were plentiful. Despite the hard, dirty work, the food was good, plentiful, and well prepared. Besides, we could always thaw out at night in tents that featured wooden pallets for flooring—luxury, no less.

This was the situation when I gave my first class on demolitions. My college speech classes helped me over my stage fright but not completely. I knew that my real salvation was knowledge of the subject and allowing the students to use hands-on training after the demonstration and lecture. Shortly thereafter I made corporal. "Off Kitchen Police at last!" I rejoiced.

A week later, the P&A Platoon moved to Enniwa and placed squad tents over the wooden frames that had been erected by civilian labor supervised by general headquarters troops. The twenty-eight-man platoon was up to strength and progress in our training was rapid after we erected our homes.

In ten days, the 2d Battalion was intact in its new homes. The shit rolled downhill shortly thereafter as future plans were revealed by higher HQs. The three regimental combat teams, 179th, 180th, and 279th, would begin a new training program designed for National Guard and reserve divisions that were called to active duty. The training would be in four phases.

After phase one, or Basic Combat Training and Advanced Individual Training, the units would move into phase two, squad, platoon, and company training. Phase three would consist of deployment by battalion and regiment. The last and least important phase would be deployment at the division level. This was to be done over a period of eight months.

To us in the P&A Platoon, the exercises became repetitious after squad and platoon training. We all agreed, however, that it was excellent training for commanders and staff people.

Before moving into deployment by companies, the P&A had a Saturday night in base camp, so corporals Hill, Zuriga, and myself departed for the as-yet-unseen bright lights of Chitose city. Eyeing me intently as he spoke, the company first sergeant briefed us on the town and, worst of all, the 2400-hour curfew.

Hill, myself, and the Indian lad skipped the cabs that hovered by the gates of Enniwa and hoofed it the entire five miles to Chitose. Bar-hopping occupied the next two hours, but when that became a bore, we walked the streets and practiced our seagoing Japanese on the local business women. Finally Hill and Zuriga returned to camp. Hardcore, I glided on. Back in the cabarets there was no short-age of alcoholic entertainment and I feasted on the deli-cious Asahi beer and Hokkaido's own Sapporo. At 2335 I finally staggered into the dim streets and began searching for a cab. No luck.

At 2350, ten minutes prior to curfew, I managed to hail a banzai warrior and ordered the driver to beat that damn curfew. The driver smiled and squealed two or three tires heading for the intersection that exited left and led to Camp Enniwa.

"Damn, this is gonna be close, driver."

"No sweat, Honcho. We make it in sukoshi time," the driver said.

The military police were three hundred yards on the other side of the turnoff and awaiting. One young corporal was born dead. Flashlights and flashing red lights were menacing on this chilly-dark night.

I yelled, "Run the son of a bitch, cabbie!" But in my heart I knew it wasn't going to happen. The Japanese were, and still are, the most disciplined people in the world. It was prayer time!

"Step out and show ID," the lawman demanded. I com-plied.

Deposited at the tent orderly room of HQ, 2d Battalion, I watched as a Sergeant First Class Gannon signed for my body and the accompanying paperwork.

At five foot, seven inches tall and 140 pounds, Gannon didn't really inspire much fear in an accused curfew viola-tor. "Get your ass to bed, Corporal Craig, and report to the first sergeant with Platoon Sergeant Van Dyke Monday morning," he said.

"You're going to turn me in for being ten minutes late, Sarge?"

"Most certainly, Corporal. It's a very serious breach of military discipline."

I lost control. "You little pipsqueak son of a bitch, how would you know? You sit on your ass behind a desk while we hump the hills and dales. For two cents I'd kick your ass right here in your castle. You look like you need some exercise anyway, asshole."

"Now you're being insubordinate and disrespectful to an NCO. Go to bed before I call the sergeant of the guard and have you placed under house arrest."

Monday morning a chastised corporal would stand at attention in front of Captain Jack Fox. The same Jack Fox who had been picked up and written up by the same MPs exactly thirty minutes after me. My platoon sergeant—Van Dyke—and I knew that as we approached the orderly room on a muddy Monday. Still, we did not look forward to the encounter. Van Dyke spoke to the first sergeant before we entered the old man's small compartment. "Corporal Craig's performance since arriving in Japan has been exemplary. His offense was very minor and could happen to anyone. Ask the Captain if that ain't so, Top."

First Sergeant Hatfield looked uncomfortable. "The captain isn't on trial here, the corporal is, Van Dyke."

"I'm asking you to ask the ole man to administer a slap on the wrist. We're short of NCOs in the P and A, and I think Craig has leadership capabilities. He's doing well as squad leader."

That was a long speech for the quiet, unassuming platoon sergeant. Hatfield nodded before unassing the desk and moving to confer with the commander. He returned shortly and motioned for the two of us to go into the chamber.

As soon as we entered, saluted, and reported, Fox's complexion began to color. I knew that I was about to receive the same treatment that the Army caste system had always perpetuated during my childhood.

"Corporal, I'm going to read you the charges and administer company punishment under Article 104. On May 13, you broke curfew, and when booked in at the orderly room were disrespectful to the charge of quarters, SFC Gannon. Do you have anything to say before I administer punishment in these obvious violations?"

"Yes, sir. How do you know I was disrespectful to the

charge of quarters? Hearsay. I don't recall that part of it. That part of the charge should be omitted, sir. I have nothing to add or delete from the first accusation." If my father had said that to an officer twenty years earlier, he would have been on his way to the stockade in a blink. Fox only got redder.

"That's mighty white of you, Private First Class. I hereby order you reduced one grade and restricted to your platoon area for two weeks. You are dismissed!"

We saluted the CO, about-faced, and returned to the desk of the topkick. First Sergeant Hatfield spoke briefly to Fox before joining us in his office. "PFC Craig, you're on kitchen police tomorrow. Report to the messhall at 0500. Any questions?"

"Yeah, Top," Van Dyke interrupted. "He's still a squad leader and his assistant will have to take up the slack. I hope this is only temporary."

"The captain did the same thing, Top," I said. Sharp glances from both NCOs quieted me.

"I suggest, Van Dyke, that you and PFC Craig have a heart-to-heart talk. In the meantime, I'll do my best for you and the platoon. Don't let the door hit you in the ass on the way out!"

Van Dyke was sympathetic to me and for good reason—I was a sharp soldier and an excellent instructor in addition to being an all-caring squad leader. Despite that, Van Dyke also knew the top soldier was right. It was time to clear the air because, if for no other reason, I was now worth saving.

Fortunately, the squad tent was empty and we seated ourselves on the madeup Army cots.

"Bill, you do great in the Army except for two or three hangups. I think it would help if we talked about that. Do you agree?"

Although I was busy cutting off my two beloved corporal's stripes with a razor blade, I paused long enough to agree. "Hell, I need to learn something besides KP, I guess."

"Number one, you have a problem with authority, especially officers. Number two, you're not much better with NCOs if you disagree with 'em. How do you justify that?"

"Jack, I was born in the Army and raised under a caste system that I did not want to be a part of. Yes, I hate officers and what they stand for, period."

"Bill, it's only for twenty-four months. Can't you set that aside for one more year?"

"I doubt it, Sergeant. Why am I being busted to private first class and that airborne asshole gets away scot-free. The system is rotten and needs to be changed. But I don't believe it'll be changed as long as the men of the NCO Corps keep their mouths shut and take that kind of shit."

"Captain Fox will be punished, but not reduced in grade. That just doesn't happen; if officers do something wrong, they fine 'em or kick their asses out. Number two, I agree that NCOs don't solve problems by keeping their thoughts to themselves. Express your opinions and maybe if you have the correct solution it'll be used. But once the decision is made, try your best to back it. Will you do that for me, for yourself, and most of all, for the people in the platoon?"

"Those are good points, Platoon Sergeant. I really hadn't given it much thought. I've managed softball, football, and basketball teams since I was twelve or so. I used to do it then, so why not now. It's a deal."

"Okay, now we're getting somewhere. My last point about the Army: Officers we can do nothing about, so let it slide. Disagree in a respectful way with NCOs and you may be surprised how flexible they are. In peacetime you would be in the jailhouse for the remarks that you made to Gannon—the asshole."

I begin to sew on my sorry PFC stripe while grinning at Van Dyke's last remark. "I'll try to cool it until the system corrects itself. What else, Platoon Sargeant?"

"Your off-duty behavior! It's not helping matters any. Do you have to get into fights and disturbances every time you go on pass? Can't you tone that down some?"

"I doubt it, Sarge. I like to live it up, drink beer, and fight from time to time. I don't see nothing wrong with that. If people say something about me or my unit, I do kinda get hostile. Is that bad?"

Van Dyke pondered the question before coming to a conclusion and answering in a somber tone. "No, not necessarily bad, but it shouldn't always lead to bloodshed. Tone it down or stay away from that sort of situation. Can you do that?"

"Top, when I get off kitchen police tomorrow, you're going to see a changed soldier boy, but I *will* defend myself on pass or leave. If I ever get another one. How's that?"

"That's a deal, Bill. You're the best demo man we have and the best squad leader in the platoon. You may not realize this, but you do like the Army; I wouldn't be surprised if you stay in. I'll try and see that you make corporal ASAP because I can't use you when you're pulling shit details. Stay away from Captain Fox, he's after your ass."

"I know that. I won't give him the opportunity to do what I know he wants to do. You have my word, Sergeant. Thank you for your time and consideration. If a few more people in my life had taken the time to talk *to* me and not down to me in my life, I'd have a better outlook on the human race."

As ordered, I pulled KP the next day, but the cooks and the troops noted the changes. I pulled my weight and joked around even when my friends made me the target of friendly jibes. I consoled myself with what the platoon sergeant had said.

Field duty for the 179th Regimental Combat Team resumed and the troops were all the better for it. We were issued very good winter clothing including pile caps, parkas, and shoe paks. Food was abundant and the morale of the 45th Infantry Division zoomed to new heights. One development helped my morale in particular: Jack Fox was relieved and transferred out of the 2d Battalion to be replaced by the commo officer, Captain Wayne Hendricks. Corporal again, I vowed—again—never to grace the messhall in a labor-related attitude. In other words, no more KP! Another development also pleased a majority of the mountain-climbing troops.

The National Guard troops whose enlistment had almost expired at the time of the call-up—mostly NCOs with no active-duty experience—were extended for one year by President Harry Truman. They had been learning their trade on the shoulders of the "go with the men you know" men and the draftees. To the delight of the men they were experimenting with, these NCOs began to leave for the land of the big Post Exchange. The 179th had just finished its last field training exercise when they departed.

The 179th RCT moved from the tent city of Enniwa to Camp Crawford on the outskirts of Sapporo, the largest city on Hokkaido. Field duty behind us, the regiment now lived in the brick, centrally heated barracks of Crawford.

The Pioneer and Ammunition Platoon had a one-story, brick barracks to itself. Van Dyke had his own room but I was still in the bay with my squad. Police details and basic classes started all over again. The NCOs and troops learned more about dismounted drill than they really wanted to know, but with the excellent living conditions, three hots, and a cot, the platoon managed to survive. It was an expenses-paid vacation for the mountain troops of the 179th RCT.

Nothing lasts forever, however, and in November of 1951 the entire division was alerted for Korea. Advance parties began to move out for the hills, thrills, and chills of the war. Between packing and menial details, we still found time to celebrate in the bars and houses of ill repute in the quaint city of Sapporo. It was in the Sapporo NCO club that I used to drink with F Company's Dan Blocker and swap lies. He'd tell me about his plans to get into show business and call me a Regular Army asshole. I promised to put him in touch with my brother Peter ("Buzz"), who by then seemed to be making a living in New York. Rumor had it that he was making that living in show business.

Dan Blocker eventually became the first sergeant of Fox Company, 179th RCT, before going on to become a television personality as Hoss Cartwright on *Bonanza*; his less-famous partner in crime would continue to march and become a Regular Army asshole, just as Hoss had predicted.

On September 15, 1951, the division's 10th Ranger Company had been deactivated. The unexplained move brought Gene Gower, one of the original "go with the men you know" troops, back to the P&A Platoon. The personnel of the 10th were given a choice in the matter—transfer to the 187th RCT in Kyusho, Japan, or back to their original unit, the one destined for frozen Chosin.

The 45th Division's 18,000 officers and men prepared to replace the 1st Cavalry Division but equipment such as vehicles, tanks, and artillery pieces would stay behind. This move saved tons of money, time, and shipping space. Although the Cav's equipment was battered by combat, the comfort of not having to drag our equipment along made the exchange worthwhile.

The T-birds had been kept well briefed on the progress of the Korean war. What we didn't glean from *Stars and Stripes* was presented in the classroom on Saturday mornings. According to many officials, the best-prepared division ever to enter a combat zone under the American flag was ready for its short, choppy ship ride.

The 179th RCT arrived in Inchon harbor in November 1951, and moved to Chorwon by train. There we stayed overnight before relieving the Puerto Rican 65th RCT. The weather was unbelievably cold.

The P&A Platoon shook, rattled, and rolled its first night on the frozen tundra. If we didn't learn anything else, we were taught the hard way to have something between the turf and our sleeping bags. The air mattresses we were issued came into play the next night. The next morning, December 10, after a cup of coffee and some C-ration biscuits, the 179th RCT was on the Jamestown line.

The United Nations spring offensive had moved the North Korean and Chinese visitors back to the 38th parallel, where the United States and its allies would eventually settle for a tie. Months of trench warfare awaited all of us newbies.

CHAPTER 5

THE 65TH RCT was no different from the other US units in December of 1951. Decimated during the offensive that pushed back the hordes, they had dug in along the 38th and were trying to survive the coming winter. Fortunately, the weekend warriors had come to the rescue.

Headquarters, 2d Battalion, 179th Infantry, moved into the well-constructed but ill-kept bunkers of the 65th. The P&A was on the forward slope of a hill that lay one ridge back of the main line of resistance (MLR). The platoon pitched a squad tent that was quickly fitted with a squad stove whose gasoline heat felt wonderful at night when the temperatures fell below zero. That the tent offered no security against the enemy's 122-millimeter and 82-millimeter mortars had not been considered by us rookies, which was brought to light on the second night of the bivouac. Surviving the shelling without any casualties, the platoon cleaned and repaired some bunkers left by the relieved unit. My squad did better than that. In two days of hard work we constructed a bunker with Korean timbers, one that would withstand just about any mortar or artillery likely to be directed at us.

Sometime later, Corporal Kubala from West, Texas, Corporal Asenap from the metropolitan area of Cache, Oklahoma, and I led seven Korean Service Corps (KSC) troops up the incline to E Company. Every person in the party had harness, individual weapon, and a load-bearing pack, and each pack contained at least one roll of barbed wire. The KSC people were older than us (we were all in our twenties) and just couldn't maintain the pace set by Kubala. Eventually I halted the single-file formation and moved up to slow him down.

Everyone got off the trail and unassed their loads. The old, brown-skinned Koreans cast glances at Kubala that could have been interpreted as critical. My mind wandered as I puffed on a Lucky Strike. I didn't want to tell Kubala, but my ass was draggin' too. I left it to Eugene Asenap to speak my thoughts out loud.

At five foot eight inches and two hundred pounds, Asenap appeared fat to the average eye, but I knew better. The Comanche sprawled next to me and looked at the overcast Korean sky while he spoke. "Corporal Craig, those KSCs are not the only ones that's hurting. It ain't doing much for me, either. These damn hills are different than the ones in Hokkaido."

"I agree, Gene. I'm hurting but Kubala seems to be having a good time."

"When we get the fence built for E Company, let's look around their positions. I think we ought to know all the line companies' areas better than we know our own, Asenap."

"Good idea, Sarge," flattered Asenap. "Let Walt take his KSCs back to the platoon area and we'll go sight-seeing."

Kubala led the forced march the rest of the way to Easy Company. Whether the KSCs could keep up or not, after our arrival and placement of a double-apron fence, they taught us a lot about building barbed-wire entanglements. One trick that saved us hours of toil was their method of tying the wire. Instead of the book method—tying fancy knots—the KSCs used a stick to twist the wires together. We used our bayonets to do the same thing. The fence was finished shortly after we consumed our field rations for lunch.

The commander of Easy came out of his bunker and thanked us for our assistance. I took the opportunity to ask permission to tour the wet, muddy perimeter and received an okay. Kubala agreed to take the Koreans and return to the platoon area.

With snow paks on our feet, web gear consisting of a first aid packet, ammo pouches, bayonets, and M-2 carbines, we moved fifty yards straight up to the bunkers and communication trenches of the well-dug-in dogfaces.

The commo trenches were five feet deep and connected the bunkers with each other. The sleeping bunkers offered overhead protection from the Chink high-angle fire weapons such as the 82-millimeter and 122-millimeter mortars and 152-millimeter artillery pieces. We chatted with the line troops we had come to know so well from Polk to Hokkaido. Like me and Asenap, they were all kinda glad to be there. The 45th Infantry Division had an illustrious past and we had all been indoctrinated into it, draftee or National Guard notwithstanding. Staff Sergeant Rie Fawbush broke up the back-slapping session. Rie Fawbush was a tall, good-looking Indian from Walters, Oklahoma. "Come on over, Bill, and watch the show!" Asenap and I didn't hesitate.

After moving to a bunker complex, Fawbush handed us a set of binoculars apiece. He excitedly pointed to the Chinese main line of resistance. The hills were straight up and down, and only a valley separated them from the U.S. MLR. With directions from Fawbush, we finally spotted the object of E Company's affections.

A squad of Chinese coolies was moving timber from the valley floor up the bare slope. As we watched, Fawbush called H Company for prearranged 4.2-inch mortar fire. The heavy weapons company responded and was right on the button.

When the mortar rounds burst in and around the laborers, they dropped their loads and scrambled for safety. We chuckled at their misfortune as the timbers rolled all the way to the valley floor. Fawbush called for a cease-fire.

Although Asenap and I had seen enough, Fawbush and a cheering E Company insisted on playing the game to a conclusion. Easy Company watched as the Chinks' masters berated their charges from safe bunkers. Back down the hill they went for the construction material.

Again, Fawbush waited until they were almost on the military crest. The mortars were again right on target, and the two-man loads were unassed once again. Because of our experience carrying barbed wire a few hours previous, Asenap and I began feeling some sympathy for our enemies. Fawbush, who was more practical, did not. We handed back the binocs. Fawbush laughed and excused us. We quickly angled over from the bunkers to a trail that led to the friendly side of the valley floor. However, once we hit the open area that led into the Chorwon valley and the Chinese frontlines, we were exposed. The 122-millimeter mortar rounds could be heard for days before their arrival, and we both hit the ground. The rounds fell short. Two scared soldiers raced for the opposite side of the slope, three hundred yards or so away. Despite weighing only 150 pounds, I did not stand a chance against Asenap. He beat me by twenty yards. We both flopped into a ravine behind the ridge in order to get our breath. The rounds fell harmlessly onto the vacated rice paddy for only a few more minutes before the bad guys gave it up.

The 158th Field Artillery Battalion proceeded to climax the duel in the mud. They pounded the Chink MLR for fifteen minutes and the plot to grease two Okies was over—for the time being.

In January and February the snow and the cold moved in on the Thunderbirds with a vengence. The average mean temperature for the month of February would flatten out at 32° below. Shades of the North Pole! For a change, the U.S. Army was ready for the onslaught. All the troops had parkas, pile caps, and long underwear, and we layered our clothing to beat the cold. Easily the greatest improvement was the newly arrived thermal boots. Any type of movement would make the insulated boots warm—would even make our feet sweat if the movement was constant, like climbing straight up. The improved equipment would help the T-birds win part one of the Korean conflict. Part two, the war against the Chinese, would be a little more difficult.

Because of the harsh weather, long periods of inactivity

were frequent along the MLR. I Corps, under command of General Mike O'Daniel, stated that patrols no larger than platoon size would operate forward of the drawn lines.

Shortly after the arrival of 1952 was celebrated with a hot meal for all, the 2d Battalion's commander came up with a new twist, organizing a recon unit composed of deactivated members of the 10th Ranger Company and volunteers. The unit would operate only at night and far beyond the battalion's MLR. High morale and espirit de corps among the citizen soldiers guaranteed a consistent influx of volunteers, but Regular Army—career soldiers—in the unit could be counted on one hand.

Airborne soldier Gene Gower, formerly of the 10th Rangers and an all-around athlete from Lawton, would head up the small unit (it never numbered over twenty personnel). After a week of training that Gower based on Ranger small-unit tactics, the unit was ready to perform. I refused to let well enough alone.

As a newly promoted staff sergeant, I had enough to do trying to keep my squad in a state of readiness to perform its assigned tasks, which had been complicated by another problem the 45th Infantry Division had inherited. For the first time in its long history, the division was being integrated with black soldiers. Inundated might have been a better word for it. We therefore would have to address the problem of overt racism ASAP.

Oklahoma and Texas, the states that supplied 70 percent of the unit, were Jim Crow states. Back there, the "separate but equal" facilities for blacks and whites kept the socializing between the two groups to a minimum. Our understanding of each other's cultures had been limited, to put it mildly. I would try to clear the air with my in-country briefing to the blacks, but only after I had briefed the white and Indian soldiers.

The only complaining I heard from the Caucasian-Indian group was that the blacks used the word "motherfucker" in a freewheeling manner. Like one Apache Indian said to me in private, "Those are fightin' words where we come from."

I was well aware of that fact and made it a focal point in my talks to the incoming black soldiers. Almost all of the blacks coming into the P&A were trained as combat engineers at Fort Leonard Wood, Missouri. They were proficient in construction and demolitions, mines and booby traps, and could contribute.

In my briefing to the blacks assigned to my squad, I emphasized teamwork and "in other words, do *not* call your Cau-Indian teammates 'motherfuckers.'" The briefing and renewed activity in the trenches had the platoon working around the clock, allowing little or no time for dissension.

One squad was assigned to Pok Hi, a small hill in no-man's-land, to help improve positions, string barbed wire, and plant mines and booby traps around the perimeter. The commander, Frank "Bud" Garrison, treated the combat engineers just like he did his own troops, i.e., they stood guard and pulled listening post (LP) duty at night. Sergeant Van Dyke rotated his squads, so one unit would not have all the fun; they all earned their Combat Infantry Badges (CIB) before the ordeal was over. Still, my adventurous nature or competitiveness—I never knew which—cried out for more. I satisfied the urge by volunteering to go with Sergeant Gower's recon unit. Upon return from those missions, I would sleep off my fatigue and then go back to work with the platoon. Neither the company nor the platoon had anything to complain about.

Gower checked all five of his patrol members before darkness set in. To protect our feet from the thirty-degrees-below weather the night promised, each of us wore the thermal boots that had been issued the day before. The patrol's mission was to snoop and poop to within two hundred yards of the Chinese MLR and observe and report any activity. One battery from the 158th Field Artillery awaited our findings and would provide some form of protection for the return trip as well.

After darkness set in, we tramped through the Chorwon

valley knee-deep in snow and exited the barbed-wire gate that led into no-man's-land. An hour of cautious deployment found us positioned on the side of a trail at the bottom of Chinatown. Despite the cold we felt no discomfort until around five in the morning; even the thermal boots could not deter the subzero weather forever. Then a Chink patrol caused us to forget our discomfort.

Gower passed the word, "Do not fire." I stiffened as I heard a patrol member's weapon click off of safe, causing me to mutter to myself.

As if on cue, the patrol stopped. The single-file formation turned and faced the snow and sparse vegetation that hid our recon unit. *I can't hold my breath forever, assholes. Do something!* I thought.

An enterprising Chinese soldier threw a snowball at our position. When we didn't react, the patrol moved on and we began breathing again.

Patrol leader Gower waited until the enemy moved away before reporting to headquarters. When the transmission was over, our patrol was ready to move back to a friendlier environment. Suddenly, two joking Chinese soldiers appeared, seemingly from nowhere. Gower greased the first one while a ton of lead put away the second one. I had not even gotten off a shot.

Gower was up and leading the patrol in a zigzag back to the safety of the T-bird lines. Our first contact was an apparent success compared to what could have been. When our small unit approached the manned positions of G Company, Gower again halted the unit. Radio contact with George Company confirmed our unit's whereabouts, and Gower left the patrol and moved down a well-worn road to the friendly entrance. He chatted with the men of the defensive complex, and only then did he relay to the recon unit to move forward one by one.

I was happy to be up and moving so the thermal boots could warm my feet, but my mind was not especially on this discomfort. *I have a cold M-2 carbine with no carbon in the breech or the barrel. Why? I'm damn sure going to find out, bet your ass on it!*

We had a hot meal at battalion headquarters, then I went back to the platoon for a few hours' rest. I had an appointment with Gower at 1800 that evening.

I was awakened in the cold, dark comfort of a dug-in complex at 1300. Asenap gave me the poop from the group. "Bill, they want you at George Company right now. They have a Chinese mine in front of their positions and they want it disarmed or blown in place, whatever. Major Worley said to tell you to get rid of it."

"Okay, let me scarf some C-ration coffee and I'll be right with you. You're going with me, aren't you?" I asked.

"I really hadn't planned on it, but hell, I guess so. What do you need?"

"Get me some quarter-pound blocks of TNT, electric blasting caps, commo wire, and an electric blasting machine. That's about all the equipment we'll need. I assume George Company has secured the area. Tell 'em we'll be there in a flash and that we're going to blow it in place. I'm not dickin' with any device that I'm not familiar with. Got it, Gene?"

"Okay, Bill, be back in about twenty. Be ready to move! Bye."

George Company, originally from Marlow, Oklahoma, occupied Hill 881 and the road that led to no-man's-land. Their commander, a captain, was a big, bad, tough ex-football star who brooked no interference from outsiders. His unit had suffered constant mortar and artillery attacks from the Chinks and had the casualities to prove it.

Brigadier General Wayne C. Smith, the new assistant division commander, was a forerunner of the Vietnam-era commanders who would evolve along with the helicopter. He commanded from the sky. Safer, you know. He flew the small command ship all over hell and half of the Jamestown Line.

One cold day in January 1952, he had landed on a small landing zone adjacent to the dug-in messhall of George

Company. The gracious Chinamen homed in on the aircraft with 122-millimeter mortars. The ensuing barrage caved in the messhall of George Company and adjusted the killed-in-action ratio of the 179th RCT. In addition, the rifle company had no hot meals for several weeks. The fact that the enemy had not touched the rotary-wing aircraft pissed off everyone from the battalion commander on down. George Company was furious but the short, fat little general seemed unaffected by it all. But his time in the barrel was a-coming.

Asenap and I climbed the snow-packed trail to G Company's headquarters bunker. The CO greeted us and turned us over to a sergeant who led our security squad to the Chink mine. Thirty minutes later, a double explosion signaled the end of the enemy mine crisis. We were walking with our security along the road to friendly lines when we heard a helicopter approaching the small landing pad. The squad leader signaled the squad to disperse and take cover before moving to our positions.

"Better get down, Bill. That sonofabitch is coming in to see the old man. He'll bring the Chink mortars in on our ass again."

We watched the chopper land but to everyone's surprise, it took off almost immediately. Our patrol returned to friendly lines without incident. At the 1800 hours meeting with Gower I found out why I admired the weekend-warrior officers more than their ticket-punching Regular Army counterparts.

Gower and I conferred in my hootch that afternoon as the Korean darkness approached. "You woulda been proud of Captain George. He told that fat little shit that if he ever landed that chopper at G Company again without permission, he was going to blow the goddamn thing to hell and back. That's why he didn't linger. We're all very proud of the captain. That little shit had the gall to fly back here and tell the battalion CO, Lieutenant Colonel Spears, to take disciplinary action against Captain George."

"I think it's great, but what's going to happen to the captain?" I asked.

"What the hell can happen, Bill? They can't send him to Korea and they won't send him home. Shit, he's not a career officer. He'd be happy as shit to be back in Marlow, and so would I, come to think of it. Screw that general!"

I continued to grin but got serious and changed the subject rather abruptly. "Gene, I didn't fire my weapon at the two slants last night because I didn't know you were going to fire, and it was all over before I could react. I feel like a damn dummy."

"Okay, I know that and I've thought about it also. It was my fault as much as yours. You also didn't test-fire your weapon before we left. That all goes back to you missing the rehearsal we had prior to the operation. I made the decision to fire and the rest of us would empty a magazine or clip after I initiated fire and then we would cut out—that's the way we rehearsed it. I should have told you. The next time you want to go, come to the briefing and test-fire your carbine. Okay?"

"Okay, I'll be ready as soon as I get the platoon caught up on those line-unit problems. I'll do better next time out."

A week later, the weather plunged to an all-time low of forty degrees below zero as the small recon unit rehearsed a mission. George Company had a small observation post (OP) manned by a platoon, and we were to act as a warning position about a half mile into no-man's-land. The OP had been harassed constantly by night patrols from Charlie Chan's finest. The night's mission would find us trying to pinpoint intruders and bring artillery and squad .50-caliber fire upon them. We were moving to the OP before dark.

We sprawled in the hasty fortifications of George's OP and received a briefing from the platoon sergeant. Officers in line companies were almost nonexistent by the first day of March 1952, and battlefield promotions to 2nd John were going beggin' for many reasons—the possibility of an extension in Korea being the foremost and a short life span running a close second.

At 2000 hours, we moved ahead of the OP next to a riverbed below. We were in place by 2100. We were lying about ten yards apart in a single-file formation when I looked up. A tall person was approaching my position. I was attentive as the man bent over to speak. *I didn't know GIs ate so much damn garlic,* I thought. Then the gentleman began to speak in Mandarin. While fear tore at my insides, it did nothing to prevent me from firing the M-2 carbine on full automatic. My first human kill, but I had no time to philosophize about it.

Gower fired a Thompson .45-caliber submachine gun at a squad of Chinks who were coming up the incline from the riverbed. Then we began receiving return fire from the far side of the river and returned it. Gower signaled the withdrawal with a grenade. Every member followed suit—throwing a grenade where the Chinese squad was last seen and only then moving toward the G Company outpost.

Gower used the PRC-10 radio to contact the men in the OP, who in turn initiated the artillery and squad .50 action on the company-size unit across the Imjin River. Under that cover, we moved back to the OP, where Gower contacted the platoon sergeant. We were given positions on the small knob and would reinforce the outpost for the rest of the night.

As I watched the tracers from the .50-caliber machine guns and as the 105- and 155-millimeter artillery rounds saturated the area, I wondered out loud, "How can anyone live through that shit? We're on the right side, I guess."

Despite all the friendly noise, the OP heard the feeble response before it even arrived, but the Chink mortars and artillery never even came close to the OP.

Around 0230, to the disgust of no one, all firing ceased. The OP went to 50 percent alert and waited for the dawn. After refusing the hospitality of a C-ration breakfast with our hosts, the 2d Battalion recon moved back to the safety of battalion headquarters.

When Gower turned in his report, he was told by the battalion intelligence officer (S-2) to report back at 1600 for a debriefing. I received permission to attend the affair. The results were not startling but did serve to enlighten us on our accomplishments. A very confident intelligence officer laid it on the line. "Last night, gentlemen, you intercepted a reinforced company from the 607th Chinese Field Army. Their mission was to overrun our G Company OP and withdraw. Thanks to you people, it just didn't happen that way. They suffered sixty-three known dead. While you saved the day for the time being, their pressure on our OP line will continue. The action last night will give us time to improve our positions in order to thwart their mission and cut down on friendly casualties. The regimental commander sends you his congratulations. Unless you have some question, you're dismissed."

I met with the executive officer and the company commander after the noon meal, and they informed me that I had been promoted to sergeant first class, E-6. Master Sergeant Van Dyke was rotating to the States and I was now the platoon sergeant of the Pioneer and Ammunition Platoon. I was also informed that no (lieutenant) platoon leader was available. My reconnaissance snoop-and-poop days were over for a spell. After my last night in no-man's-land, I refused to fall apart over the fast-moving events. Besides, I had a twenty-seven-man platoon to take care of. But with three draftee squad leaders who had been in the platoon since Fort Polk, I was in good shape.

The battle of the outpost lines had begun and would not end for the 2d Battalion until after the memorial battle at Pok Hi. The P&A was scattered among the battalion's outposts and would stay on site until they finished their assignments—the laying of barbed wire and mine fields, construction of or reinforcing of personnel bunkers and weapons positions, and the like.

The bitter Korean cold moved slowly into the history books and the battalions begin rotating, forty-two days up on line and twenty-one days back in reserve. In the latter part of March 1952, the P&A Platoon took its first shower in three months. New fatigues, socks, and underwear were also furnished. Despite the lack of bathing facilities while on line, the unit had suffered no trench foot or any other disease associated with dampness or filth.

A few days after this event, I left my platoon for the first time in a year: The chance for rest and relaxation in Japan was just too tempting to turn down. The R&R program started in March 1952, and five hundred T-birds a month enjoyed the warm weather and hospitality of Japanese society. Still, I felt a pang of guilt as we boarded the C-46 aircraft at Seoul's Kimpo Airfield for the short ride.

All GIs fastened their seat belts as the World War II–vintage aircraft's engines sputtered and coughed into action. I watched and noted fear of the coming event spread across many of the young faces, but I felt nothing but joy and exhilaration in anticipation of my first flight. The cargo aircraft cleared the runway at Kimpo and banked; the fear on the faces of some GIs increased while I continued to grin. The C-46 landed a few hours later in Tachikawa AFB, just outside Toyko. We were hustled aboard a fast-moving train for our final destination.

At Otaru, a resort city on Japan's Pacific coast, the locals eagerly awaited the free-spending troops. After being assigned rooms at a spacious hotel, OD-clad soldiers descended on the bars and beaches of Otaru. I shed my choir boy image of the last five months, and held back nothing. Another Okie and myself teamed up, just the way the briefing officer had said that we should, and stopped in the first bar available. Six days and nights of drinking beer and chasing the *ojosans*—young ladies—had begun but we quickly noticed that the chases were of a very short duration. The beautiful ladies of the night were in a class by themselves. Trained from childhood to please the male homo sapiens, they treated the Korean vets to their lore. The old cliché, "Opposites attract," held true in this case.

Trained by their families to accept a life of male dominance, the ladies clashed head-on with American culture, which insisted that women be placed on a pedestal. The resulting relationships were not only safe sex, but a feeling of trust and admiration on both sides as well. Many soldier boys went to sleep from an overdose of drink and lovemaking while stuffed billfolds lay on a coffee stand. When they awoke, not only was the business lady present, so was the billfold. Despite the fact that the world's oldest and second-oldest professions lay together in sin, the Japanese ladies made a lasting impression on the transient GIs.

Matrimony? This thought was often close to the surface for the soldiers stationed in Japan PCS (Permanent Change of Station). Of course the armed forces had an answer for that problem—paperwork! Yes, paperwork and other roadblocks that would drive a reformed alcoholic to drink. If a soldier started such an asinine adventure, his twenty-three-year-old commander would begin the paperwork drill. In extreme cases, the GI might be shipped back to the States. In effect, the Army was condoning shacking up and illegitimate children but saying no to marriage. When the GI was shipped back to the States, the children would be left in Japan and shunned by Japanese society. But their good looks and drive would frequently overcome the handicap of their mixed-race heritage, and many became entertainers, banding together to avoid the harrassment by the two societies that shunned them.

In the R&R bull sessions, the commander of the 187th RCT (Airborne) came up time after time. According to the paratroopers, the colonel was death on soldiers who wanted to marry Japanese. Apparently rank gives some people knowledge far beyond their education and experience.

To me the issue was simple. "What the hell does Westmoreland have against marriage? He's married and it's perfectly legal. But how do the marriages to the Japanese work out, provided the individual goes through the red tape and gets to the finish line?"

The answers from the Regulars very seldom varied. "Only a few have made it through the bullshit the embassy and the Army can dream up, Bill. Of the ones that have made it, I know of not one divorce nor of anyone who regretted going through with it. Westmoreland? He's no different from the others. 'A marriage to a Japanese will ruin your Army career.' Bullshit! An officer's career, yes, but an enlisted swine's? Often it preserves it. The officers know best, William, that's about all I know about it."

Of course, we didn't know it but that can of worms would plague American forces for decades to come.

I learned more on R&R than just the Army policy on freedom of choice in the field of marriage. After only a few days, I began to miss my platoon. I worried about the men and even the Japanese beer could not take my mind away from my adopted family. "Maybe Blocker was right. I just can't believe I'm going to stay in the Army, but I'm ready to go back to my unit, like right now."

On the fifth day I and most of my companions sobered up for the trip home. A short train ride to Yokota AFB, then a Gooneybird (C-47) was airborne and heading for the slow-warming climate of Korea.

Processing back into a unit was a science by then, and little time was wasted. When I strolled down the streets of HQ Company, then in reserve, I waved and hollered back the greetings from my friends. Deep down in my gut, I now knew that I was just what Dan Blocker and a few others had called me.

I was a candidate for Regular Army enlistment as well as a candidate to follow in the footsteps of my father.

CHAPTER 6

THE 2D Battalion moved out of reserve and again occupied part of the Jamestown Line complex. The P&A Platoon moved one squad and ten Korean Service Corps troops onto Hill 200, later known as Pok Hi. The outpost was a thousand yards in front of the friendly MLR and not much farther from the not-so-friendly Chink lines.

I accompanied the squad with Sergeant Kubala, who by now was an old pro in building fortifications. Company F, 179th RCT, Captain Frank "Bud" Garrison commanding, occupied the small hilltop perimeter. Garrison was well-known in the battalion and admired as the all-American boy of the unit. Always the picture-book officer, with spit-shined boots and immaculate appearance, he was looked up to by the enlisted personnel. In return, he catered to their every need.

I shoved aside the shelter half, stepped into the bunker, and talked to the CO while Kubala lashed at his Koreans. The KSCs would respond to his slave-driving by surrounding the entire hill with a double-apron fence in one day. No mean feat.

"Who built that two-holer sitting dab-smack on top the hill, Captain?"

"The dumbasses we replaced, Bill. I had rather dump in my longjohns than allow twenty-one thousand Chinks watch me defecate."

"Hell, I never thought about that," I grinned. "Shit, sir, might be good publicity for you."

At the end of the warm and humid day, two exhausted

NCOs laced the fence with daisy-cutter picket bombs. Kubala took his people back to battalion while I stopped off at the rear headquarters of F Company. The date was May 25, 1952, and 1st Sergeant Dan Blocker was busy briefing replacements. When I got there, the teenage draftees were being held spellbound by the immense soldier's war stories. Dan waved at me but continued.

The enemy began shelling at 2245 that night. That was followed with a ground attack by eight hundred to a thousand troops on Pok Hi. The men of the P&A Platoon monitored the battle from the safety of their sleeping bunkers. There would be no more sleep for anyone in 2d Battalion that night. Company H was furnishing close-in mortar support, and the other line companies were on 100 percent alert.

While the 158th and the 45th Division artillery answered in kind, the Chinese were enveloping a small hillside commanded by Frank Garrison. I monitored the PRC-10 radio and chatted with Walter Kubala. Our innards tightened every time a 152-millimeter artillery round crashed near our haven. Fighting Fox Company battled on throughout the night while helicopters awaited the dawn to carry away the friendly dead and wounded.

From the radio, the entire battalion knew that Frank Garrison was down. It was not lost on me or Kubala that we had only two weeks to go in-country. Kubala pointed that out vividly when a large-caliber arty round caused our bunker's timbers to groan and shake.

"Lord, we're too tired to die. We're also too short to die!" Kubala prayed, looking skyward.

"Don't be praying for me, I don't wanna die at all," I retorted. "You'd better pray for Buddy Ryan and his pals in Fox Company, they're short too, you know!"

The sound of small-arms, machine-gun, and mortar fire from Hill 200 accentuated the pleas. At six in the morning on the 26th of May, it was all over. Kubala shouted, "They held, Bill, they held. Let's drink coffee then go help 'em bring out the dead and wounded."

Our help was not needed, however; the choppers removed the six dead and thirty-two wounded from the small hill without incident. Platoon Sergeant Buddy Ryan counted 132 dead Chinamen around the U.S. positions. Three prisoners of war were escorted back to battalion by the tough foot soldiers. The battle for Pok Hi was over.

Quiet settled over the Jamestown Line by the end of June. The T-bird outpost line had repulsed twenty counter-attacks and administered 3,500 death sentences on the men from north of the Yalu. A Chinese field army of 21,000 to 30,000 men just wasn't getting the job done.

The phasing-out of the original 45th Division troops had begun in April and the last of us would depart on or about June 6, 1952. Sergeants Ryan, Kubala, Jim Hill, Gower, and myself were eager to begin the journey. One sergeant scheduled to ship out from G Company would beat us home, but in a body bag. He and his replacement were outside of their bunker discussing the situation on a sunny afternoon when an 82-millimeter mortar round landed between them, killing both. When the news reached the short-timers, it made us cringe and stay bunker-bound for days. Stomach muscles were so overworked that many had problems gagging down the hated C-rations.

A large contingent of Thunderbirds boarded the ship on June 5, but not without incident. Tank commander Roberts from Walters, Oklahoma, and myself were lined up and ready to board, but from his throne on high the keen-eyed captain of the troop ship spied our handlebar mustaches. "No handlebar mustaches allowed on this ship." The commander had gotten our immediate attention. The line continued to move toward the gangplank.

"Don't worry, Bill, I have some small scissors in my duffel bag. Can do easy," said Roberts.

As soon as Roberts whacked my stash, he handed the instrument to me and I did the same to him. With a couple of thousand T-birds and 40th Division California soldiers, the ship departed for a six-day trip to Sasebo, Japan. After a night of liberty in Sasebo, we continued on to San

Francisco, arriving twelve miserable days later. When the ship docked, the captain didn't have his way. "All T-birds move to the other side of the ship, so the Californians can greet their kinfolk." The captain's message caused a minirevolt. In fact, the T-birds on the port side of the ship rushed to the starboard side to see the native prune pickers.

Camp Stoneman, a welcome-home speech, and steak dinner awaited all of us who had beat the elements and the Chinks, or at least broken even. Then followed the three-day train ride to Fort Sill, Oklahoma, and one week of processing, a vacation for the Okies and Texans.

A ton of civilians awaited us, with Fort Sill furnishing the band. Not even in World War II had the Army post witnessed such a display of affection. To my complete surprise, even my mother and T-4 (Ret.) Roamey T. Craig greeted me when I detrained. Oklahoma had, somehow, made sure that none of her native sons were slighted.

During the week of processing, the weekend warriors were transferred from active duty to the control of the Oklahoma National Guard. For the next twenty-four months, there would be the two 45th Infantry Divisions—one in the Sooner State and one in Korea. The division in Korea would not be deactivated until September 25, 1954.

Those released went about putting their lives back together and I was certainly no exception. Despite working odd jobs, I managed to throw away some of the $1,800 I had saved in Korea. However, I had placed some of the cash in the bank for future use.

All I knew about the first eighteen months of my life was fed to me by my mother. I begin visiting her, now that she again lived in Lawton, and from these visits I obtained all the information I needed to make my next move.

I called Dr. Brown at Barnes Hospital in St. Louis, and, to my surprise, received an appointment for the coming week. Brown assured me that he was just as anxious to see me as I was to have an appointment. When the subject of money was brought up, I was assured that any examination or action would cost no more than what I had stashed away—by then a thousand dollars. A room close to Barnes Hospital ended my 666-mile nonstop motor trip. My used Chevrolet held up well and I rested until my appointment the next day.

The receptionist greeted me with a smile in the small office that led to the examination room. My file folder lay on the lady's desk. The wait for Dr. Brown's attention was short. The intercom sounded off and I walked through a door. An examination chair surrounded by white-frocked physicians awaited me.

The six doctors nodded before a heavy-set, partially bald man stepped forward and introduced himself. "Bill, I'm Dr. Brown, and it's good to see you after twenty years or so. You look fine, glad you grew the mustache, too."

"I grew it in Korea, sir. It's good to see you also, sir. My mother has told me so much about you."

The boxlike room was lined with glass cabinets but my attention was on the dental chair. Brown motioned me to be seated before he recited a short history from my file. The student doctors were from the Philippines, Taiwan, West Germany, and the United States. When Brown stopped he directed his remarks to me.

"What problems exist now, William, and how can we help you?"

"Sir, my nose is all over the place from a kick in the face, and I can only breathe through one nostril. I would also like you to see if everything else is in order."

At a nod from Brown, the students began to tape measure every feature of my face. When they had finished, Brown looked inside my mouth and placed a suspended X-ray machine next to my face. After the pictures were snapped, the examination was completed.

"Bill, your mouth is fine, but you need to pay closer attention to your teeth. How did you let your nose get in that condition?"

"Sir, I was kicked in the face playing high school football. All the doctor did was tape it, and it's been that way ever since. I think it would improve my speech if I could get it fixed properly. Don't you?"

"Yes, I do. And we need to straighten it, so you can breathe. That would remove the nasal sound from your very good speech habits. You have a tooth that is growing up through your gums, and that has to be extracted. In addition, your nose is a little long, and I would like to correct that for cosmetic purposes. I will then place your upper face in a cast until the entire structure heals. When can you be ready?"

"Sir, I came up here ready. Let's get the show on the road."

"Then pay attention—we're ready also. Be here Thursday at eight in the morning and we'll put you in the hospital for pre-op tests, then operate the next day. Is that fast enough?"

"It's great, sir. How long will I have to remain in the hospital?"

"Bill, I understand you don't like hospitals but you must be here at least three days. I'll release you then but I want you to remain in the St. Louis area for about a week to ten days. Okay?"

Three days later, I was admitted to Barnes Hospital and pre-opped for the next day's ordeal. The only disagreement I had was with the anesthesiologist. I wanted to be out of it all the way, but Dr. Brown insisted on local anesthesia.

"Doc, I don't want to watch such a thing, you know that."

"You won't see it or feel it. The lights will be so bright that you'll keep your eyes closed. Any time a person is deliberately made unconscious, there are too many things that can go wrong. I just won't have it any other way!"

Dr. Brown was not absolutely correct in his every assessment. I kept my eyes closed as he said I would, but I damn sure felt it, especially when the needles penetrated my forehead, upper lip, and nose. My profanity made the room sound like a night on the town by a bunch of GIs. Brown, as always, solved the problem. He dismissed the female nurses and used male students instead.

I gritted my teeth in anticipation when Brown placed a two-pronged forklike instrument up my nose to straighten it. No pain, but when he began to chip away at the end of the nose bone, the chisel slipped and I came unglued. Brown apologized and continued. Mercifully, the doctor finally sewed the skin back over the bone structure of the face and the operation was over. I was moved back into the convalescent ward and slept the entire day and following night without interruption.

Awaking the next morning, I screamed in fear when I couldn't see a damn thing. Almost instantly, student doctors were at my side, explaining that I had not lost my eyesight; my eyes were just swollen shut. It was three days before I was handed a mirror. Dr. Brown watched as I slowly brought it into position.

Unable to see my nose because of the cast, I concentrated on the skin around the eyes. Squinting through cracks in the swollen skin, I inspected the black-and-blue area surrounding my eyes and grinned for the first time in a week. "You beat the piss outta me, Doc. Hell, I'm used to that."

"Your language was bad enough to warrant a beating, young man. We all think the nose is going to be fine. It'll improve your speech. I hope." He grinned. "And it'll do wonders for your self-esteem. I'll release you tomorrow but I want you to stay around the city for a few more days. I'll have a doctor in Lawton take off the cast and submit photos after I release you. You're going to be fine."

I treated myself to a St. Louis Browns–Cleveland Indians baseball game a few days later. With a cast covering my nose and cheekbones, I was conspicuous even in the crowded ballpark. I watched as Satchel Paige, in the sunset of his career, got knocked out of the box by the Indians. Dale Mitchell, the Oklahoma University star, and Al Rosen, former OKC Indian, kept my interest high. When Rosen climbed up in the stands after a fan who deserved it, I moved higher into the bleachers of Busch Stadium; I was satisfied Rosen could handle the problem.

In just a few days, the Chevrolet was heading south. Rolls of cotton up both nostrils prevented my nose from functioning, so even cigarettes were tasteless.

A week later, in Lawton, the cast came off and Dr. Brown was proved right again. My nose, shortened though it was, was straight as a string and my morale soared when I looked into a mirror. Despite being flat broke, I still agreed with the resident doctor. "Money and time well spent, young man."

My discharged buddies and me took our first few months of the freedom to do nothing constructive. After my facial reconstruction, I moved in with my mother, stepfather, and younger brother in downtown Lawton. I worked odd jobs for my stepfather and the local sheriff in my spare time. I encouraged my buddies to go back to school but made no such move on my own. My campaign was an apparent success. I escorted Buddy Ryan to Stillwater and he was awarded a four-year football scholarship. He would go on to become an All-Big Eight tackle and a successful football coach in the pros. Ranger Gene Gower would do no less, and would enter the education field after graduation.

Pleas from my parents and friends in respect to my own situation fell on deaf ears. Two incidents in the fall of 1952 finally stirred me to move. Former Ranger Billy Ray Mathis called me on the eighty-ninth day after our release from active duty. "I'm going back in the Army today. Want to come with me, Bill?"

"Why?" was my only response.

"Bill, if you don't enlist within ninety days after discharge, you lose one stripe. After one year, you lose two. I'm not going to lose any. Come go back as an SFC with me."

I said no, but my negative reply left me wondering what I really wanted to do.

CHAPTER 7

COMPANY F, 179th Infantry Regiment (NGUS) was activated as a state unit in the fall of 1952. I accepted the job as unit administrator of the newly formed unit.

The unit administrator is a full-time job and the recipient is paid by his state, not the Federal government. Fort Sill, Oklahoma, leased a building to the state for the new Thunderbird unit in the World War II training area located on Sheridan and Craig roads.

Though I wouldn't admit it, I was happy to be back in uniform, and I proved it by the meticulous manner in which I wore my olive drab and khaki uniforms to work. After lining the oblong classroom and headquarters structure with wall lockers, desks, and orderly room equipment, I was ready for business.

File records of T-birds released from active duty were used to notify the veterans of their new assignment. Those combat veterans would form the nucleus of the new unit, and I was appointed first sergeant by the commander. The weekend warriors started their State Guard unit with 100 percent combat-experienced NCOs and officers. It was time to fill the line platoons with newbies. I planned to begin the recruiting close to home.

Joe Bob Craig, in addition to being my youngest brother, had been a popular high school track and football star at Lawton High School. He was now performing the same functions for Cameron Junior College, also in Lawton. Word of his decision to enlist somehow reached both schools, and recruiting of his fellow students took off.

The first weekend drill kept me and my warrant officer boss busy with paperwork and swearing-in ceremonies. High school and college recruits were lined up to take advantage of the good deal—each day of drill would compensate the new soldiers with a day's prorated Army pay—excellent compensation for three hours of military classes. The satisfaction for the unit administrator and first sergeant did not end with the recruiting success.

In the following months of preparation for summer camp of 1953, the reception of subjects at the drills was phenomenal. Weapons and wearing of the uniform received an unbelievable amount of interest. My perception of National Guard units would be forever formed from the effort and attitude of those young warriors. They insisted upon learning everything about their part-time profession. From these revelations came an axiom that would be espoused by the officers and NCOs of the new unit. "You learn by doing, you master by teaching."

By the time the summer camp rolled around, F Company was one of the larger units in the 45th Infantry Division of the Oklahoma National Guard. The second Fox Company was still in Korea and would not be deactivated until 1954. While the Foxes in Korea were thawing out from another bout with the most miserable weather in the world, Fort Hood, Texas, and a tent city awaited the stateside unit of the same name.

After three days of garrison life, the training shifted to the sandy, blackjack game–studded outskirts of Fort Hood. Saturday night found the young Thunderbirds and some of their brave cadre in Waco. The town wasn't ready for that and some of the troops apparently weren't either.

The partying weekend warriors gathered on the Waco courthouse lawn for their ride back to Hood at 2300 hours. Despite knowing that I had had enough beer for two men my size, I saw them off and taxied to the gin mills on the outskirts of the large Texas city. Around one o'clock in the morning, the party was over and I found myself at the wrong end of a club wielded by an offended bartender.

Shortly thereafter two deputy sheriffs roughly hustled me into the waiting patrol cruiser.

Back at the courthouse where it had all begun, I was escorted to the jail cells on the top floor. An older police officer told me to empty my pockets. When both hands were in my pockets at the same time, he pinned my arms and the two arresting officers did the rest. The beating was over in a few minutes and I was tossed in a cell.

Monday morning a captain from Fort Hood's military police escorted me back to camp and released me to Captain Hendricks, my CO. After a brief explanation, I cleaned up and went back to work and the rest of the week was busy and ended without further incidents. I was a long way from justifying my behavior not only to myself but also to my superiors. That my job lay in the balance worried me not. At the end of the two-week summer camp, I had no regrets about leaving Texas and the good times behind.

Still, I was not fired and went back to work the Monday after returning. But to prove that I had learned absolutely nothing from my recent experience, I proceeded with a repeat performance. This time, however, I was not prepared to stand idly by while the police administered a beating— and proved it.

The fight started in a bar in downtown Lawton after a customer objected to the language I used to the lady bartender. I had been living with the lady and objected to his interference so I told the entire bar to fall outside. To my complete surprise, about half of those present did so.

When I had them lined up in an orderly fashion, I faced my first adversary and was greeted by a blow that knocked me up against the plate glass window of the American Bar. I came away quickly from the falling glass and the riot was on. Although I was outnumbered a tad, help was on the way.

My youngest brother, Joe Bob, and a car full of the Cameron Junior College boxing team were cruising down the street. The police and the boxing team arrived on the scene at the same instant. My Army buddy Leland Keel and the adventurous crew parked the car and joined the melee. The real problem for the police now centered around the attempted arrest of one William Craig. Just as the Lawton Police had me in the cruiser, the National Champion boxing team struck a blow for freedom. I unassed the car and the riot continued. It was now a struggle between myself and the boxing team against the Lawton Police, the Highway Patrol, and Fort Sill's finest. Despite the odds, the street was jumping around many prone bodies, and the fun continued for about thirty minutes.

Finally, with the help of the Oklahoma Highway Patrol, my brother and I were thrown into jail. The next morning, Joe Bob was released. Not so his wayward brother. That afternoon, charged with four misdemeanors, I appeared before a judge and several policemen and was fined two hundred dollars.

Joe Bob floated a loan from our heartbroken mother and I was released on bond. But not for long. When we came out of the small jail into an alley, I kicked over a garbage can, spilling the contents into the asphalt street. An alert military policeman spied the thoughtless act and well ... this time I was arrested for damaging city property and placed in confinement. My cellmates chided me for my paucity of free time. Joe Bob dutifully went for my bail money. By this time, my mother was for disowning her oldest son, but I was again released on bond.

That same day, the chief of police and my mother had a long talk at the Malt Shop. The chief knew me pretty well, and he told my mother that he was afraid I was going to jail if I didn't change my ways. He knew that in the meantime I'd been fired from my job at the 45th National Guard armory. Mom pointed out that I wasn't even living at the house I'd bought for her and Joe Bob on the G.I. Bill. They ended up with the chief saying he'd ask Sheriff Ed Gartrell to talk to me.

Although the small bar was on Lawton's outskirts, the bartender knew who his customer was. Everyone who read the local rag knew who I was. Three laughing GIs entered the gin mill.

I glanced at the three and resumed chastising myself. *What the hell is wrong with me? No job, few friends that would own up to it. Where do I go from here, Lord? Why don't I go back in the Army like deep down I want to? Just because my friends will say I told you so? That's not much of a reason, I must say.* The phone broke up my soul searching.

I glanced at the barkeep and noted he was talking to someone but kept staring at me. "Is your name Bill Craig, mister? The sheriff wants to talk to you."

I moved to the telephone behind the bar. "Yeah, Ed. How are you?"

"Bill, I need to talk to you, like alone. I'm going to Geronimo on a business trip. I'll pick you up and we can talk on the way over and back. It shouldn't take us over an hour and I may need some help over there anyway."

I had to laugh despite myself. "You mean I'm gonna help the law for a change. That's a twist."

Sheriff Gartrell chuckled. "So I've heard. Yeah, you owe us. Be ready in five. We need to talk, Bill!"

"What's the call in Geronimo about, Sheriff?" Geronimo is small township in Comanche County located eleven miles from the county seat.

"It's a damn family squabble, as usual. They're the worst kind and I hate 'em. The forty-five-caliber pistol is in the glove compartment if you need it. I don't think you will, though. Let's talk about you for a spell."

"Go ahead, Ed. I need some talking to, I reckon."

"Ever since your folks split up about ten years ago, you've been an unhappy person. For two years the Army got you into a constructive frame of mind, but now you're heading for hell in a handbasket. You don't know the answers—hell, I don't think you know the questions!"

"I've been thinking the same thing, Sheriff. Carry on!"

"Bill, your problem is very simple. You don't like yourself and the aggressive behavior stems from that. Unless you come to grips with yourself, you'll very shortly self-destruct. You know that much, don't you?"

"There's something wrong, Ed, I know that. I shouldn't be getting into trouble and embarrassing myself and my folks."

"Bill. Let me explain the problem as I see it, and on the way back we'll talk solutions," said the graying older man. "You should be talking to your dad, though, not me."

"We're not close, Ed. He's still brooding about getting outta the Army."

"Some of this, I really never wanted to tell you but you won't tell yourself the problem, so I will." The sheriff of Comanche County glanced from the dirt road to me, but I stared straight ahead and said nothing.

"You were born with a harelip and cleft palate that have been repaired, and you look fine. The mustache you wear now covers the scar and many people can't even tell it. You were teased by the kids when you were young and you took it for a while, then you became like a little puppy. If you tease a puppy long enough, he grows into a mean, aggressive dog, and will fight back. About that time your folks split and remarried, and your security was lost.

"You went into the Army and were happy for a while because your companions took the place of your family. But you've regressed back to your childhood behavioral patterns. Well, here we are, cover my back but stay in the car."

The farmhouse was separated from the road by twenty-five yards. A car was parked in the driveway of the wooden home that had all lights glaring. The sheriff approached the car and ordered the young occupant out. While he lectured the driver—a thin, young man—the front door of the house opened. A slim, older man with a shotgun in his grasp stood observing the proceedings from the front porch.

Upon command, the younger man obediently got back into his vehicle and backed out of the driveway. Sheriff Ed Gartrell turned to talk to the father.

"It'll be okay, John. He won't be back tonight, but call

me if you have any more problems. Get some rest, those cows need milking bright and early."

On the way back to Lawton, Ed took up his saga where he had left off. "Everybody has problems, Bill, you're not an isolated case, you just approach yours differently. Your appearance isn't the problem. It's time for you to make up your mind about life and what you wanna do with it. What do you want to do, Bill?"

"I don't know, Sheriff, but I know I have to make up my mind. Now!"

"When you got off active duty, what rank were you?"

"A sergeant first class, E-6, Ed. Not bad for just two years."

"Why don't you reenlist, son? I think you have a future there. Go on back in the Army and don't worry about what your so-called friends say. It's your life at stake, not theirs. Whatta you think?"

"The Lord only knows I've thought about it, but I keep holdin' back for some damn reason. What about going back to college, Ed? Hell, I'm a second-semester junior with only a year and a half before I finish."

"School on the GI Bill wouldn't be a bad deal. Just be sure it's what you want. But the chief of police wants you outta town, like right now."

"I know; Mom told me. Tomorrow, I'm gone. I'll let you know what I decide and thank you very much, Sheriff Gartrell. I'll always remember your help. May God bless you and your wife."

I went over the details of my departure with my mother, down to the car payments and placing the house in her name. The last move was for tax purposes, if nothing else, as I would continue to make house payments. The 1950 Chevrolet was serviced and loaded and I was headed for Miami, Florida, that same afternoon. Whether school or the Army, I would take a while to make my decision. After the nonstop trip to the balmy state, I found a boarding house and slept for twenty-four hours.

The politicians who wrote the GI Bill had made sure that

the vets who fought to correct their mistakes could not afford to go to the University of Miami. Retiring to the boarding house and doing my math, I found my ambition to be financially unsound.

The Korean War GI Bill did not pay tuition, books, and fees as did the World War II bill. The allowance just wouldn't cover your room and board in addition to school expenses; unless you could sponge off of your parents or work part time, there was no way. But the facts did not deter me from enjoying a two-week vacation in Miami. With its many palm trees and beautiful lawns, Miami was never more gracious than in the late summer of 1953. I did manage to get turned down for a night watchman job because of my proposed full-time student status. Still, I stalled. After explaining to the house mother my inability to stay, I was traveling north with nothing on my mind and very little on my stomach.

Working for the railroad in Chicago for six months did fill my stomach but little else; loading and unloading boxcars gave me time to ponder a bleak future. One dark, bleak night after work, I suddenly ceased procrastinating and packed my meager belongings. A twenty-four-hour drive back to Lawton and a short talk with the recruiting sergeant was all that separated me from my second hitch in the United States Army.

On March 12, 1954, a veteran could not enlist in the Lawton recruiting station. I was told that I had to go to Fort Sill and I did just that and received a briefing from the recruiter. "The inactive National Guard time counts for pay purposes only. Because of your over-one-year break in service, for pay purposes you'll be enlisted as a corporal with over four years. After processing, your application for the 101st Airborne Division will be honored." I nodded as the recruiter rambled on.

"You'll take a physical, an IQ test, and jump school PT test. You should be on your way to Fort Campbell, Kentucky, in a month."

The month would deteriorate into four years.

CHAPTER 8

THE PHYSICAL at Fort Sill's Station Hospital went fine except for the dental exam. The dentist laid it on the line so that even a corporal could understand it.

"You need three front teeth pulled, and a partial plate in their stead. Fort Campbell doesn't have the dentists that we do here at Sill. Jump school will have to wait for a while."

Back at the post recruiter: "There's only one outfit on post in need of your job title, the 522d Infantry Battalion (Separate). That'll be your assignment until you can pass the airborne physical. Sorry!"

"That's an all-black unit. Hell, I'm not black. No thank you!"

"Yes," said the recruiter, "they *were* an all black unit. A white guy from Waco, Texas, was assigned there yesterday and you'll be the second white boy. In six months you should be gone, anyway. If not, the unit should be racially representative by that time." He grinned.

Corporals Bruce Roberts and William Craig were the first whites ever to serve in the 522d Infantry Battalion. In addition to carrying out menial post details, the mission of the battalion was to support the Field Artillery School.

Two white boys' inprocessing into their unit was as big a shock to the blacks as it was to me and Roberts. I was a step ahead of Roberts before the week was over, however. I received permission from the commander to live off-post because I owned a house in Lawton. Roberts was not over-joyed with that development, but he also had an advantage over his white-boy sidekick—while a military policeman in Europe, he had learned the language of his new associates.

At my first formation with the 522d's Pioneer and Ammunition Platoon, Master Sergeant Magee welcomed two newcomers. After the laudatory speech, I did not understand a word said for the rest of the formation.

Roberts folded over at the expression of bewilderment on my face. "Shit, how was I to know they spoke a foreign tongue?" I asked.

"Let's eat and I'll teach it to you. At least I know the lingo," Roberts said.

While we ate the worst chow I had ever eaten in the Army, Roberts proceeded to do just that. "In a month, you'll talk it like they do," said Roberts.

"That's what I'm afraid of. All I knew was 'motherfucker,' and that's a no-no in Oklahoma. Remember that, Bruce. Now I know how they must feel when they're shoved into an all-white outfit. Like damn outcasts."

The next two months in the black unit taught me and Roberts more than we ever wanted to know about segregation, integration, and civil rights. The lessons would never be lost on us Jim Crow white boys. Between trips to the dentist, I was also very aware of my surroundings. Less than a mile from where I was born, the Infantry billets were luxurious. Built by the WPA during the Depression era, the three-story stone buildings featured tile floors and all the modern conveniences.

To the south and rear of our billets was a forested area and across the street to their front was the post baseball diamond. To the north of the ball diamond was the officer's club. In the summer months of my youth, I had accepted handouts from the backdoor of the establishment from my mother, who had worked there as a waitress, as well as bacon rinds for crawdad fishing in Medicine Creek.

In my opinion, the personnel in the 522d Infantry were far below the standards of my Korean unit. Education was close to nonexistent. My squad leader gave a class one day and to the surprise of no one, not only spoke a foreign language but misspelled his name on the blackboard. The dress and military bearing of the black soldiers, however, equalled or surpassed that of their white counterparts in the Artillery. I liked this aspect of the assignment and became meticulous in dress in order to keep up. The advent of large, white First Sergeant Hill from Houston, Texas, changed the unit's point of view almost overnight. The chow became edible and discipline was unquestioned. The First Soldier was followed by Captain Eads, the former commander of H Company, 179th Infantry Regiment, in Korea. Roberts and I watched our status rise with each passing day.

Shit details always found the two white soldiers at the front of the line but we expected it. In private we often said, "We're the niggers, now." But white soldiers continued to integrate the 522d, and the situation for Roberts and me eased somewhat. Between details we ran the demolition portion of the infiltration course, which was a welcome relief after the menial work. The impressions for my partial dental prosthetic were sent to Fort Sam Houston, Texas, for processing. Fort Campbell and jump school should not be far off, I thought.

One day, I was called to the Hill, as the orderly room was now called, and ushered into the commander's office. Captain Eads told me that I would be promoted to sergeant (E-5) effective the first of the month, but the real purpose of the visit came shortly after that welcome news. Eads proceeded with a motivational speech about Officer Candidate School, Fort Sill's pride and joy.

Eads's friend had recently taken over the school, and I was assured of a slot in the next class if I would only apply. First Soldier Hill nodded his approval while I listened in dismay.

I didn't want to slight the captain, who had gone out of his way to accommodate a young sergeant. So I was diplomatic for a change. Even so, Hill and Eads were dumbfounded over the refusal.

"You can go to jump school after you finish," Hill said. "It will disrupt none of your career plans."

"I'm sorry," I said, finally getting it out in the open. "I'm not cut out to be an officer, Top. I want to be a first sergeant like yourself." The obvious flattery saved me from further sales pitches. This episode was apparently over but fate was not to deal me the hand I desired.

The phone rang in the small three-bedroom house located in southwest Lawton. I cursed before placing the half-shined boot on the floor and answering. My brother Joe Bob chimed in immediately.

"I'm at a gin mill at Second and Bell, drinking beer. How about a ride home, Bill?"

"It's almost eleven and I have to work tomorrow, you dumbass. Hold what you have, and I'll be there in ten."

Arriving as promised, I entered the noisy den of iniquity and refused all offers of 3.2 Oklahoma beer. Joe Bob made his farewells, then insisted on driving the Chevy home. I wanted to get back to the house ASAP and gave in. Only a block away from our departure station, it happened. The Line of Duty and Misconduct Status would read as follows:

DD261 dated 25 July 1954, Craig, William, T. Corporal, RA 25700157 at 2318, 19 July 1954, while a passenger in a civilian vehicle which collided with another civilian vehicle at the intersection of Bell and 3rd street, Lawton, Oklahoma. Medical diagnosis: Multiple rib fractures, Multiple fractures left humerus, bilateral hempnema-thorax, Multiple lacerations and abrasions.
Remarks: Provisions of para 7a and/or SR 600-140-1 have been considered. Vehicle was owned by Cpl Craig, but at the time of the accident his brother was driving. Vehicle collided at intersection with another vehicle and Cpl Craig was thrown out of the vehicle sustaining the above mentioned injuries. As a result of the accident Cpl Craig could not remember any details of the accident, therefore an accurate interview was not possible.

II. Findings XXX. Line of duty not due to misconduct. Signed: Charles E. Baxter, 2nd Lt Inf 01879909.

Only a few yards from where I was born, I was not given a chance to live. The second night of my fight for life, the P&A Platoon stood vigil outside the hospital. Whether the all-night vigil and prayers did any good, I will never know; but when I did finally hear about it, I was deeply touched. Still, I fought the odds and lost ground.

Finally, after an enterprising old Army doctor used his surgical scissors to hook the rib that was puncturing my lung and tied it to the bed frame, I could begin a long comeback. My mother broke down and cried once again when I refused the last sacrament of the Catholic Church. My "I ain't going nowhere, Father," ended the request. I was right for a change.

For six months and three operations I remained at the Station Hospital. I began to move around after a bone graft and silver-plated humerus began to heal my left arm. When both broken shoulders healed, I was back in my unit in time for basketball season. First Sergeant Hill appointed me the athletic and recreation NCO of the by now almost all-white infantry battalion. The job got me through the winter and just before summer rolled around, I was again assigned to the P&A Platoon.

When the first sergeant went on leave, I also filled in on his job while the company E-7s continued to get over on the system. First sergeant was then an E-7 position because the E-8 and E-9 supergrades hadn't been instituted as yet. While logic dictated that I not take on all the unit's responsibility for the same pay as a platoon sergeant, I simply viewed the opportunity as good experience.

However, when I flunked my airborne physical again, this time because of my arm, I once again considered becoming a civilian. The doctor buoyed my spirits somewhat. "In a year, you could have all the movement back in both shoulders as well as your arm. Work at it, it's just not going to be easy, though."

In the meantime, a flashy-blonde love affair was not going as I had intended either. While I was thinking of a casual romp in the hay she was planning something more permanent. I started thinking of faraway places. I initiated paperwork.

Just before my thirtieth birthday, I said farewell to the 522d Infantry, my folks, and the blonde. I went to Fort Myer, Virginia, to complete a ten-week Spanish-language course before setting sail from New York for the Canal Zone. I arrived at the School of the Americas, Fort Gulick, Panama Canal Zone, ten days later in April 1956.

The ship ride to Colon, port city on the Atlantic side of the Isthmus of Panama, was a picnic compared to the trip to Japan in 1952. An eight-hour layover in Puerto Rico to deliver Puerto Rican soldiers being discharged emptied the confinement facilities of the ship, making for a roomy, carefree trip the rest of way to the Canal Zone.

My first visit to the tropics opened my eyes as well as my pores. The steamy heat was oppressive, even to the Canal Zone homesteaders, and there were plenty of those to contend with. The brick-masonry barracks at Gulick, and elsewhere in the Zone, had a pipe running a few feet from the ceiling. There, with the aid of a long stick you hung your coat hangers and clothes. Footlockers were fitted in a floor stand with a place for boots and shoes also provided. The in-heat briefing emphasized the importance of keeping clothing and equipment off the floor or even near it for that matter. Mildew being what it is, newcomers only needed a few days to realize the practicality of the practice.

I was assigned to the engineer division of a school that taught officers and NCOs from South and Central American countries. I would teach demolitions under the able tutelage of a young Medal of Honor winner, Lieutenant Rodriguez. As we were both veterans of Korea, a rapport was quickly established. Although our relationship was close and trusting, it proved to be of short duration. I was impressed and amazed that Rodriguez never told me how he'd won the

Medal. Of course, I was quickly told by the clubhouse lawyers who infest every Army barracks.

The officer-in-charge of the division, Major Nono—not his real moniker—was another matter. The major had enough smarts to leave the Medal winner alone, but he could and would screw with Rodriguez's assistant. My attraction to Nono's secretary, Miss Tinga Ling, added nothing positive to the feelings the OIC and I had for each other. Miss Ling, of Chinese extraction but a Panamanian citizen, was a tall, lanky, twenty-five-year-old beauty. Her English was exquisite and the combination made the offices of the division a happier and brighter place to frequent.

My Spanish, especially written, was not as good as it should be. This gave me all the excuse I needed to lean on and talk to the major's secretary, who was quickly aware that I was the only single male in the division. I was not married but, thanks to Miss Ling, was getting younger every day. Despite Nono's sarcasm and the increased work load he heaped on Miss Ling, the affair was reaching the serious stage when an incident happened.

My night life had quieted down somewhat, thanks to my meager pay—$127 a month plus overseas pay—and lessons learned elsewhere. One Saturday morning as the summer of 1957 neared, Headquarters, School Division, had an in-ranks inspection. I easily won the sharpest-soldier award, and a number of us went to the nearby NCO club for a celebration.

While I was laughing and joking with the NCOs at the bar, Sergeant First Class Johnson—an old soldier like my father had been—was observing from a booth in the corner of the establishment. When I brushed off a mention of the award with a funny remark and easily changed the subject, Johnson was not amused. He ambled over. "Bill, I want to talk to you alone. Like right now."

My smile froze in place as I followed SFC Johnson to his hidden drinking place. After being seated, I took a drink of Balboa beer and waited patiently for his lecture.

"Bill, you're just short of amazing. You joke about being

the sharpest soldier in the unit when you should be braggin'
about it. You play yourself down, chase women, and drink
when you should be trying to make something outta yourself. What's your problem, anyway?"

"I enlisted for the airborne, Sergeant. After I got hurt at
Sill, I did kinda give up the ghost. I guess I'll never get
there."

"I figured that was your problem. You're feeling sorry
for yourself. Hell, your arm and shoulders are healing.
You'll pass the PT and physical next time—maybe you
could right now—but you have three years to do over here,
first. How much education do you have?"

"I'm a five-semester junior in college."

"Good," Johnson said. "How much education did your
father have, Bill?"

"Oh, about the fourth grade, I reckon. Get to the punch
line, dammit!"

"The day of an uneducated NCO corps is just about over.
You have to have an eighth-grade-level education now, and
the requirements will go higher. You have that part of it
whipped. What else are you doing to improve yourself? Not
a damn thing. Here's my advice. Start taking correspondence courses with the series-ten officer prep course as a
starter."

"I don't want to be an officer, dammit!"

"It's just a tool to better yourself. Forget about officers.
We need NCOs that they can't humble and treat like shit.
The officer corps has been the elite for too long. Stay with
your education for the rest of your life. You'll go far, I
promise."

I also promised, and finished the ten-series lessons as fast
or as slow as the U.S. mail could send them to the Canal
Zone.

I moved from the troop billets to the top floor of the two-
story engineer building. Being the only occupant on the
floor, it offered some after–duty-hours security, and I enjoyed
the privacy. My pet boa constrictor watched me do my

homework each weeknight. The pet snake was tolerated by the powers that be only because they were unaware of it.

Baby Boa had been rescued during one of my many forays into the jungles surrounding Fort Gulick. Some South American troops had killed Baby's twelve-foot mother in a moment of panic. The six children had scattered but Baby came to me and was rewarded with a new parent and a home as well. Both of us learned from our unusual relationship.

I had to go to the books to learn about the Boa's diet and living habits. Boa had to adjust to living on a concrete floor, taking a bath in his drinking water, and sleeping on a GI cot. Both of us made the transition without any life-threatening situations. But a Saturday night incident ended the relationship permanently in May 1957.

I had finished my rounds of gin mills in Colon and was heading for the bus stop to return to Gulick. Thinking of a good night's sleep, I was walking on a brick-surfaced street behind a line of drinking establishments. A back door to one of the bars was open and the interior lights dappled into the street.

A tall, well-built American had his arms on the swinging door and was observing my approach. Other U.S. soldiers came to the back entrance but returned to the bar, after a glance into the rear and mumbling something to the door hanger. "Why don't you use the main street like everyone else, soldier? Somebody looking for you?"

"Mind your own business, shitface. I can find my way home. If I need any help, I'll holler. Okay?"

The fellow moved into the alleyway and confronted me. "You've already hollered enough!"

I was also not prepared for the beautifully executed roundhouse that landed on my jaw. The blow sent me sprawling on the damp bricks. Before I could get comfortable, a well-aimed kick landed on the eight-inch scar of the plated humerus of my left arm. I was unable to suppress a scream but was fast to rise and my quick hands and boxing experience had the GI reeling shortly.

Although I continued to rearrange the man's face, I couldn't floor him. The fight came to an end in a very military fashion when someone called "The MPs are on the way" from the exit end of the bar. The aggressor hauled his bloody face back where it came from and I moved to the bus stop.

The next morning I drove to the Army hospital's emergency room. Both my hands were X-rayed and then put in casts. On my return trip to Gulick, a bus passed and a smiling bandaged face waved. I waved one of my casts at the happy soldier. "At least he don't hold a grudge," I thought.

Since hands in casts are not suitable for rowing small boats, Lieutenant Rodriguez had a transportation problem getting to the small island that served as a demolition training area. So he loaded the vehicle, told me to board, and he did the rowing. His gracious attitude made me feel worse about my predicament.

"I heard about your Saturday-night brawl, Bill. Some of my friends witnessed the affair. I know you were only defending yourself, but when Major Nono gets hold of it, Lord save us." He had my complete attention.

"Why should he get ahold of it, sir. Hell, 'I fell in the parking lot' was good enough for the doctor. He don't need to know what you know. Who was that asshole, anyway?"

"He's a young lieutenant at the Jungle Warfare Training Center at Fort Sherman, Bill. He accepts full responsibility for the affair but that won't keep down the uproar over the incident. Major Nono probably knows about it by now, so expect the worst. He's more worried about Miss Ling's virginity than he is about your ass. Expect some repercussions."

That afternoon at closing time, the school's engineer division NCOIC confirmed the lieutenant's suspicions. "Report to the major at 0800 hours, tomorrow. I don't know what it's all about. Dismissed!"

"Thanks, asshole," I murmured, leaving the office. I hoped I'd be able to count on Rodriguez and his CMH. I didn't appreciate how the NCO corps was taking up for its people; apparently right or wrong didn't make a difference. Not one to back off from aggravation, I went directly to Miss Ling's small cubicle.

"Hi, Bill. Been hearing about you all day."

"Ting-a-Ling, how about you and I going out to dinner, tonight? I'll meet your folks or whatever it takes."

After the shock passed, she said, "Bill, my folks are very particular whom I date, and when and where. I'd have to see them and get their permission. Maybe then we could do that. Okay?"

I went to the messhall in a pissed-off state of mind. Between bites of Army chow, my eyes stared into space while I pondered the significance of it all. Attempts by other NCOs to draw me into a conversation were not successful.

Hiding Baby Boa in my sweat-soaked fatigue jacket, I went to the jungle behind the barracks and released the snake, which had just finished his meal. The daily ritual lasted about thirty minutes. As Boa frolicked in his natural habitat, I stayed around to insure that no wildcats confronted him. When Boa returned to my feet, we went back to the billets to await our fate.

"Sergeant Craig reporting as ordered, sir." The tall, heavyset major returned the salute and ordered me to be seated. He swiveled from side to side behind the gray Army desk before he began. "It's been reported to me that you've been fighting with officers in Colon during your off-duty time, Sergeant." Nono glanced at the casts on my hands.

"My medical records will not bear out your facts, sir. But, yes, I defended myself Saturday night in Colon. The rank of a person dressed in civilian clothes was never a consideration when he attacked me."

Major Nono was not pleased. "Your conduct set a very bad example for the NCOs and enlisted personnel, Sergeant. This school did not profit by your hasty reactions to a bad situation."

"I was not trying to set an example, sir, just trying to stay alive. I did not know his rank or I would have run away." That was a lie, of course. "There is no official paperwork on the fight, so why not drop it, before the officer gets in trouble." I was trying to get the upper hand, but the ploy failed.

"I want you outta this division within a week, Sergeant. You have the next five days to find a home. The infantry brigade at Fort Kobbe on the Pacific side of the Isthmus has openings for your job title."

"Sir, I was assigned here by the Department of the Army. If they want me to move on, all they have to do is issue orders and I will comply. I've done nothing that I would not hesitate to do again. Why should I look for a new home? I like it here."

"If you haven't found a home in five days, I'll find you one, Sergeant. You're dismissed!"

I saluted and did an about-face. I found out more about myself than I had bargained for during the exchange. I had actually enjoyed the give-and-take. The officers corps had lost a "yes man" for the duration and six months.

A search of the infantry brigade at Fort Kobbe turned up several possible assignments—as well as an idea about the reception a rowdy Korean veteran was likely to get. Stopovers in the Kobbe NCO Club revealed a selection of jobs that would welcome my talents and leadership skills, and wearing the Combat Infantryman Badge on my khakis enhanced the possibility of an assignment with the ground forces of the Canal Zone. But after meeting with sergeants Silvernail and Krueger, I decided to pass on an Infantry assignment—Major Nono had reacted much faster than I had. His Army Engineer connections soon had me outta sight and outta mind. Friday at noon, I was handed orders transferring me to the 551st Topographic Survey Company at Fort Kobbe.

Saturday, I sadly released Baby Boa to his natural environment, packed my bags, and reported to my new unit. Given a room to myself, I was instructed by the charge of quarters to report to the first sergeant Monday morning. I unpacked my belongings in the two-story stucco building while eyeing the NCO Club that was just a football field away. At that point I was pleased with the arrangements.

Dance time found me at the Fort Clayton NCO open mess only twenty miles away, where two of my language-school NCO pals and their wives welcomed me to their table. Around midnight, one NCO complained that every time he danced with his wife, a black soldier attempted to cut in. In 1957, the hillbillys were not ready for the Equal Opportunity Program.

"Dance with me, Mrs. Gross," I said. "If he tries that again, I know a secret." Rum and coke has many more mind-altering possibilities than I was aware of. But Mrs. Gross accepted the ill-conceived plan and the fun was on.

The black soldier was my size at five foot ten and 150 pounds. He tapped me on the shoulder during the slow dance number. I responded at quick time. "Go away, black bo. Find your own shade to dance with!"

Mrs. Gross was moving back to her table when a left hand decked the black man. I was gloating when another black soldier hit me from the blind side, knocking my head into the stone building support. Blood begin to flow from a cut eyebrow. Now I faced two vengeful African-Americans. The doormen and bouncers had a ten-minute struggle before getting the miniriot stopped.

I drove back to Kobbe and had my eye stitched. Once again the medical slip read, "Fell in the parking lot."

CHAPTER 9

I ENTERED the orderly room Monday morning and was greeted by a grinning Specialist Fifth Class Bruce I. Luttrell. "Have a seat Eye, First Sergeant Davis will see you in a minute."

While going over the fun-filled weekend, Luttrell and I couldn't contain our laughter and it apparently got the first sergeant's attention. "Send him in," he bellowed, breaking up our party.

Davis draped the small swivel chair and glanced at his notes as I entered. Despite the white surgical gauze that graced my eyebrow, he liked what he saw. Large, at 225 pounds, six foot two inches, Davis had never been accused of being a choir boy. Even so, he had not okayed the transfer until he had checked the records. My Infantry background had impressed him, and the fact that Major Nono didn't like me didn't hurt my chances. And, like Davis, I had the CIB.

I was barely seated as he began his spiel. "The 551st Topo Company has the mission of establishing triangulation stations over the Isthmus of Panama and the Canal Zone. These stations enable the map makers to perfect the maps already in existence. Bench marks, or sea-level vertical distance, are our concerns also.

"For about a month you'll be trained here in the company area with theodolites and engineer transits, and in recording procedures. You'll then be moved to the field for your on-the-job training. Any questions so far, Sergeant?"

"No, First Sergeant," I replied.

"We have here in this unit a group of draftees and first termers, most of whom are college dropouts. They're above average in smarts and don't particularly care for the Army, or for that matter, authority. I need you to keep them in line and they need you to remind them that they're in the Army. Finally, you need them to teach you the basics of the map-making trade. I have three other NCOs who are old soldiers, but they're professional map makers and lack your type of experience. I expect you to be a positive influence on the young people. Can you handle that?"

"I hope so, Top, but with these sutures above my eye, I'm not off to a very good start."

The first sergeant grinned. "I never said I wanted an angel. In fact, I don't; an NCO will do. Want to tell me about your eye, and the reason Nono wanted you outta his hair?"

"Sure Top, why not? Topkicks always find out anyway," I replied. I gave him my version of the reasons I was seated in his office, careful to skirt around Miss Ling, of course.

"Bill, be diplomatic with the officer corps. They can ruin your career in an instant, regardless of your guilt or innocence. You were born in the Army, you should know that by now."

I nodded as Davis continued. "You were fighting with two off-duty military police at the club the other night. One of them was the welterweight champion of Panama. I'll see that they don't harass you, but don't drive your car off-post until I say it's okay. If their first soldier doesn't agree, I'll punch that bastard out—or worse, I'll tell him I'm gonna let you go out for the boxing team."

We both laughed, although I really didn't want to. The briefing was over.

I supervised the cleaning of the billets and policing of the outside area in addition to receiving my informal classroom instruction, keeping me busy for the next month. Classes on recording procedures and the T-2 Theodolite filled the steamy daylight hours. Before lights out at 2300, I generally had a few beers at the NCO Club where Bruce Luttrell, Les Silvernail, and I would settle the problems of the Army and the world over the only pastime we could afford. Punching out the jungle warfare officer had made me an instant hero with my new friends. Les Silvernail was a formidable sergeant first class at six foot seven inches and 230 pounds. The likeable giant was normally very quiet but would talk when he had something to say. And one night he had plenty to say about my attitude.

"Bill, you aren't too old to go to jump school. I graduated with a forty-year-old my own damn self at Fort Bragg. Be in good physical shape, and the age and maturity will help you through the constant petty shit they throw at you. That type of harassment causes some students to quit, but not anyone who wants it bad enough. I was in Special Forces when I was shipped down here and I thought it was—and is—the best unit in the Army. Damn hard to get into but damn well worth the effort. Think about that when you get outta jump school. You guys aren't married and that helps, because in Special Forces you're away on assignments constantly. I'm going back when I leave this sauna bath. Hope to see both of you." This conversation piece stayed with Luttrell and me for our entire tour in the Canal Zone.

After completing garrison training, I bid my friends farewell and began a two-year exile in the jungles and on the islands of the Republic of Panama. It would not be boring.

Panama stretches east and west for 400 miles, connecting South and Central America. It varies from 30 to 120 miles in width, and is bathed by the Caribbean Sea on the north and the Pacific Ocean on the south. The troops therefore watch the sun rise over the Pacific and set in the Atlantic. Although Colon and Panama City, near Fort Kobbe, house more than half of the two million Panamanians, there is a frontier to the republic—one sparsely populated, mostly by Indians. The frontier embraces the dense rain forest of Darien Province in the east and thick forests that blanket the Atlantic coast between Colombia and Costa Rica.

During the first month of 1957, the topographic survey company sent me and a six-man crew to the east coast of

Panama for our first adventure. Just off the coastline of
Camarca de San Blas lay the many small San Blas Islands.
More than 150 of these 300 islands are home to the Carca
Indians.

At that time, the messhalls of the United States Armed
Forces in Panama hired, almost exclusively, San Blas Indians as kitchen help. I was told that unlike the majority of
the ethnic groups of Panama, the San Blas tribe had not
mixed with former West Indian slaves or with Europeans. If
these gentle, kind people have a fault, it's intrafamily
mating—fathers siring children by their daughters and so
on. The many albino kitchen police are good indicators of
these relationships. The albinos were unable to live in the
bright sun and seldom ventured outdoors in daylight hours.
Their pink eyes and white skin just wouldn't stand up to
the damage under the tropical sun.

Specialist Fourth Class Eugene L. Dahlman and I were
selected to leave base camp at Ailegande by boat and be
dropped off at a very small, remote island twenty miles
from base camp. The target island was so small that one
family of Indians was a basic load for the sandy, palm-tree-
studded diamond. We were to establish a tide gauge there
and read it every hour on the hour for seven days and
nights. Ten days of field rations would see us through the
ordeal.

After pitching our only pup tent, we set up our gauge at
the edge of the small piece of land. Our tent was stationed
very close to the two or three bamboo huts that were home
to the twelve inhabitants of the island.

Each morning the brown-skinned males would depart in
their canoelike craft for fishing and marketing on the mainland. It would often be days before many of them returned.
This gave us an opportunity to eye the ladies left behind.
To our surprise, the ladies were making more observations
than we were.

Dahlman's Nordic-blond hair and my Scotch-Irish
reddish-brown hair attracted the most attention. Although
the small-boned Indians were not interesting to Dahlman

and me, they seemed very attracted to us. To prevent unwanted attention, Dahlman and I learned to stay out of sight.

One dark night while the native males were absent, we were resting in a vacant shack when a large sea turtle invaded the island. It was so large that the ladies and children could not handle it alone and came for help. With no warning, a very old woman rushed into the shack and pulled the blanket off me as I lay naked, sleeping.

I leaped up and started grabbing for my clothes while the great-great-grandmother openly stared at my nakedness. Mumbling profanity, I finally got my pants on and helped rope and corral the dinner, breakfast, and supper from the beach.

Later, while we awaited our landing craft for the ride to the mainland, I commented to Dahlman. "I've learned three things out here, anyway, Dahlman. One, that story about white men never having stayed overnight on a San Blas Island is bullshit. Two, their women are never too old to want to make love and cause waves. And three, that would be a piss-poor reason to die!"

The tide-gauge information was soon on its way to Fort Kobbe and another bench mark was available for the map makers of Central and South America.

We arrived at base camp in time to help the small crew of GIs eat a sea turtle they had purchased from an enterprising native. I was hesitant, but after ten days of C rations, found myself easily persuaded. To my disbelief, it turned out to be the best meal that I had ever eaten. I made a mental note that the next sea turtle that I had to Tom Mix would be my own.

Dahlman and I lollygagged around the small base camp for three days before our next assignment. We would fly to another island that afforded a small airstrip and set up and shoot reciprocal vertical and horizontal angles with two triangulation stations on the mainland. A piece of cake and my first airplane crash.

The small, two-engine Otter took off as I watched the

very nervous captain who was flying it. We were airborne only a few minutes when the aircraft made a pass at the small landing strip on the sea-level island. Dahlman and I noted the three-foot-high dam that guarded the approach. Dahlman also noted that the pilot had spied the dam and was chattering about it to his copilot. "If you can't land it, let me and the sergeant try it, you gutless bastard," was only one of Dahlman's helpful comments.

Despite Dahlman's generous offer, we didn't make it. The front landing gear scraped the wall and the aircraft pancaked on one strut and spun on down the runway. Dahlman and I gritted our teeth and prayed a lot. One of Dahlman's prayers was apparently not addressed to God— "You gutless sonofabitch! If you're afraid of your profession, get the hell out and into another line of work."

The spinning top came to rest at the end of the small island and airstrip. The pilot had succeeded in wrecking an Army plane with no explosion or loss of life. That was some consolation, but tempers continued to flare while we unloaded our surveying equipment. Grinning locals were also admiring the Americans' discomfort, but a couple of them found time to help unload the aircraft.

At dusk a helicopter came for the pilots and a passenger presented me with a message from the American Red Cross. It was obvious that the Sergeant First Class Anslin from the topo unit knew the contents but he waited until I had finished reading the leaflet before commenting.

We regret to inform you that your Father, Roamey T. Craig, died of cardiac failure on Jan 8, 1958 at Ft. Sill Okla Station Hospital. He will be buried Jan 11, 1958 at Ft. Sill, Okla Post Cemetery. Your presence is requested by the family.

"The old man said to bring you back on the aircraft if you wanted to attend the funeral."

"Sergeant Anslin, you and the old man didn't read the damn thing too well. Hell, he was buried three days ago.

Do I want to go home? What the hell for? No! Tell the American Red Cross someone goofed. See you around."

We moved to our triangular marker, set up our instruments, and exchanged shots with two other stations before retiring for the evening.

In the privacy of my jungle hammock that night I pondered my recent loss. Technician Fourth Class Craig had served twenty-seven years and fifteen days before retiring. He had lived twelve years after that. I pondered Dad's lack of education, our relationship and conversations. After an hour of mental gymnastics, I broke down and sobbed for the first time. I thought that I should have been there, at least I owed him that much. "Fucking Army! You bastards ain't gonna treat me like you did him and his family." I unconsciously aimed my rifle at the Army's caste system. The trigger would stay cocked and ready for the next eighteen years and would provide some entertaining moments in various parts of the world.

About then our small survey crew moved back to Fort Kobbe for a two-week break. We were given physical examinations, and time to clean our gear and take care of personal matters. After I remitted my car payment to the States, Silvernail, Luttrell, and I wore out the NCO club for several nights before embarking to Panama City. The bright lights, alcohol, and ladies of the night soon had this soldier ready to move back into the boonies—a trip that would complete my tour in Panama and the Canal Zone.

Kobbe's NCO club was filled with soldiers from different units on the night before the topo platoon's departure. Luttrell, Silvernail, and I occupied a booth on the side of the large barroom. In the adjoining ballroom, a Jamaican band blared. I was openly admiring the slender, beautiful Jamaican waitress named Marie when Silvernail jolted me out of my reverie. "Get your mind off women for a few minutes and tell us how you're doing on your pullups, pushups, and situps. It won't be long before your airborne physical and physical training test, you know."

"I'm still having trouble with pullups, Les. That damn

left arm doesn't seem to want to come around. When I get to base camp in Almirante, I'm going to be lifting weights for that arm. Pushups and situps I can do all day. I should be ready when I get back."

"You'd better get with it, boy," Silvernail said. "Jump school waits for no man."

"I'll be ready. You coming with me, Bruce?"

"Yeah, Bill, I'll be right behind you but I'm not buying Fort Campbell. Fort Bragg's for me. I always wanted to be in the Eighty-second All American Division and here's my chance."

"I was given a choice in the matter, Bruce. I volunteered for the 101st at Fort Campbell, and that's what I got," I said.

"We'll all end up in Special Forces at Fort Bragg. Bet on it," said Silvernail, eyeing yours truly.

At that time the topo platoon occupied a tent city just outside Almirante, in the heart of the Republic of Panama. The GI camp was composed of a squad-tent messhall, headquarters tent, and a supply tent. Living quarters consisted of three more squad tents that formed the squared, fenced-in compound. My survey squad did not have much time to enjoy our new surroundings; we were flown south from the province of Bocas del Torro in northern Panama to the infamous Coiba Island shortly after arrival.

Like other island penitentiaries such as Devil's Island and Alcatraz, the penal institution on Coiba Island houses the violent and political criminals of Panama, where they are guarded by the Panamanian National Guard. Escape just didn't occur—"If we don't get them," the commander said, "the sharks will."

The topo troops used the convicts for labor during our short stay. We learned from the inmates that the island had three different camps: for murderers, for homosexuals, and for political prisoners. We used only political prisoners and murderers for labor, but managed to visit each camp during our three weeks of exile.

We entertained the guards and prisoners by showing

movies in each camp, and the prisoners appreciated the attention. Number one on the Coiba hit parade was easily *Red River* starring John Wayne. It made me kinda homesick my own damn self.

In addition to raising their own crops, the prisoners picked bananas and coconuts to export for the greedy commander. The doomed men opened their minds and hearts through their mouths to the very few people who would ever leave the island.

"There have been two U.S. prisoners that I know of on this island, amigo. They were both convicted of murdering a Panamanian. Neither lasted two years.

"One was killed by guards as he tried to hide on an aircraft at the landing strip you came in on. The other built a raft and died at sea. He came about as close to escaping as anyone else has. The sad part was that they were abandoned by their own country. There is no escape, amigos."

The conversation came about as close to describing available leisure pastimes on Coiba as anything I can think of. Needless to say, the movies were therefore out of this world to those men and women. My topo squad was not saddened when we had to leave for the base camp in Almirante.

When we were not climbing the wet, steep mountains near the Costa Rican border, we would frequent Almirante's three or four bars. Here I managed to meet a West Indian named Winston Brown and we quickly became close friends. Brown, of Jamaican descent, challenged us GIs to a softball game. I accepted the challenge and recruited my club. The game filled the small Almirante ball park, which had been constructed by the United Fruit Company.

My pitching was not enough to put the GIs in the win column but it kept the results in doubt until the final moments. The entire community and the American soldiers became closer because of the contest. That night Winston Brown told us that he was a professional baseball player who would be pitching for the Dallas team of the Texas

League the following year. And he invited us to watch him play there.

We all found this very surprising. I said I'd try because I'd be home in June and then go on to Fort Campbell for jump school. "The best of luck to you, babe. I wish I was that talented in baseball."

"You don't do that bad, just need some practice, Bill. I'll get homesick in Dallas—come see me."

The last two weeks in Almirante served to remind me that I was still at war with my profession. By that time all NCOs but myself had flown to Kobbe, leaving me in charge. When they returned, the platoon safe was, according to the platoon sergeant, short $128. I did not sweat the small shit because I did not have the combination to the safe. Regardless, the investigation by a second lieutenant came to the conclusion that I was at fault.

I screamed to high heaven. "I didn't have the combination. How in the hell could I have taken anything?" A little thing like facts or proof made no difference to the blame-someone board of officers. The $128 would be deducted from my $135-a-month pay.

My last week at camp, I took a crew of hired locals to clear a hill near base camp. At the conclusion of the chore, I pocketed my $128 from Class B funds allotted to pay the help (one of the laborers gladly signed the receipt). I had decided that if I couldn't win, I was damn sure I wasn't going to do worse than break even.

First Sergeant Davis and Luttrell helped process the paperwork when I passed the physical exam and airborne PT test. My arm, plate and all, managed six pullups. A very happy soldier signed the papers that promised eighteen months of jump status if I survived jump school at Fort Campbell, Kentucky, and an assignment to the famous 101st Airborne Division. My secondary military occupational specialty (MOS) of combat engineer earned me a place in the 101st's 326th Combat Engineer Battalion.

A plane ride Stateside and a thirty-day leave found me at

a gravesite at Fort Sill's Post Cemetery. On my knees, I said a prayer to God before speaking to my father.

"Sorry I couldn't be here at the end, Dad. I was thinking about you, though. I know you wanted me to be an officer, but I just don't agree. I'll make you proud before it's over, just you wait and see. Stay with me. I may need your help from time to time. Bye, now."

I saluted the gravesite of the veteran of both world wars and walked slowly back to my transportation.

CHAPTER 10

I WAS thirty-two when I left Lawton on or about the sultry day of June 2, 1959. Thanks to my Panamanian exile of two and a half years, I drove a paid-for 1956 Ford convertible to Memphis, Tennessee. Exiting to Highway 79, I never dreamed of stopping for a night's rest.

Clarksville, Tennessee, brackets Fort Campbell on the south and Hopkinsville, Kentucky, sandwiches the military reservation on the north. Departing State Highway 41 had me at the main gate of the home of the Screaming Eagles the very next day.

At the replacement company, I wasted little time making my bunk and occupying it until roll call the next morning. The red tape of in-processing took only three days to unwind, allowing me to report to Company B, 326th Engineer Battalion, across the street from jump school.

A short, overweight first sergeant handed the paperwork to his clerk before the interview. Both of us were dressed in khaki uniforms, but there was still a difference: The first soldier wore his jump boots bloused; I wore low quarters. I consoled myself with the fact that I wore the CIB—the first sergeant didn't and probably never would.

The top soldier broke up the mutual inspection tour and started the conversation off just as I thought he would.

"You're a little old to be going to jump school, aren't you, Sarge?"

"Yes, Top. I had some bad luck a few years back that delayed the deal somewhat. I'll do okay!"

"Okay, Sergeant Craig. You stand formation and do PT

with the 1st Platoon. After completion of details each morning, you're on your own to work out. We have a gym here on post, class fifty-six will start ten days from now. For that period you'll be assigned to jump school. Good luck."

I did not meet the company commander, but I noticed that he was not in his office. I toured the post for the rest of the day. Fort Campbell reminded me of Camp Polk in 1950—few permanent buildings and very little housing for enlisted married personnel. I had a hard time relating it to Fort Sill and the Canal Zone, what with their stone, brick, and masonry structures. *This is the home of a Strategic Army Command unit in the U.S. Army? Makes you wonder,* I thought. In 1959 STRAC units in the Army were alert units, ready to move on a moment's notice to any hot spot. However, the barracks were comfortable and the food was out of this world. Just a few days of wallowing in food convinced me that it was STRAC, Jack.

Despite sitting at the NCO table in the battalion mess, I was befriended by no one. The silent treatment came to a head one day in the chow line.

"What part of the fried chicken do you want, Sarge?" the cook asked.

"The leg." I grinned. "Leg" is a derogatory term for non-Airborne personnel—which is what I was and why I hadn't been making any new friends. I hadn't proved myself yet. Anyway, the specialist fifth class clerk standing behind me apparently couldn't resist the chance to make an amusing remark.

I said quietly, "Listen up, fat boy. I'm a leg but I can and will whip ten fat bastards like you any time, any place, and anyhow. Take it to the bank, fatass!"

The flushed soldier did not reply. Any thought of laughing and joking with me went by the boards that day in the 326th Engineer Battalion.

Leg or no, I was awakened by the charge of quarters of B Company the Saturday before jump school began. I sported an Airborne haircut, no mustache when I went to early chow that day. In other words, I looked like a victim of the Indian Wars.

To the surprise of no one, the jump school cadre administered another airborne PT test to the students before issuing student numbers and platoon assignments. The test was nothing like the other three the students had been subjected to. This leg sergeant learned many things that day in 1959 under the hot Kentucky sky.

In only ten minutes at my first station—pushups—I knew who would not pass, regardless of physical strength. The thoughtless soldiers not clean-shaven, with belt buckles and boots not shined; Displaced Persons who spoke little English; those with holes in their T-shirts—those people were all gone.

Elimination was a simple affair. The instructor would single out people destined not to graduate and simply not count their repetitions (for being "incorrect"), so they'd have to repeat them. After five hundred incorrect pushups, even Superman would be unable to pass the requirements. Four pullups, thirty-two situps, twenty-two pushups, and the one-mile run in under eight minutes trimmed Class 56 down from 500 would-be paratroopers to 404 just before high noon.

The class learned that military bearing would count as much as stamina and intestinal fortitude. The cadre were all NCOs who demanded—and received—respect from every student regardless of rank. A daily inspection in ranks by your cadre platoon sergeant was routine. He would look critically at haircuts, shaves, starched fatigues, belt buckles, boots, and military decorum.

At the conclusion of the first day's test, the survivors formed the student company. The student commander, Colonel J. Collins, stood at parade rest as the school sergeant major approached his location.

The six foot four, 220 pounds of lean, mean Polish-American stared at the middle-aged, smallish officer. "Sir," said the sergeant major, causing Collins to come to attention and slap his arms and hands against his sides. "You look just like shit, sir."

"Yes, Sergeant Major," was his only defense.

Number 173 of the 3d Platoon almost laughed aloud. Only the close proximity of a cadre NCO prevented my indiscretion.

The ranking EM called Class 56 to attention and turned it over to the jump school commander, Captain Vranish, who informed us of the schedule covering our three-week assignment to the school, which would start Monday morning.

"Inspection in ranks at 0700, PT at 0730, and classes begin at 0800. You'll be formed in your present formation and dismissed at 1600. No walking in the school area by anyone, double time at all times. Each platoon is assigned one of the C-130 cargo aircraft mockups to your rear for breaks. Pushups will be administered for any violation of performance standards or regulations."

I, number 173, glanced at my cadre platoon sergeant, Sergeant Marple. I stared at his clean-shaven neck for the rest of the speech. The tone of voice and demeanor of the much younger sergeant during the PT test had alerted 173 that not all personnel necessarily wished to indulge me in the fulfillment of my dreams. We would meet under different circumstances in different locations. However, because of jump school, it would take two or three years for us to become friends.

Sunday night, the students checked fatigues and T-shirts and shined their boots before retiring. I had a light beard and therefore usually shaved the night before. I pondered the scar in the middle of my lip and vowed that when jump school was over I would never shave off my cosmetic mustache again, Army or no Army. This is the procedure for turning dreams and vows into prefabricated untruths. In June 1959, Monday came too quickly for Class 56.

Students in fatigues with bloused boots double-timed into the school area. Helmets fastened down with the Airborne chin strap, we went directly to our break area. I was surprised to find Colonel Collins already in the mockup, and smoking with the troops, no less. Also to my surprise, the colonel spoke to me as I lit up. The fact that we all had a common enemy, the cadre, gave me the courage to speak my mind to the soon-to-be-general.

"Sir, you didn't have your fatigues cut down, that's why they just hang on you."

"I didn't know I had to, Sergeant. Do you think I should?"

"Sir," I drawled, "that's why the sergeant major said you looked like shit on Saturday, goddammit!" (careful to keep my voice low, of course).

"It'll be done this afternoon, Number 173, and thanks for the advice."

My mind whirled before the cadre whistles and loud-mouths broke up the smoke break. *Here I am giving advice to a full-bull colonel who should know better. The Green Machine is changing my outlook on the universe. What next?*

Next came the ritual of the daily in-ranks inspection. I did not receive a personal demerit, or "gig" during the ordeal, nor would I during the entire course. Many of the students, new officers fresh out of Officer Candidate School or enlisted men just out of advanced individual training, did not fare as well. As for myself, it was important not to have to knock out pushups before the physical training started; at my age, that could be detrimental to my health and welfare.

Physical training started slowly the first day but increased in intensity with each session. The last Saturday of ground training it culminated in a five-mile run.

The third day and the jump tower increased the dropout rate of Class 56 dramatically. The tower is a boxlike structure thirty-four feet from Mother Earth that simulates an aircraft door. A cable runs from in front of the door of the tower to the ground. The trainee's harness is hooked to the cable by a static line just before he makes a vigorous exit out the door in a jump attitude, i.e., head down, both hands on the side of the reserve chute, and feet and legs together.

In real life, that position will keep the prop blast from throwing the jumper around.

After counting one thousand, two thousand, three thousand, four thousand, you look up to simulate checking your parachute canopy, only to find yourself sliding down the cable to the ground below. This simulated aircraft exit still washes out more would-be paratroopers than any other single factor. Many people refuse to go out the door, period. You have to make a minimum of five satisfactory exits to be qualified for the real thing, and it was a daily class for all.

By the end of the first week, I was jump tower–qualified and spent my class time observing or running the unhooked cable back to the tower. Many students never made it at all. On the first day of this thirty-four-foot drill, I met more people coming down than I did climbing the stairway to heaven.

It was on this very day that the colonel pulled another, "I don't know the enlisted" maneuver. While the class was taking a smoke break in the mockup and berating the cadre, Collins lit up and handed me his cigarettes. I already had one lit so I passed them on to the platoon. The pack never came back, of course. I had to warn the colonel to stop trying to be one of the boys because he'd be taken advantage of. He'd have to be himself.

Saturday before jump week, the five-mile run proved to be an insurmountable obstacle for many, and for some it was their last opportunity to quit before their first jump in flight from an aircraft. A few took advantage of it, but most did not. I was certainly having my problems with it, and the cadre were not helping the situation a helluva lot. The pace was slow, then speeded up, then slow and exhausting, the idea being to run for the entire fifty minutes allotted. Regardless of rank, students helped each other to survive by dragging or holding up the faltering. I received no assistance but Sergeant Marple did burden me verbally. "You ain't gonna make it, one-seven-three. No guts, one-seven-three, drop out, quitter."

It would take me five years to forgive Marple for those remarks, but I finished the run. All that was left was exiting a C-130 cargo aircraft five times in the coming week.

When the survivors finally reached the C-130, many of them were in an aircraft for the very first time. We had one thing in common—none of us would land in the damn thing. My mind was churning as usual.

The cargo aircraft was 1,250 feet above terra firma. The four props roared in unison, creating a powerful prop blast for the C-130's scared cargo. Both doors were open and gave us newbies a ton of noise to contend with. When the first command came from the cadre jumpmaster, my mind went into the deep freeze. Using hand and arm signals in addition to his loud mouth, the jumpmaster gave his command to stand up. After the big, bad paratroopers complied, he gave his second command. I was thirteenth man in the stick and eyed the door as I hooked up my static line. *You gotta be a dumbass to be doing this,* number *one-seven-three,* I thought.

"Check your equipment!" was the third command.

I've checked it forty times, you dumb shit. But we all complied without hesitation.

"Sound off for equipment check!"

"Number twelve, okay. Number thirteen, okay." *Number thirteen? Hell, I'm gonna die.* I knew it, why else would I be number thirteen? *It's the end of the line for me.*

"Stand in the door!"

Hell, how can all of us get in the door. Let's get this over with. At least, I'll make my own funeral.

When the light on the side of the door turned green, the man standing in the door was slapped on the butt by the jumpmaster. "Go!" *That's a legal order, soldier.*

The stick shuffled forward and I knew I couldn't stop or I would be stomped to death. My mind froze a tad again after I exited the aircraft. The next thing I knew, I heard voices from the ground that sounded familiar. The cadre's profane instructions brought my mind back to my predicament. I checked my chute and grinned, then looked at the fast-approaching drop zone and the smile faded. I hit the ground hard, recovered, and collapsed my chute. I was laughing with joy as I turned in my first jumped parachute and noted that only one or two of my classmates had been carted off by an ambulance. That only made me feel happier, to be among the living and uninjured. "I can do it! I can do it!" I shouted.

The day of the fifth and last qualifying jump, General William Westmoreland handed each enlisted paratrooper a check for 55 big ones, $110 for the officers. The division commander also shook the hand of each of the 297 soldiers who had completed the trying course. It was the first time I had ever met the future Chief of Staff of the United States Army and I was very impressed, especially with the military bearing "Chesty" displayed to the four NCOs of Class 56. I had finally met the former commander of the 187th RCT of the Korean War days.

In the 101st Airborne Division, NCOs and officers who finished jump school were automatically enrolled in the jumpmaster school upon graduation. The first sergeant gave me my orders and briefing. "Do not take this program lightly! The flunk-out rate is well over fifty percent. In fact, the 326th Engineers has not had an individual successfully complete the course in the last eight months."

I was astounded. "Why such a dropout rate, Top?"

"You must 'rigger-check' each jumper before he enplanes. It's the most important job a jumpmaster has. If the chute is not on correctly, and if the static line is misrouted, a casualty could result. To make it short, if you can't rigger-check, you can't pass that course, nor can you be a jumpmaster in this outfit. If you have one major malfunction on your final test, you're out. So pay attention."

The briefing alerted me so I worked hard on checking proper fitting and wearing of the parachute once the course began. The night jump and equipment jumps came off without incident. The final performance test allowed the student two minutes to rigger-check three individuals. I was nervous as a prostitute in the front pew but passed the tough exam;

60 percent of the class did not. A very proud NCO, I came back to my unit at the end of the course jumpmaster-qualified—and with a total of only eight jumps; but something else very important had taken place during the course. The few who survived the course now had confidence in jumping; the fear of it had all but been eliminated.

Across the street from the jump school area, Company B, 326th Engineer Battalion, had a new squad leader in the second squad of the 1st Platoon. At thirty-two years young, I was the third-oldest person in the unit. My second squad had a twenty-one-year-old assistant and ten teenage Airborne soldiers.

The physical training formation on the first day of duty in my unit opened my eyes. Personnel who lived off-post—that included all officers, platoon sergeants, and most other NCOs—were conspicuous by their absence. Though astounded, I marched my people to police the assigned area, took PT, then went to breakfast.

The work formation at 0730 opened my eyes even wider. My platoon sergeant, a veteran of the Battle of the Bulge, took the report, assigned the work details, and we saw him no more the rest of the day. The assistant platoon sergeant braced me in the meantime. "Did you police around the boxing ring this morning?"

"Yes, Sergeant, but that was two hours ago."

"It looks like shit, do it again!"

"I said that was two hours ago while you married people were still in the rack at home," I said, slowly.

The red-faced NCO said, "Do it again, and do it right this time."

The word streaked around the unit that the new sergeant didn't go along with the status quo. I became the enemy to the off-post personnel and a hero to my young squad of barracks-bound Airborne soldiers.

The next afternoon I went to my room to prepare for supper and was greeted by NCOs lined up by the orderly room to look at the bulletin board. "What's the problem?" I asked.

"The damn duty roster isn't up yet. We're waiting to see who's on kitchen police and charge of quarters tonight and tomorrow," said one anxious NCO. "The first sergeant's wife does the duty roster and I guess she's late."

"I don't believe this shit," I said, walking away. Three more days passed before I met the commander of this STRAC unit, ("A Commander is responsible for what his troops do, and for what his troops do not do").

The captain took the formation from the first soldier and grinned strangely. It did not go unnoticed that the first sergeant moved back to the billets.

The company, less the married personnel, was given a right face. "I'm gonna show you some real PT, now," the captain said. He did. Eleven miles later, the unit was scattered all over Fort Campbell and half the state of Tennessee. The NCOs who made it were few. Fresh out of jump school, I survived; most of the company did not. At least I met the stupid sonofabitch.

While cleaning up for chow, I noticed that my feet were bleeding from the marathon. When the married personnel came in for work formation, I asked to talk to the platoon sergeant and was granted an audience by the gracious Czech expatriate.

"Vot is the problems?" opened the Displaced Person veteran.

"The problem," I said, "is that we have a morale problem. That fucked-up CO didn't help matters much this morning. Physical training is not supposed to be an endurance contest, it's a conditioning drill. I don't care how bad he thinks he is, he ought to be jailed for that performance; he screwed up the unit."

The platoon sergeant was momentarily aghast but finally grinned. "Yes, he's a tough old bird. If you can't take it, just quit!"

It was my time to get steamed up. "Goddamn it, Platoon Sergeant, I was there. Where were you? Home with Mama?"

"I am taking you to the first sergeant, Sergeant!"

When I faced the paunchy old soldier, First Sergeant Homes was red-faced also. "For a new man, you're making a lot of waves. I'm like your platoon sergeant—if you can't stand the heat, get outta the kitchen."

"First Sergeant, my leaving is not going to solve your problems. Why do married people have different hours from us barrack rats? Why do we have to wait in line to see who's on charge of quarters? Who is the commander? I've seen him once in three weeks and then he had my squad scattered all over this fucked-up place."

"Would you like to talk to the CO, Sergeant?" asked the Top.

"That's up to you, Top. I'll only repeat the questions I've asked you."

The next day, I no longer had a room by myself. The black soldier sported sergeant first class E-6 stripes and stood a slim six foot three inches in his stocking feet. Sergeant First Class Mcalvey spoke in a soft, lilting voice. "Hi, Sergeant Craig, I'm your new roommate. The first soldier has warned me about you, so go ahead and tell me what's on your mind."

"Sit down, Mac, and tell me what the fat bastard said."

"He said that you were a troublemaker and from a Jim Crow state, therefore, you wouldn't like me 'cause I'm a 'nigger,' as you white boys say." Mac was still grinning as he seated himself and waited for a response.

"Mac, I'm glad to know you. I hate to pass my troubles on to you but I have no choice, I reckon. What was your last assignment, and what's your job here?"

"I'm in from West Germany, and I have the third squad of the Third Platoon."

"Welcome to the most screwed-up unit in STRAC. First of all, I've served with more blacks than the topkick's ever seen. I was a white boy in an all-black infantry battalion. *Sooo*, he's full of shit. I have never had a black as a roommate, however, so we both should learn something. I don't call blacks 'niggers' unless they call me 'redneck' or 'whitey.' The first sergeant is trying to piss me off again. You and I have too much in common not to get along."

I went on to explain the unit sitcom. Mcalvey, being free, black, and single, understood where this white boy was coming from and we were instant friends.

A week later, the unit again faced the commander of Company B. Work formation was given open ranks and First Sergeant Homes followed Captain Cull for the unannounced inspection. Second squad received not a demerit, which seemed to anger the CO as well as his topkick. They approached me. I was still at rigid attention. The captain got right into my face just as I knew he would.

"Who told you you could wear that mustache, Sergeant?"

"No one, sir, only the regulations!"

Cull flushed. "It will be shaved off before the morning is out, Sergeant."

Homes noted the order on his clipboard before moving on. "Report to me after formation."

Again standing in the orderly room, I listened up to my superior. "He's a salty old bird, ain't he, Sergeant?"

"I wouldn't know, Top, I never see him but once a month." The remark got the job done.

An angry NCO raised his voice a tad. "He has his ways and he is the CO. Hair will be no longer than one half inch on top and no facial hair. That goes for your mustache, go shave it off! *Now!*"

"I will, Top, but his policies are against Army regulations. I'm gone." I meant it in more ways than one.

I told Mac my tale of woe before I saw my platoon sergeant for permission to visit A Company. First Sergeant Royal of Company A, 326th, listened intently to me, then told me to put in a 1049 for transfer, and that he'd tell the battalion command sergeant major that I was acceptable to A Company. The fat was in the fire.

The pentomic concept of the U.S. Army of that day trained squads to be deployed individually and to be able to fight and survive as small units on an atomic battlefield. The entire division was working on that premise as the C-130 approached the drop zone. As squad leader and jumpmaster, I stood 'em up and let my assistant, Sheets, bring up the rear of the stick. Once we were on the ground and assembled, I gave Sheets the azimuths for the overland trip to company headquarters. Sheets selected a pace man and the second squad was off to the races. To the disgust of the commander and first sergeant, who had trucked in, we were the first of the unit to complete the equipment drop and the compass course.

Homes gave the second squad its sleeping area and guard duties. I staggered the pup tents in a tactical manner only to be shot down by the first sergeant. "We don't do that in the Airborne. Line those tents up in a military manner!"

"Sorry, Top. I thought this was a tactical problem."

After ten days in the field, the tactical move back to Campbell proper was in good order. The platoon sergeant told the second squad that the umpires had rated them highest in the engineer battalion. All the young soldiers were elated at their performance rating. Cleaning and exchanging damaged field gear occupied the rest of the morning.

Sheets approached me at two that afternoon. "Sarge, they all have their equipment cleaned, including their bods. They sure want to go to the Post Exchange, though."

"Okay, young man. Let's inspect them now, and if they're okay, they can go."

I dismissed them at 1500 and was told immediately thereafter to report to the platoon sergeant at 1515 hours.

"Vere is your squad, Sergeant?"

"I gave them the rest of the day off, Platoon Sergeant, for a job well done."

"Did you check with me, first?"

"No. If I can jump 'em into an area and take care of 'em for ten days without any help, I figured I could give 'em two hours off."

The platoon sergeant disagreed. "You will check with me first, Sergeant Craig."

* * *

Two Special Forces recruiters were eating in the 326th messhall. An interested squad leader, I sat at the NCO table and observed Major Parmley and Sergeant Major Denton intently. *Very sharp-looking soldiers. Silvernail tried to tell me, but I know everything. Shit!*

My enlistment was within six months of expiration so I reported to Sergeant First Class Paddy, the unit recruiting NCO, for the reenlistment spiel. I knew that Paddy was waiting out retirement. I also knew that he cared about the enlisteds, and I felt the same way about the short, feisty Irishman.

"Well, Bill, how's the war in Bravo going?"

"I'm losing, Paddy. You can't beat the system. How can A Company be so different from B Company?"

"Easy. A commander and a first sergeant. Reenlist for Awful Alpha. That way they have to take you." The recruiter smiled.

"What happened to my 1049 to A Company, Paddy?"

"That's easy, too. Neither the battalion CO nor the command sergeant major would go for it. It'll work this time, Bill."

I thought a few minutes before replying. "Naw, Paddy. I think I'll give 'em nine years and go back to school. I made a mistake coming back in the Army. I'm a slow learner, I reckon."

"You're a dumbass in more ways than one if you give 'em nine years. Tell you what, Bill, I have an idea you might go for. Wanna hear it?"

"What the hell have I got to lose? Shoot, old soldier."

"Special Forces is recruiting now. First time I've seen that in years. Here's the qualifications and the best I can tell, you meet all of 'em. Pay attention, I may ask questions later! You must be an E-5 or above and possess one of the following military occupation specialty qualifications: 11B light weapons leader, 11C heavy weapons leader, 11F operations and intelligence, 12B combat engineer, 05B radio operator, and 91B medical specialist. In addition, the soldier must be Airborne-qualified, preferably with combat experience, have an IQ of 110 or above, and twenty-one months to serve. How does that grab you, young soldier?"

"Tell me more."

"They stay in the field most of the time and after being awarded a "three" suffix to their MOS, they get some challenging assignments. You will not die of boredom although you might expire from other causes. No chicken shit, no wiping the noses of a bunch of kids, and no time to feel sorry for yourself, like you're doing now."

"I tried to transfer to A Company and it was short-stopped, so how do I know it won't be short-stopped again?"

"The only ones who can act on this 1049 request are Department of the Army and Special Forces. I think you both need each other. Give it a shot!"

I made up my mind quickly. "Let's go for it, Paddy. What have I got to lose?"

"Only a three-year enlistment, provided you're accepted, Bill."

A month later, the entire 326th Combat Engineer Battalion jumped into a training area and was constructing an emergency landing field. The second squad was deployed in defensive positions along with the rest of the platoon when the call came. "Squad leader of the second, report to the first soldier!"

"You're to report to battalion headquarters at Campbell. You've been transferred to the 77th Special Forces Group at Fort Bragg, North Carolina. A jeep is waiting for you. I didn't know you asked to go to Bragg and Sneaky Petes."

"I reenlisted for it, First Soldier. It can't get any worse. I'm not happy here, you know that!"

"Yeah, maybe it's best. Good luck to you." His reply was unexpected and I took it with a grain of salt.

Back at Campbell and the battalion personnel shop, the fat specialist fifth class acted amazed or confused—I couldn't tell which. "Whatsa matter, fat boy, can't you find my records. I want outta here, like yesterday!"

"You have no priority that I'm aware of, Sergeant."

"If I could get you out in the woodshed, I'd make my own priorities, junior."

A master sergeant E-8 broke up the wordplay and finished the outprocessing. The Ford convertible was packed and I moved it to a pawn shop just outside the confines of the Airborne post, where I hocked my watch and ring. Leaving behind my squad and roommate, in my haste I gave little thought to my new post and the 77th Special Forces Group (Airborne).

CHAPTER 11

SPECIAL FORCES, despite its detractors in the Army, was allowed to recruit 240 NCOs in September 1959. That would bring their strength, worldwide, to 1,100 personnel stationed in three groups covering the entire free world. With only 200 souls, the 1st Special Forces Group (SFG) blanketed the Far East from the home base in Okinawa. The 10th SFG claimed Europe as its hunting grounds and had about the same number of personnel. With its 240 new men, the 77th would constitute the largest unit of the groups. Of the 240 new candidates, mostly from the 101st and 82d Airborne Divisions, only 80 or so would still be around Fort Bragg a year later. Constantly at war with the Army, this was my unit of choice I joined forces with in early October 1959. We would, down through the years, win some and lose some.

Smoke Bomb Hill consisted of a two-story HQ building for the 77th and a parade field two hundred by one hundred yards wide. The field faced north to the billets, classrooms, and administrative buildings of the unit. To the south of the 77th lay the Psychological Warfare School for officers who wanted to be psy-war specialists or who just wanted to get their tickets punched for promotion. All of the buildings were the standard World War II wooden structures, unlike the modern facilities of the 82d Airborne Division, which was also located on the post.

When I signed on Friday night October 17, 1959, the briefing on my unit of choice began. To his credit, the officer of the day (OD) broke it down to where I could understand it.

"You are—like all new personnel—assigned to FC One, and further to FB One for inprocessing and training. Good luck!"

I couldn't—and wouldn't—let him off that lightly. "Could you break down that FC and FB business for me, sir?"

"That'll be done during your orientation week, Sergeant Craig," the first lieutenant replied.

I moved into the barracks belonging to Field Detachments C-1 and B-1. Few NCOs were yet visible in the billets. Because of the Airborne requirement, the majority of the 240 new Special Forces NCO recruits were from the 101st and the 82d, and had a reporting date of November 1, 1959. Those people with enough funds had gone on leave. Special Forces orientation and training would begin on or about the reporting date.

FCs in SF were company-size, about 165 officers and enlisted men. Each company-size unit contained three FB detachments, which in turn contained three or four FA detachments. In a short time, the Field Detachment C designation would be changed to Company. FB-1, in the meantime, fell out Monday morning, and forty troops faced 1st Sergeant Kettleton. After roll call he marched the undersized unit to the police area of FB-1.

Regardless of the unit they came from, the NCOs were very familiar with police call. What we were not in tune with was having to bend over and pick up the cigarette butts and trash left by unthinking troopers. Most of the newbies went along with the drill, but some did not. After the boring procedure a few of the West Point NCOs—elitists—felt demeaned by having to police so they went to Kettleton and requested to return to their parent units. The weeding-out process had started earlier than most of us cared to believe. "Obviously not from the 326th Engineers," was only one remark that was heard from the ranks.

Kettleton, a slim-waisted master sergeant, directed the

quitters to the C Detachment sergeant major's office and continued to march. Calling names in pairs, he directed us to report to Psychological Warfare School headquarters after formation. "Come Friday, you and an assistant will give demolition classes to the officers enrolled in the psy war course." The uproar could be heard at Fort Campbell, but me and Buck Sergeant Daniel O'Connor uttered not a sound. Many of the NCOs said they knew nothing about the subject, and some even dared to say that they couldn't give a class, regardless of the subject.

Kettleton attempted to quiet the dissension. "If you read and heed instructions, you have four days to rehearse the damn thing. You should be ready by Friday." That sounded plausible to O'Connor, a young Ranger graduate, but apparently to many in the group it did not. So the FC-1 sergeant major processed the disgruntled back to their parent units. I remarked to my assistant instructor, "Jesus, O'Connor, in four days we could give a class on a nuke." O'Connor smiled in agreement. By the end of class rehearsals that day, the strength of the 101st and 82d had climbed somewhat, while the number of prospective SF operators had tumbled.

Sergeant O'Connor and I practiced and rehearsed our "field-expedient" thermite grenade class for four days. The ingredients that made up the metal-penetrating heat device could be purchased at any store or pharmacy throughout the country. We were ready for the psychological warfare class on D-day.

To demonstrate the grenade's penetration capability, we would start the class by detonating an issue thermite grenade on a steel plate. I then gave a briefing to each class of officers, ranging in rank from 2d lieutenant to major, then broke them down in pairs. I and the assistant instructor moved among the tables in the Pine Tree area of Smoke Bomb Hill and supervised the assembly of the devices. When both of us were satisfied that the grenades had been assembled correctly, the students were allowed to detonate them using a blasting cap and a time fuse. The smiles of satisfaction displayed by the class proved to O'Connor and me that the class had learned something about unconventional explosives. Probably unknown to the students, the two of us had learned the most.

Special Forces, the unconventional arm of the U.S. Army, began orientation for all of its newbies on the Monday following November 1, 1959. The briefings were given by NCOs and field-grade officers (major and above). The Special Forces mission statement read something like this: "Trained for deep infiltration into enemy territory by land, sea, and air to conduct unconventional warfare, sabotage, and escape and evasion. To operate as small teams for extended periods of time with minimal support, to organize, train, and equip guerrilla forces, conduct sabotage operations, support resistance movements, and to evade, and if necessary, escape from enemy forces."

After a smoke break, a historical résumé on Special Forces would enlighten us about why we were sitting in the psy-war theater.

According to the U.S. Army, Special Forces are the descendants of the 1st Special Service Force. This unit was a combination of Canadian and American forces known as the Devil's Brigade. This highly trained conventional unit, more like the Ranger companies of the Korean conflict, made an awkward comparison to the unconventional warriors of the 1950s. Actually, because of the mission, relayed to us in the previous hour, the obvious predecessor of today's Sneaky Petes is the Office of Strategic Services (OSS).

The OSS was organized in 1942 by Major General William J. "Wild Bill" Donovan. When he insisted that the United States should have a military unit devoted to guerrilla warfare operations, immediate opposition not only formed but mounted daily.

Opposition from the chiefs of staff of the Army and Navy did not surprise him, but when the Federal Bureau of Investigation chimed in, he was shocked. The FBI had planned to form an international intelligence organization under its own control.

Regardless of the military dissent, Donovan believed the unit should be military. Throwing up both hands at the military disagreement, the general played his ace in the hole, going directly to Franklin D. Roosevelt. Donovan and the President had a long-standing friendship that paid off for the general. Roosevelt issued orders for the activation of the OSS. General Donovan wasted little time on his flight to merry ole England.

The British Special Operation Executive (SOE) gave abundant assistance in forming the unit. By that time, the SOE had two years' experience in occupied Europe. Their agents behind German lines gathered intelligence information and organized and trained members of the resistance movements in "G" warfare. In addition to furnishing the OSS with information on the training of agents, the SOE eventually agreed to joint operations. The backbone of European operations was the thirty-four-man teams dropped behind enemy lines in Italy, Greece, Asia Minor, Yugoslavia, and France. These operations were generally successful and helped the allied invasion of Europe.

General Douglas MacArthur would not allow the OSS to operate as a unit in the Pacific theater. Despite Roosevelt's friendship, Donovan received no help in bucking "I'll be back, Mac." Still, the China-Burma-India Theater would set the stage for one of the OSS's most successful forays.

Captain Ray Peers, later a lieutenant general, led a group of OSS men in training the Kachin tribesmen of northern Burma to engage in guerrilla war against the Japanese. By the end of the war, this unit would number over ten thousand and claim the destruction of near that number of Japanese. The Kachin losses would be under 300. The Kachin tribesmen often proved their body count with the ears of their enemy. It would take Captain Peers and his OSS troops over six months to stop the happy, fierce, tribesmen from carrying their divide-by-two body count in their bamboo tube storage containers.

Besides the high attrition rate of Japanese, the CBI theater commanders admitted that 90 percent of their intell came from the OSS and their Kachin Rangers.

Unfortunately, when President Roosevelt died, so did the Office of Strategic Services. In existence for three years, it had been a resounding success just as Donovan had stated it would. The hierarchy of the Army, Navy, and FBI finally won one. President Truman ordered it disbanded in 1945. Ironically, the CIA today considers its origins to be the OSS and Donovan to be its founding father.

The first morning of our orientation ended on that note. The briefers had gained the class's complete attention.

As the briefings and presentations moved on, the realization of what they might be getting into overcame some NCOs who had been schooled in conventional warfare: Light-years away from home and family; living among and fighting alongside people of a foreign culture; realizing that when you go to sleep at night, it may be your last time. The fear of the unknown began to take its toll. At the end of the scare tactics, two or three more quitters departed Smoke Bomb Hill.

The swimming test would take up the afternoon of our first day of orientation. I had been briefed on the exams before leaving Fort Campbell, so they held no surprises for me.

The weather being the way it is in November in North Carolina, we carried our bags on the bus. Each bag contained an entire change of clothing including jump boots.

To my momentary relief, the fifty-meter swim with fatigues, boots, and headgear would be the first event. Once the boots and clothing became soaked, we all slowed down a tad. To tell the truth, I was exhausted at the finish. The fact that my companions were no better off helped me not. We were given a twenty-minute break before the final, then were permitted to change into swim suits or jockey shorts.

The two-hundred-meter swim was freestyle with no time limit attached and that's the way I took it—my time, that is. I finally got there, but a bunch of treading water and dog paddling was the norm. We bussed back to the billets, ate supper, and used the GI bunks for their intended purpose. I wasn't surprised at the lack of quitters. Airborne!

FC-1's work formation, preceded by breakfast on the hill, was at 0730. Field Detachments Bravo-1, 2, and 3 fell out for the second day of orientation. We were informed that we would take our qualifying physical training test after the morning briefing and the noon meal. FB-1 occupied the center of the formation that marched the ten minutes to the theater. We had been disbanded as a unit at the end of the previous day's session and looked forward to discovering why we had arrived at Fort Bragg in 1959. The briefers didn't disappoint us, and resumed where they had left off the previous day.

After the big one—World War II—and despite events in Europe, unconventional theories opened no doors and few minds. One advocate, a Colonel Volkmann, who had headed up the guerrilla movement on the Japanese-occupied Philippine island of Luzon, stayed in the Army and was sent to Fort Benning, Georgia. Volkmann produced two field manuals (FMs) on the subject but previously slammed doors failed to open.

In 1949 and 1950, the possibility of the USSR's invading Europe raised a few questions in the Pentagon. At the very least, the Army realized that a basis for a resistance movement should be established. In the summer of 1950 the Korean war demonstrated the brass's lack of planning.

Ruling out the use of nuclear weapons left MacArthur in a bind. He watched as his forces were harried from behind their trenchlines by North Korean guerrillas. He possessed no capabilities to counter that tactic so he played out his only ace. Volkmann left his literary life at Benning when ordered to MacArthur's headquarters in Tokyo. There, he was ordered to take command of all operations behind enemy lines.

To his credit, Volkmann began tapping key personnel, but he became ill just after the planning and basic organization were completed. He was medically evacuated to the

States. What followed his removal could not be classed as guerrilla warfare. Most of the veterans who were involved in the operations felt they achieved zilch. By 1952, even the Pentagon was convinced that a different approach was needed. In other words, one should not wait until a war starts to begin unconventional operations—planning, selection of personnel and specialized equipment, support organization, and training were required in advance. General Robert McClure stepped into the breach. He had under his control a psychological operations staff unit, which contained a special warfare division.

McClure recruited the best unconventional warfare specialists in the Army, including the now-recovered Volkmann. Others included Colonel Joe Waters, formerly of OSS and Merrill's Marauders; Colonel Aaron Banks, former OSS; Colonel Robert McDowell, former OSS; and several other experienced unconventional warfare specialists of the European and Indochina theaters during World War II.

McClure started selling a proposition of establishing a permanent special forces group in Europe. History was repeated by the opposition. When McClure's group was finally making headway, he discovered other, tougher, opponents. New establishments—Air Force and CIA—along with the State Department presented their own unconventional ideas.

President Truman's intervention resulted in the Army's receiving the guerrilla warfare and special forces mission; the Air Force was charged with air resupply. McClure received approval for total peacetime strength of 2,500. Still, the Pentagon never gave up its opposition. In April 1952, Colonel Banks was sent to Fort Bragg to establish the Special Forces Group. He was directed to the recently established Psychological Warfare School to set up his unit. Despite objections from Banks and Volkmann, that's where it was formed.

On June 20, 1952, the 10th Special Forces (Airborne) was formed. The training was intensive and the trainees participated in major U.S. Army/Air Force exercises. But, after disrupting several maneuver situations with their guerrilla tactics, they were removed from any role in the local war games. In November 1953, the 10th Special Forces, seven hundred strong, embarked for Bad Tölz, West Germany.

The 77th Special Forces was formed immediately after at Fort Bragg. In June 1956 three officers and thirteen NCOs formed the 14th Operational Detachment and were sent to Hawaii. From there they were sent to Thailand to assist in training the Thai Rangers. Then they went to Taiwan and Vietnam for the same purpose.

Five officers and seventeen NCOs then formed the 8231st Army Special Operational Detachment, which was sent to Japan. One year later both units were moved to Okinawa to form the 1st Special Forces Group (Airborne). The Far East was finally receiving as much attention as the European theater. As we sat in the psy-war auditorium in November 1959, the three groups were hard at it and exchanging personnel for cross-training. That concluded our third orientation session.

The PT test was administered at a nearby track surrounded by wooden bleachers. The group and the events were broken down as follows: Section one, pushups, twenty-five qualifying; two, situps, thirty-two in two minutes; three, chinups or pullups, four minimum; and lastly, the mile run in under eight minutes. If I just did the minimum acceptable number at each stage, I would end up with 250 points; that wouldn't get me anywhere near the 300 points needed.

Due to the plated humerus of my left arm, I would do only the minimum in stations one and three. Pullups were not my thing. In the mile run and situps, I would go for broke. The plan worked to perfection. Only after doing sixty situps in under two minutes did I complete the mile run—jump boots and all—in under seven minutes. I totaled just over 350 points for the day and was ready for my fourth day of the week-long orientation. Did we lose any prospects over the menial exam? Of course, two or three went back to the 82d or the 101st after their scorecards were signed by Major Lee Parmley of FB-1.

I was very suspicious of these individuals, and for good reason. I personally knew of no Airborne people who could not pass a test of this type. I suspected, as I did in jump school, that many quitters did so because they did not want to change their routines in Army life. For myself, I was ready for the fourth enlightening day of our orientation. This would be the last day in the conferencelike atmosphere of the psy-war theater. The fifth day was reserved for a paper drill and records check at the group personnel shop.

Before the briefing on our unit designators began, we were told once again that being flexible was a key to understanding. The instructor then began with the FC terminology. I was very interested, because the designators FC-1, FB-1, and FA-1 had me stumped.

The 77th SFG (Airborne) was composed of FC-1, FC-2, FC-3, and Group Headquarters. The speaker answered the obvious. "The FC stands for Field Detachments C-1, C-2, or C-3. If you're from an infantry unit, compare it to a line company headquarters. The composition of the FC detachment will help your understanding."

We were handed slips that broke down the FC by personnel and job descriptions. The paperwork was to be returned before the day was out. The class followed the briefer as he read the information, and made comments about each position.

Field Detachment C

1	Commanding Officer	Lieutenant Colonel (O-5)
1	Executive Officer	Major (O-4)
1	Adjutant (S-1 Personnel)	Captain (O-3)
1	Intelligence Officer (S-2)	Captain (O-3)
1	Operations Officer (S-3)	Captain (O-3)
1	Supply Officer (S-4)	Captain (O-3)
1	Sergeant Major	SGM (E-9)
1	Intelligence Sergeant	MSG (E-8)

```
1  Operations Sergeant.....................MSG (E-8)
1  Assistant Supply Sergeant ..........SFC (E-7)
1  Radio Operator Supervisor .........SFC (E-7)
1  Radio Repairman..........................SSG (E-6)
4  Radio Operators...........................SGT (E-5)
1  Administrative Supervisor...........SSG (E-6)
```

Even before the briefer concluded the seventeen FC positions from *Table of Organization and Equipment* [TO&E] 31-107, the NCOs were impressed with the rank in such a small unit. The briefing on the Field Detachment B would be just as impressive.

Field Detachment B

```
1  Detachment Commander.............Major (O-4)
1  Executive Officer.........................Captain (O-3)
1  Adjutant (S-1 Personnel) ............Captain (O-3)
1  Operations Officer (S-3).............Captain (O-3)
1  Intell Officer (S-2) ......................Captain (O-3)
1  Supply Officer (S-4) ...................Captain (O-3)
1  Sergeant Major.............................SGM (E-9)
1  Intell Sergeant (S-2)....................MSG (E-8)
1  Operations Sergeant (S-3)...........MSG (E-8)
1  Demolition Sergeant.....................SFC (E-7)
1  Heavy Weapons Sergeant ...........SFC (E-7)
1  Light Weapons Sergeant .............SFC (E-7)
1  Medical Specialist........................SFC (E-7)
1  Radio Supervisor ..........................SFC (E-7)
1  Supply Sergeant (S-4).................SFC (E-7)
1  Administrative Supervisor...........SSG (E-6)
1  Assistant Supply Sergeant ..........SSG (E-6)
1  Medical Specialist........................SSG (E-6)
1  Demolition Specialist ..................SGT (E-5)
4  Chief Radio Operators ................SGT (E-5)
```

The conclusion of the Field Detachment B class left me impressed once again. The enlisted positions furnished ample opportunity for promotion, regardless of one's specialty.

All of us in the audience awaited the briefing on where we would—more than likely—begin our Special Forces careers. The Field-Detachment A segment concluded the organization briefing.

Field Detachment A

1	Team Leader	Captain (O-3)
1	Executive Officer, Team XO	1st Lieutenant (O-2)
1	Opns Sergeant, Team Sergeant	MSG (E-8)
1	Intelligence Sergeant	SFC (E-7)
1	Heavy Weapons Sergeant	SFC (E-7)
1	Light Weapons Sergeant	SFC (E-7)
1	Medical Specialist	SFC (E-7)
1	Senior Radio Operator	SFC (E-7)
1	Assistant Medic	SSG (E-6)
1	Demolition Sergeant	SSG (E-6)
1	Demolition Specialist	SGT (E-5)
1	Junior Radio Operator	SGT (E-5)

Closing his orientation on the twelve-man A Detachment, the briefer explained that eight-man detachments were on operations at that time. In fact, the OSS and the British SOE had used three-man "Jedburghs" during the big one.

The last hour of the fourth day of the orientation was presented by the C-team adjutant and administrative NCO. Most NCOs were turned off by the subject but changed their attitudes when we realized how vital our military occupational specialty (MOS) code was in relation to our future. We were given a handout from Army Regulation 611-201. Unlike the other material, we were allowed to keep the printed matter. It pertained to enlisted skills or jobs in the Special Forces field. My MOS upon arrival at Fort Bragg was 12B.67.

The first three digits identify the MOS and skill level. I was a combat engineer skill level B. The fourth character is a number. With the first three characters, it shows skill and grade level. I was grade level six and could become a staff sergeant E-6. The fifth character was then a number (later changed to a letter), and identified me as parachute-qualified. My goal was to be a 12B.63, or a combat engineer, Special Forces qualified. Other MOS's that would affect our training were 11F, infantry operations and intelligence; 11C, infantry heavy weapons; 91B, medical specialist; and 05B, radio operator. Exactly how these specialties would affect obtaining a 3 (or S) qualifier would be explained in the fifth and final day of our briefing.

The operations and training (11F) NCO from the Field Detachment C-1 laid out the training for the next four to five months. Because of the complexity of the coordination required—in some cases—the dates were rather vague. None of the wannabe's seemed overly concerned.

Each specialty would be schooled in his MOS for the first six to eight weeks. Almost all of these six fields from engineer to radio operator would be schooled at Fort Bragg. The only exception would be medics (91B) who did not have the basic course. They would spend their apprenticeship at Fort Sam Houston, Texas. That affected very few of the medics as it turned out. All training would be suspended during the week of Christmas and New Year's due to the nonavailability of training facilities. We all understood this, because the Army went on the half-day schedule kick during that period. When our MOS school was over, we would be assigned to A detachments in FC 1. The cross-training in all SF subjects would begin at that time.

"The cross-training instruction will be given by two sources; the C team training committee or your own A detachment," the briefer promised. Once again, we were told to be flexible on the times. Hopefully, the cross-training would be over in eight to ten weeks. As per usual, we would all be tested before going any further.

Mountain and ski training were to be combined at Camp Drum, New York, or Camp Williams, Utah. Other terrain-survival exercises would be held at Camp McCall and Green Swamp, South Carolina. At this time we, and our A detachment, would be ready for an Army training test (ATT) at the mountain phase of Ranger School in

Dahlonega, Georgia. The survivors would be ready for the 3 suffix. Again, we were told to be flexible about times.

In my estimation, the last part of the orientation brought out two very good points. In 1959, jump prerequisites were that you had to jump at least once every ninety days to be eligible for jump pay. If you transferred from one Airborne unit to another, you had to start your count anew. In other words, my last jump at Campbell in October did not cover me for November because I was in a different unit. Stupid! It would take years, the Vietnam conflict, and General Westmoreland to straighten this mess out in the middle of the sixties. To put it bluntly, we all needed a pay jump. Not to worry.

The very knowledgeable master sergeant laid it out for us. If facilities permitted, we would no longer jump in the daylight. Night jumps would be our thing. I wasn't too thrilled about that, but the chief hurried on without me. "Most of your jumps will be on Friday night, enabling you to sleep in Saturdays." We all liked that part, at least. His last bit of instruction enlightened us on another innovation the Army would take ten years to duplicate.

"After December of 1959, you'll no longer be paid across the board." After that sunk in, he hurried on to his main point.

"You will be paid by check or direct deposit. When you leave here this morning, you'll be given a form to fill out and turn in. You must state how you want to be paid. For direct deposit, you need a banking institution and an account number. The quicker you turn the information in, the better. Special Forces does not know where you'll be from one day to the next, much less on paydays. No exceptions."

Again, it would take the Army more than ten years to fully institutionalize this feat. My new unit was showing me something this first week of November 1959.

For the NCOs who had remained, orders were cut and we began schooling in our basic military specialty the first of the following week.

CHAPTER 12

TWENTY-FIVE students began the five-week demolition course that would graduate a week before Christmas 1959. The class was greeted by the best enlisted instructors in the U.S. Army—or any other army for that matter. We were also greeted by a class load that would send us to a study hall every night until the ordeal was over.

The wooden barracks that housed the would-be Special Forces operators were of the two-story variety and were cleaned each morning by the NCOs. After police of the outside area and depositing the pine cones in one pile, chow was served. The mess sergeant, Norman "Porkchop" Racibor, got the troops' attention the second week.

A young PFC pulling kitchen police gave the huge man a ration of back talk and was rewarded with a backhand to the mouth. Things ran smoother in the mess hall for the rest of the day, and in addition, Racibor and I became fast friends—a friendship that is active to this day.

A basic math refresher course consumed almost all of the first week of the classroom instruction, followed by the demolition formulas in the metric and U.S. system that would make the first ten days go by quickly. Everyone in the class felt as if we were back in college, but we took the training much more seriously than we had the academics of school. The Army had the attention of most of us, for the first time in some cases, but a few in the class didn't feel that way and were conspicuous by their absence in study hall. The younger ones were cautioned by older NCOs but some chose to ignore the warnings.

The third week we spent on the demolition range constructing home-made explosive devices and detonating them. The observation of safety regulations was a must. Failure to observe them was another cause for PCS to Washout City.

In the fourth week, we examined nukes. The class learned more nuclear theory than the crews who dropped devices on Hiroshima and Nakasaki ever wanted to know. Three days of testing awaited the students before graduation. Seventy percent in all phases was the standard and no exceptions were tolerated.

The first day of the finals consisted of written exams that covered formulas, military explosives, and home-made devices. In the main, students who had observed the study periods struggled successfully through the four-hour block. When grades were announced the next morning, a few more stragglers hit the road.

Day two consisted of practical exams at the demolition range, where students had to perform without assistance. In addition to carrying out a task, we had to present a short spiel about the demonstration before proceeding. I explained and gave four live demonstrations for my evaluation: First, prime and detonate nonelectrically a quarter-pound block of TNT; second, prime and detonate electrically a pound block of C-4 plastic explosive; third, detonate four quarter-pound blocks of TNT electrically and simultaneously; and fourth, using a mine detector, locate and disarm a land mine.

To my knowledge none of the students went by the wayside during that phase of the exam.

The remaining candidates were now certain of a graduation certificate since a night jump, with equipment and a simulated nuclear device, was only a formality. The simulator was broken down into three parts, each weighing around sixty pounds. Me, O'Connor, and Asa Ballard, also formerly of the 326th Engineers, were designated a team. After assembling from the night jump, we were to set up the device to the satisfaction of the cadre. The exercise turned out to be problematical for the entire class, as well as the military and civilian security police.

Our first problem arose when high winds blew us away from Drop Zone Sicily. I had the simulator in a Griswold container and had planned on releasing it at a hundred feet from the ground. The twenty-foot release strap was secured to my harness and would stop the descent of the Griswold, but wouldn't do a helluva lot for my back or intestines. I spied the pine trees I was heading for after my vigorous exit, and decided to ride the Griswold container in, simulator and all.

I crashed into the trees, but with the added weight of the simulator managed to break through to the ground below. I hit the ground and lay stunned and bleeding from the impact and the ungrateful limbs. "This has got to get better," I gasped.

I also heard my partners crash and burn in the trees and spotted one hanging about fifty feet above the ground. In about thirty minutes, we had joined up and assembled the device, and waited for our graders. But the cadre were having problems as well.

The civilian police allowed no traffic to stop on Highway 77, despite the fact that one jumper had slammed into the pavement and was injured. As they awaited medical coverage for the injured trooper, his equipment was secured by the military police. The news media would have had a ball if they knew part of an A-bomb had landed on public property—simulator or not.

It would be almost dawn before the MPs and cadre found us three battered and bruised tree-jumpers and our assembled device. Three bloody soldiers awaited their final exam.

"Get it broken down," the cadre ordered. "We need to lock it up. We have half of the state of North Carolina looking for that damn thing. Break it down!"

We were not pleased by the orders and said so. "How about us?" asked Ballard. "Don't we count for something?"

"Not a helluva lot. Let's go before the FBI and CID get

involved. There's nothing wrong with you guys that a quart of iodine and plastic surgery can't fix. Move it!"

Of the original twenty-five, twenty-one happy NCOs graduated from the Demolition course. We looked sharp in our dress greens, bloused boots, and overseas caps. The only discouraging remark came from one of the spectators. "Those guys look like they should receive a Purple Heart with their graduation certificates." Many of us graduates felt the same way. Cross-training was next on our march to the coveted "3" suffix.

The elation that we felt evaporated the next week shortly after the final grades came out. SFC Murphy was first in the class with 89. O'Connor was second, and I was third at 83. This was as it should be—then came the incident.

Murphy was called in and told that he could proceed no further, as he had been convicted of selling moonshine while in his teens in Kentucky. This was—and still is—a felony. His security clearance was therefore denied. The entire class was furious and Special Forces suffered because of a dubious, inflexible regulation.

Twelve of us fifteen barracks rats spent the Christmas holidays alternating between the billets and the Main Post NCO club. Due to the negative reception some of us had received there in the past, few of us ever strayed to the plush 82d Club. Money being in short supply, us single men pulled charge of quarters duties for a few bucks and wished the holidays of 1959 into the history book.

The first Monday of the New Year, all of us newbies were inserted into twelve-man A detachments. I went to Detachment A-4 and would remain there until the qualification course exhausted itself or the potential operators. Only a few unique situations distinguished our training from the conventional conditioning.

Cross-training was a constant activity during our instruction. Team members gave classes in their specialties to their detachment and we discovered that the more classes we presented, the more our own expertise grew. Of course, the remainder of the group was enlightened by the process as well.

Master Sergeant Art Fodder was young for an E-8 team sergeant. Straight out of the 82d Airborne Division, this NCO had problems relating to the unique soldiers he had on board his schooner. He was much younger than me (I was thirty-three), and my being treated like a private in the rear ranks often chafed. So much so in fact that I often told Fodder to lighten up and quit oversupervising. So we grew apart during the training cycle.

A Lieutenant Colonel Tate was now the commander of FC-1, 77th SFG (Airborne), and the company would spend five weeks in and around Camp Williams, Utah. The colonel had made a name for himself during World War II, but was out of condition and made a less than favorable impression on the old soldiers under him—and on the younger ones as well.

All echelons began preparing for the excursion to Camp Williams, a few miles south of Salt Lake City off of Highway 68. Thirteen miles south of Camp Williams awaited the small city of American Fork. In addition to ski training, the five-week program included a one-week survival problem and a two-week field training exercise. As anyone who has ever experienced them can testify, conditioning for such activities can never be overemphasized. Skiing accidents could put a soldier out of action for months upon end. Poorly conditioned skiers are a broken leg or ankle looking for a place to occur. Detachment A-4 and its commander, Lieutenant Perry, were determined that A-4 would not wind up with arms or legs in traction just because of Utah's rough terrain and the idiot sticks on the operators' feet.

Detachments continued cross-training in the demo, medical, intelligence, and weapons fields, as that was an essential task if the members were ever to be qualified as operators. But each afternoon in the humid North Carolina February, the classes ceased for conditioning drills.

Staff Sergeant Willie E. Stark, a Korean veteran, was my partner in the conditioning marches. The slight, blond, Nebraska boy hoisted his forty-pound rucksack to his back and shoulders; I did the same. "You may be six years younger,

Willie, but I'm gonna bring smoke on your ass today. Ten miles in under two hours, that's just a brisk walk for us dogfaces. Shit!"

"It's not as easy as it sounds, Bill. Betcha we end up running to get in under the wire. Remember, we've got to make it as a team or do it again."

"Can Fodder, Wilson, and Wofford make it, Willie?"

"I'm not worried about it, Bill. You're the oldest, at thirty-three. Hell, if you can make it, why can't they?" Stark grinned.

"Thanks a lot, pal. Let's go. We'll see who's old, you damn kid." We went.

We always completed the ten miles in the time allotted but, just as Stark had predicted, would end up jogging part of the way. Every team member looked out for his PT partner and the rest of the detachment as well. Lieutenant Perry led the way and the team sergeant huffed and puffed while bringing up the rear. We eventually got the time down to one hour and fifty minutes, but no one was eager to break any world records.

Orientation classes on the fitting and wearing of skis, winter clothes, and accessories were given before the big birds from Pope Air Force Base dropped A Company on the unsuspecting populace of Camp Williams and the state of Utah. We stood at the runway with our chutes, waiting to load, when Lieutenant Colonel Tate entered the lead aircraft with his headquarters personnel (we line soldiers called them pukes). It provoked a remark from another Oklahoma native, Staff Sergeant Burl Wilson. "Sir, why doesn't GG lose some weight?"

"Sergeant Wilson," said Perry, innocently enough, "who in the hell is 'GG,' for God's sake?"

"Garbage Gut Tate, sir," Wilson answered.

"Sergeant Wilson, that's disrespect to a commissioned officer," Perry admonished, but not too sternly.

"I know, sir," Wilson said.

We loaded the aircraft and began a typical SF adventure.

CHAPTER 13

THE THREE C-130 four-engine aircraft flew in formation over the cloud-darkened skies of Utah in March 1960. Ground winds ranging from sixty to seventy miles an hour had caused cancellation of the scheduled night jump, so we landed at Salt Lake City and were trucked to Camp Williams by the Utah National Guard. We were in our beds and barracks before midnight.

Camp Williams had ten or so troop billets, a messhall, and a small club and recreation center. All structures were at dress right dress and of brick construction. Sidewalks fronted the billets and led to the other facilities. Twelve to fourteen inches of snow covered the area at the time. The barracks reminded me of the one-story brick hootches of Camp Crawford, Hokkaido, Japan. Each long, narrow building housed three A detachments—thirty men; officers lived in the bachelor officers' quarters (BOQ). The first morning out, Sergeant Porkchop Racibor and his highly trained staff treated a subdued company to a nutritious meal.

At our 0800 work formation, instructors from the Utah National Guard's Special Forces and Lieutenant Colonel Tate awaited the newly winterized soldiers, with Tate speaking first, of course. He spoke, in the main, of his pet peeves.

"The sidewalks are shoveled free of snow, use them. I do not want you trampling on my lawn." He pointed to the foot or more of snow. The speech went on at some length but mercifully ended in time for Utah's finest to point out

127

the training areas for the detachments. The weather was only around freezing so we were stripped down, just long johns, fatigues, pile caps, and thermal boots. It had taken a while, but thanks to the Korean conflict, the U.S. Army could dress appropriately for terrain other than Europe. Nor was the fact that Tate had suddenly acquired Camp Williams lost on us stupid enlisted personnel.

In quality, the instruction was far and beyond anything I had ever received in Hokkaido. The weekend warriors from winterland knew the art of skiing, whether uphill, downhill, or cross-country. The National Guard from Utah spent the entire day teaching us Regulars how to put on skis, how to stand, walk, and snowplow. At one phase of the training we were soon very adept—learning how to fall properly. Without being facetious, the instructors admonished us that this seemingly natural phenomenon would, if done properly, save us from serious injury.

By the end of the work week, we probably couldn't have entered the Olympics, but at least we could get from point A to point B. It did not escape Detachment A-4 that many pointers given by the instructors were disregarded by the all-knowing company staff.

"Never ski over six hours a day. You are using more calories, up to 7,200, than you can possibly replace. Injury, or worse, can result." Of course, the company staff had us skiing an eight-hour, or longer, day. Racibor and his crew of mess mates tried to keep us up with the calorie count at mealtimes but diminishing waistlines and weight loss told us we were losing the battle.

The second week, all us unconventional warriors were allowed some downhill antics with weapons and rucksacks on board. Some of the falls that resulted were of the gut-busting variety. We'd given up the idea of not laughing at our teammates' misfortunes. Besides, we could console ourselves with the reality that they were laughing at us as well, and things always seemed to even out.

The instructors expressed open amazement at our detachment's lack of injuries, major or otherwise. They thought we were the best-conditioned people that they had ever trained. Remembering the ten-mile speed marches at Bragg, we tended to agree with their assessment.

Week three was survival week. Each of us was allowed to take one pound of any desired foodstuff and no more. After being airdropped into a night landing zone (LZ) a short distance from Williams, the pound of goodies and a loaded carbine were to see us through the six-day exercise. There would be ski gear for each detachment but it would be dropped in a separate bundle. What did we select for our one pound of cuisine? We shall see!

Jumpmaster Fodder got the detachment out the door of the aircraft after kicking our ski equipment bundle out on the first pass. Night assembly, a difficult task, went off well, and we found how tiring it could be without our slats while searching on foot for the door bundle.

We breathed a sigh of relief upon finding our bundle and fitting the Army-issue cross-country skis. Det A-4 skied for several hours in the dark before pitching pup tents for the night. Before dozing off, I mentioned to my tentmate that if I had known as much about winter living when I was in Korea as I had just learned, it sure would have helped me a ton.

At 0800 the next morning, Lieutenant Perry stated the mission. "We are to move to the pickup point fifty miles away in an alert situation. Our side missions are to survive, conserve energy, and live off the land. Friday, if we live that long, we'll be trucked back to Camp Williams. Any questions?"

"Yes, sir," piped Burl Wilson. "Can we visit the towns around us? I could survive a heck of a lot easier that way. I have money."

We smiled at the soldier from Oologah, Oklahoma. "No, Sergeant Wilson, all Highway Patrol and town cops have been alerted. If we're caught in or near the roads or villages, we will spend five days in jail and be fed nothing. No roads or towns, please."

Team Sergeant Fodder was heard from. "What one-pound item did everyone bring?"

The answers came from around the seated circle—peanut butter, rice, oatmeal, bread, jelly, flour . . .

My selection drew a few stares and unsolicited remarks. "Flour?" asked Wilson. "What in the hell are you going to do with flour, Bill?"

"Yeah," chimed in Stark, "you're going to look silly as hell eating flour, you dumb Okie."

"I'm going to bake bread to go with the meat we kill. I'm a baker of the first water."

Head shaking and mumbled oaths showed that my teammates were less than impressed with my selection. Flour and all, the detachment skied on in the direction of the pickup point.

Snowshoe rabbits are plentiful in the hills, dales, and the slopes of the snow-covered mountains around Camp Williams. The carbine rounds made sure we did not want for meat. Each of us became proficient in skinning and cooking them, but after three days of rabbit, cross-country skiing a ten-hour day, the ski troops were complaining by the noon meal on the fourth day.

"Let's try it raw, Bill," Wilson suggested.

"Get serious, meathead! I'm cooking mine!" I said. "I'm gonna top it off with a tasty piece of homemade bread from my flour."

"You still haven't used that flour? Hell, I've been outta oatmeal for two days," Stark said.

"Tough shit," I said, while my team watched me mix the flour with melted snow and cook it over the team's open hearth. The flour blossomed into a toasted bun in no time at all. Team members eyed it hungrily but I was quick to remind them of their earlier remarks.

Thursday, the detachment was at our pickup point, lighter but happy that our ski training had enabled us to make the deadline. The only negative aspect of the exercise was our new but deep hatred of snowshoe rabbits—or any other kind of rabbit. A trip to Camp Williams and Saturday night at the small club or Salt Lake City would be our reward for devouring half of the snowshoe population in Utah.

Party time would be followed by a bunkside inspection of billets, weapons, and equipment, and a Monday-night jump into Sawtooth National Forest for a two-week exercise. There, all teams would conclude a ski-training exercise before returning to Fort Bragg, North Carolina.

Wilson and I saved bus fare by hitchhiking to Salt Lake City. The Mormons of Utah were impressed with the green uniforms, spit-shined boots, and overseas caps with the glider patch of the Airborne. The first male driver to pass motored us to the bright lights of Salt Lake City on Highway 68.

The bars and gin mills of Salt Lake were subdued compared to what we Fayetteville gentlemen were accustomed to. Both of us Okies acted like the natives, drinking our beer and talking to everyone in sight. At two in the morning, we boarded the Camp Williams Special—driven by a master sergeant—at the bus station. Happy, laughing, and full of beer, among other things, our cohorts were in the same mood. None of the mature individuals caused or participated in fights or disturbances.

On Monday morning Detachment A-4 had its field equipment and weapons uniformly laid out on bunks and footlockers. We stood at rigid attention as Lieutenant Colonel Tate approached with Lieutenant Perry at his elbow. The barracks was just as immaculate as was our equipment. Tate moved quickly until he stood in front of one demo sergeant. My eyes looked straight ahead and refused to focus on my new antagonist. To the surprise of everyone but me, the agitated colonel began a one-sided conversation.

Only glancing at the spotless field gear, he picked up the M-2 carbine. "So, you're the tough guy? Are you really a tough guy?"

"Yes, sir. I'm tough enough!"

Not pleased with my refusal to beg, Tate continued. "We'll see how tough you are, badass. You could start out by learning how to clean a carbine." He slammed the weapon back on the bunk.

Despite myself, I flinched at the remark. I knew, as the overweight colonel knew, that there was nothing wrong with the weapon; it was free of carbon, grease, oil, or dirt. I also guessed that I would be under the gun because of a Saturday night incident when an old SF NCO and I had exchanged words on the bus. I had, therefore, taken pains with the cleaning.

When the colonel moved on to the next barracks, the men relaxed. "GG don't like you, Bill," someone said.

"Yeah," chimed in another teamy, "you can't be all bad."

Stark brought the crisis into focus. "Keep your eye on Garbage Gut, Bill. He don't like you at all."

"Yeah, and the feeling is mutual," I managed to mumble, dejectedly.

It was left to Lieutenant Perry to bolster my sagging morale. Picking up the carbine from my bed, he only glanced at it. "There's nothing wrong with this weapon, Sergeant, so don't sweat the small shit. Everyone get ready for the field exercise. We jump in at 0200 in the morning. Cloud cover will make it darker than hell, so be ready for a long night. The team sergeant will brief you on the operation, so let's get it together or it will be two long weeks as well."

At that point Sergeant Fodder took over the briefing. "We'll jump into the Sawtooth National Forest from a C-130 at this landing zone." Fodder pointed to a map sketched on a blackboard. "It's composed of small, snow-covered hills and very few trees. We'll make three passes at the LZ, one for the pilot's orientation, one for kicking out three door bundles, and one for us to unass the aircraft from 1,250 feet, actual. We'll assemble on this small hill in the center of the LZ, spread out to recover our bundles and be off the LZ before daylight. Any questions so far?"

"Are the bundles marked?" Wilson asked.

"Yes," said Fodder. "Each one has a flashlight attached that will be turned on before it goes out the door."

"What's in the bundles?" Stark asked.

Fodder looked exasperated but replied. "The three bundles contain our rucksacks, field rations for two weeks, and snowshoes and skiing equipment. What else?"

"Where is Sawtooth National Forest?" Blackmon asked.

"Goddamn!" Fodder exploded. "Don't you people study your maps? It's near the Idaho border, north of here!"

"We don't have maps, Top," Stark said.

Fodder quieted somewhat. "The briefing will continue after the packing of equipment and issuing of maps. This isn't going as I had planned." He stomped out of the barracks onto Tate's white, white grass, followed by Perry.

The detachment was apicking and agrinning. Medical Technician Blackmon summed it up for the peons of A-4. "If there has been any planning, it escapes me. Things can get worse!"

After a delicious meal in the house that Porkchop Racibor built, packing three bundles and the issuing of ammunition and maps, the briefing continued.

"Listen up! The C-130 aircraft will turn on the green light at zero two hundred in the morning. We have one hour to assemble, recover our bundles, and move out.

"We'll recon this area for ten days and set up an ambush at LA 240566 on the last day. When the ambush is over, we'll be trucked back here. Any questions?"

From 1,250 actual feet above the ground, the parachutes billowed below the four roaring engines of the aircraft. Our T-10 personal chutes had followed three cargo chutes that carried the team supplies. The ground wind was nil and the ten-foot-deep unpacked snow cushioned our parachute landing falls. Detachment A-4 assembled quickly and put on skis after stowing the chutes on the drop zone. The Utah National Guard would recover the chutes the next afternoon.

All the dropped bundles were recovered but one: Despite a frantic search, the food bundle was not recovered within the hour allotted. Rucksacks on our backs, we sadly trudged away from the drop zone and a ten-day supply of field rations. The mumbling and complaining could be heard in

Salt Lake City. "No food for ten days. Thank God we have live ammunition. The snowshoe rabbit population will pay for this screw-up!"

The instructors from the Utah National Guard had cautioned us about two dangers in skiing—don't ski over six hours a day and do not ski after dark. Our detachment was on its way to our first reconnaissance mission and the violation of both commandments.

At dawn, Blackmon and Buie were dispatched back to the drop zone to look for the food bundle. They returned in three hours with a negative report. We had a long way to go and a short time to get there, so we moved out. A deserted forest ranger station many miles away was our first target.

Day one went quickly. Expending 7,200 calories apiece in our eight-hour cross-country trip, the detachment was in the night location at dusk. Not a living creature was spied during the entire ski trip; some snitch had apparently warned the snowshoes away from us hungry, armed renegades. Wilson and I pitched our shelter halves and complained about the lack of nourishment before we fell asleep. We awoke at dawn to the sound of gunfire.

Team Sergeant Fodder had downed a rambling snowshoe. He and Perry had the culprit skinned and turning over an open fire before half of our eight-man detachment arose from their slumbers.

Wilson, Stark, and I eyed the six-pound prey. Willie Stark said it all. "That's about four bites apiece for all of us. We can't ski all day on four lousy bites!"

Four bites and ten hours later, we approached the abandoned ranger camp, set up in our night location at 1700, and awaited the dawn in a starvation attitude. Wilson spied a porcupine climbing a small pine tree and shouted. We both moved through a six-foot snowbank to a tree-covered area where the first shot from Wilson's carbine hit the animal. The porcupine did not even lose its grip on the small pine tree. The animal defecated, reached back with one paw, filled it with his own excrement, and stuffed the wound.

"I'll be damned," I exclaimed. "He's not impressed with your carbine, Wilson!"

"I kinda hate to kill the tough little bastard," said Wilson. Somehow, our stomachs overrode our remorse. With a head shot, I blew the porcupine, shit and all, into the snow below. Wilson handled the spiny creature carefully and we snowshoed back to the small encampment. Very carefully, we skinned the creature and stood back and admired our upcoming meal.

Stark spoke for the remainder of the detachment. "There'll be no days when I eat porcupine, even if I'm starving."

Wilson and I disagreed and we alternated boiling the entire night. Come breakfast time, the team was once again given a shot at the delicacy. Again, they refused our gracious offer. Eating with our God-given utensils, Wilson and I finished the little fellow off in only minutes, but our stomachs churned and rumbled.

"Well, how did it taste, you big dummies?" Stark asked.

Wilson was still busy turning three different colors so I stepped into the breach. "It, ah, it tastes just like Crisco. Lard, that is." There were weird, rumbling noises coming from the pit of my stomach. "It was truly awful."

Breaking camp, Det A-4 moved to surround the abandoned ranger station. After thirty minutes of observation we moved through the summer facility. I took off my skis and went into a latrine marked WOMEN and spied the trash-filled receptacle. I searched the container meticulously, and counted the moldy cookies before stuffing five of them into my parka side pocket.

Four snowshoe rabbits fell to the invaders before we pitched tents at the foot of a snow-packed hill. Sparse pines shielded us from aerial observation. Wilson and I were again paired up in a pup tent. We still had our clothes on but removed our thermal boots before lying back on our air mattresses. My hand strayed to the side pocket containing the moldy sweets.

In the darkness I feigned a yawn, plopped the cookie into the open gap, chewing extra slowly so Wilson wouldn't notice. The ploy just didn't work.

Wilson sniffed at the delicious odor and glanced at my slow-moving jaws. "You bastard, you've got something to eat. Where? How? And give me some!"

"Quiet. I got five cookies out of that trash can at the ranger camp. Fifty percent of five is two, so here's your share."

Wilson joined me and also chewed slowly and smiled before softly speaking. "Bill, you're a good scrounger, but your math ain't worth shit."

After a three-bite breakfast of rabbit and a cup of hot water, three two-man recon patrols were dispatched. Stark and I drew a two-day job to recon Highway 30 near the small towns of Park Valley and Rossette, Utah. Fodder's briefing was short. "Observe Highway 30 for traffic density. Stay out of towns; the Highway Patrol has orders to arrest us on sight, as do the local police. We're the enemy. You should be there by tonight and return tomorrow. Any questions?"

"Yeah," said Stark. "What the hell do we use for food? That's a fifty-mile round trip on skis, carrying a thirty-five-pound rucksack. We'll look like refugees from Dachau by the time we get back."

Fodder flushed. He knew that we resented his over-supervision. He also knew we blamed him for not returning to the drop zone to recover the food bundle. What he probably didn't know was that the detachment wished he was back in the straightlaced 82d Airborne.

"Eat what you find along the way; the mission comes first. We're no better off than you two."

"That's not much consolation, Team Sergeant," Stark said. "If we're dead from starvation, what happens to the mission then? Let's go get that bundle and eat like human beings for a change." I nodded in agreement while Fodder stomped off.

We both spent four hours sidestepping up a steep slope that was covered with Utah grass before reaching the plains that led to Highway 30 and the two small towns. By 1600, we were camped only four miles from Park Valley. After camouflaging our pup tent, two tired, hungry troops built a fire. "If you're gonna starve to death, no use being cold, too," I said. No game had been sighted all day and our hunger pains were acute. We stared at each other and came to the same conclusion at the same time.

"How much money do you have, Willie?"

Stark smiled. "I have seven bucks, Bill. How much do you have?"

"I counted it before we left. I have nine. Here's the plan—screw Fodder. I'd rather be in jail than dead. We'll flip a coin to see who goes into town, gets sixteen dollars' worth of goodies and splits back here. Whatcha say?"

"Deal me in. But what if we get caught by the cops?"

"No problem, the other survivor waits until dark, then skis to town and throws himself on the mercy of the court. They have to feed us."

I flipped the coin, making sure Stark won. While heating water to shave, we broadened our plans. "My cover story bothers me somewhat, also," Stark said. But we worked out the problems before 1730 and Stark's departure.

"Two outdoorsmen are on a skiing vacation in the National Forest and just dropped in for supplies. They're camped on the south side of Highway 30. They have plenty of deer meat, but need some condiments to round out their diet."

"Mention diet to me, Willie, and I'll choke you."

"I'll buy bread, peanut butter, and candy bars by the ton. I read one time of a guy who lived for weeks on peanut butter," Stark said.

"Go for it, Willie. I also read somewhere about these mountain folks eating their companions to stay alive. That's an idea."

"Yeah, it is," Stark said. "I wonder how Fodder is gonna taste?"

I watched Stark ski off to Park Valley and the first super-market he could find. The sad part of the recent conversation, I thought, was that we were serious about Fodder. He'd make a platoon sergeant in the 82d; an SF team sergeant, he was not.

Staff Sergeant Stark skied the four miles cross-country to Chow Town, Utah. Finally, he spied a snow-packed road that led to Highway 30 and food. He sidled over until he was on the road and only two hundred yards from the wargame enemy. Then, throwing caution aside, he skied to the intersection and noted the small food mart that hugged the state thoroughfare.

Looking down the highway, he could see the entire small city. A few parked cars were visible but no humans. Quickly removing his slats and placing them on the wooden porch of the store, he entered the establishment.

An on-the-spot inspection by the pretty lady on duty told her all she needed to know. To make matters worse, Stark knew she knew. "You had better git gone. They've been looking for you GIs. Watcha want?"

Stark quickly removed the rucksack while the lass assembled his foodstuffs. Paying the lady, he packed the goods and was back on the road to camp in good time.

Over a campfire, we two would-be SF troopers devoured the bread and a jar of peanut butter. The candy bars were in no danger of spoiling and would see us back to base camp, a long twenty-five miles away.

As we entered base camp just before dark, a beautiful sight greeted us. The deer was skinned and ready to be cut into portions and placed over the roaring campfire. Morale in the detachment had zoomed.

The team leader, Lieutenant Perry, helped the morale process along the very next day and did not do it surreptitiously. The epochal announcement came after a breakfast of deer meat and a candy bar for all.

"We'll move back to our drop zone and attempt to recover our food bundle, then press on to our ambush site, to conclude the exercise."

Everyone but Fodder cheered the good news.

Recovering the bundle of field rations proved to be an easy task in the daylight and preserved the lives of many a snowshoe rabbit. Three days later, we successfully ambushed the buses that transported us back to Williams. Only a trip to Fort Bragg and a field training exercise (FTX) in Georgia separated us survivors from our "3" qualifications. My teammates and I would take four weeks to recover our lost weight.

CHAPTER 14

THE CHARTERED buses sped through the North Carolina countryside on State Highway 19. A scheduled stop at Morgantown interrupted, momentarily, an all-day trip to Dahlonega, Georgia, for the three SF A and support detachments. Khaki uniforms and bloused boots entered the fast-food chain restaurant but lingered only seconds because two black soldiers were refused service by the petite lady behind the counter. That experience on a day in April 1960 served to open the eyes of thirty-four Caucasian males. We loaded up again on our buses and sped on.

Leaving Morgantown on Highway 76, the buses were shortly in the foothills of the Chattahoochee National Forest. Taking a hard left on Georgia's Highway 60, we were at the Ranger camp in time for supper.

The camp provided instruction and exercises for the mountain phase of the Army's infamous Ranger School. We were quick to note that the camp was not built for comfort. The small wooden structures surrounded the center of the forested area with a messhall dominating the terrain. I spied the 1st lieutenant as soon as I entered the galvanized-tin building.

Lieutenant Dewitt Adkins, late of E Company, 179th Infantry, and Walters, Oklahoma, was concentrating on his meal as I seated myself opposite him on the picnic table. He looked up and was startled into a war whoop. I grinned and noticed, for the first time, the shiner below the blond officer's eye.

Years before, Adkins had been the All-Army boxing

champion at 118 pounds. When I surprised him at Ranger School, his five foot seven frame was carrying 135 pounds. We shook hands across the table before I began to lecture to the younger man. "Dewitt, you're an officer and a gentleman now. You are no longer a vulgar enlisted swine. You cannot go around getting into barroom brawls, like we used to. *Que pasa?* And what the hell are you doing here?"

Adkins glanced left and right to make sure everyone's mind was on the cuisine. Pale blue eyes and a broken nose above a grinning smile finally came up with an answer.

"Bill, I'm here to grade your detachment's performance. If you're on the team, I know damn well you'll have had the meat. Second, I had a few beers in a joint down the road a piece the other night and some cracker called me an Okie, among other things, so I decked him. His buddies didn't take to it, so I just did the best I could with 'em."

"I'll say one thing for you, Lieutenant. That battlefield commission didn't straighten you up any. You still act like an NCO. Where have you been for eight years, for Christ sake?"

"I was in the 11th Airborne Division in Europe for a few years after leaving Korea but I screwed up so much they sent me to Special Forces and I've been here ever since. How 'bout you, ole pal?"

"Fort Sill for eighteen months, Panama for three years, the one-oh-worst for a while, and now the 77th Special Forces Group. When this is over, I'll finally be qualified as an SF operator. How do you like Special Forces, Dewitt?"

"It's the only outfit in the Army for me, Bill. You learn something every day. Some of the assignments really put you in peculiar situations, but I wouldn't trade it for the world. When's the last time you were home, Bill?"

"Oh, about a year ago. Saw a lot of the guys. They're never gonna leave that damn place. Hey, don't be too hard on my team or I'll black your other eye, asshole."

"Bill! You can't talk to officers like that!" Adkins laughed.

"I know. I wish the hell I could, though. What's gonna happen to us here, anyway?" I asked.

"Your team is going through the mountain phase of Ranger School and then a graded field training exercise. We, the umpires, will give you assignments in the field and grade you individually on how well you carry them out. No sweat, GI!"

"My ole T-bird buddy is going to shaft his pal. Asshole!"

Adkins smiled at the mention of the four-five boys. "Damn, those were the good ole days, weren't they? Guess I didn't realize when I was well off."

"I told you not to take that battlefield commission but you wouldn't listen. See ya in the boonies, sir!"

The rappelling and the slide for life went well for the detachment. A cable over the Chattahoochee River fitted with a twelve-inch pipe had the soldiers hanging on for dear life despite knowing that the riverbank would cushion their sudden stop. Since we had practiced the procedures before leaving Smoke Bomb Hill and Fort Bragg proper, none of the exercises proved to be much of a challenge. Even so, the instructors impressed us with their military bearing and expertise in the subject matter.

Before moving out for our one-week FTX, Stark and I tried to lighten our load as much as possible. Fatigues, jump boots, and soft baseball caps were a must, as was just basic web gear—pistol belt, harness, two ammo pouches, first aid packet, and two full canteens tucked into their aluminum drinking cups. To save two ounces and arouse his packing partner, Stark eliminated one drinking cup.

We proceeded to lay out the equipment on our steel bunks before placing the gear in the aluminum-framed rucksacks. Our lightened loads would include the following items: Three pairs of OD socks in the outside pockets, jungle hammock, poncho and liner, five cans of C rations, cleaning rod, oil and patches for the carbines, six packs of cigarettes with C-ration matches and coffee packets from the field rations, and a roll of parachute suspension line.

Toothpaste and brush in the zipped top flap concluded the packing of the lightened rucksacks.

After we had war-gamed a few ambushes and been ambushed, I was given an assignment that would conclude my part of the test. "A dam located at GE350640 must be blown. You'll recon the area, take the measurements, and bring back a drawing containing your solution. The drawing must include the amounts, type, and placements of charges as well as the formulas you used to derive your solution. All law enforcement units in the area have been alerted and you must complete the assignments without detection. Are there any questions?" the briefer asked.

Stark and I studied our maps and planned our approach route. We finally concurred that the major problem in the exercise was completing the recon without detection by outside sources. The dam was downstream from Ainicalola Falls and only two hundred yards upstream from Highway 60 and a small picnic area that presented travelers a scenic view of the dam.

Securing harnesses, rucksacks, and the idiot sticks— carbines—we were off and running on a route that was up and down the damp Georgia countryside. So much so that some heavy breathing and slow walking preceded our noontime chow break.

Despite the welcome smoke breaks, we managed to be nestled in the dead leaves and pine-needled forest by 1700. We slung jungle hammocks under the pine canopy, and our overnight campsite was established.

The dam was thirty yards across and deeper than we had expected. From our view adjacent to the dam, we spotted a highway patrol car. The officer parked in the picnic area and was lounging on one of the cement benches. Stark and I were two hundred yards from being spotted, so we withdrew.

The patrolman left the area by 1800 and was replaced by transients—parents and two children who dawdled over their fast food and looked up at the dam from time to time, not knowing they were also being observed. By the time darkness had set in, the area was deserted. We then completed measuring the height, thickness, and length of the barrier.

"We'll sack out now," I said, at a few minutes before midnight. "I'll do the sketching, formulas, and placement of charges after we rise and shine."

The morning hours found me working out in my GI-issued notebook. Willie Stark was not dawdling either. He warily approached the picnic area, careful to look for sign of movement, and dutifully taped a sheet of paper on every table and bench in sight before retreating. Visitors to the area that day found signs that read:

ATTENTION, WOULD-BE PICNICKERS OR LAZY HIGHWAY PA-TROLMEN. THIS FACILITY HAS BEEN BOOBY-TRAPPED BY THE DEVIOUS GIS FROM DETACHMENT A-4, 77TH SFG (ABN). DO NOT SIT AT OR USE THE TABLES HERE. YOUR LIFE IS IN DANGER IF YOU ELECT TO IGNORE THIS WARNING. IN ORDER FOR THIS FACILITY TO BE SAFE AGAIN, CONTACT THE EXPLOSIVE ORDNANCE DETACHMENT AT FORT BENNING, GA. THEY WON'T KNOW WHAT TO DO EITHER. HAVE A BLAST! SIGNED: THE FOXES OF A-4.

The foxes were still a-grinning when we loaded up and retreated to our safe area. I turned in my sketches and smiled at the thought of visiting Fort Bragg once again.

The umpires briefed our detachment on their successes and near misses, concluding the briefing with their overall grade of satisfactory. Each individual was also graded and given a rating. Everyone was pleased but the team leader, Lieutenant Perry, who had received a message reading "Report to the camp commander." That was also the approximate choice of words that greeted Stark and me, twenty minutes later.

A large, balding major eyed us as the first sergeant escorted us into the Old Man's office. Stark and I reported to the major, but we also had eyes for the Georgia Department of Public Safety official who stood by his side.

The major glared at Perry before turning his attention to us. Stark and I weren't intimidated by the commander as he shoved our picnic bulletin toward us.

"Did you two compose that bit of wisdom, soldiers?"

To Perry's consternation we grinned. "Yes, sir," I replied. "What's the problem, sir?"

"The problem, sergeant, is that you two scared the wits out of the police and civilians of this area. That's the problem!"

"War is hell, sir. It was just a war game. He," I pointed to the policeman, "was after us. Payback is always hell, sir."

"Were you alerted that these men were in the area, Officer?"

"Yes, sir," sputtered John Law. "Had orders to arrest any GI I might see loitering around the dam or the highway. Didn't see none, though, and besides, a threat is a threat."

"These men carried no live ammunition or explosives, Officer. Seems like their only offense was trying to outwit the enemy, and I use the word wit rather loosely. You people are dismissed unless the lawman has thoughts to the contrary."

"No harm was done, I reckon. I was ordered to make sure there was no explosive devices left in the area, sir. Reckon, I'm convinced there wasn't."

A happy Detachment A-4 rode a chartered bus back to Fort Bragg and was given a three-day pass to boot. We single men enjoyed the main NCO club while the married personnel enjoyed their families.

On Wednesday, after the brief respite from the boondocks, we were handed our orders. In accordance with Special Orders # 103, dated June 3, 1960, we had all rappelled, starved, and climbed our way to the coveted "3" suffix.

The summer of 1960 didn't prove to be the fun and games indulged in at Dahlonega, but no one could blame the foxes of Detachment A-4.

With a new team sergeant on board, the team participated in a Special Forces Group parade on D-Day, June 6. When the khakis, jump boots, and overseas caps of the 77th SFG (Airborne) crossed the finish line, they had changed the history books forever. The 77th Special Forces Group was no more.

Team Sergeant Stanley Reed led his charges past the reviewing stands after the 77th's colors were retired. The 7th Special Forces would be organized along the same lines, but a lot of the gobbledegook of World War II would be retired along with the old colors. Having learned all we could learn from our OSS, European, and Canadian predecessors, Special Forces was striking out on its own. And we added another word to our mission statement—counterinsurgency!

Field Detachment C-1, or FC-1, was now Company A, 7th Special Forces Group (Airborne). It maintained its basic components, however. The twelve-man A detachments were still the operational elements. Administration, logistics, and tactical employment would remain the responsibility of the B and C detachments. In the years to come, under the guiding hand of Colonel William Yarborough, Special Forces would change the entire United States Army.

Charge of Company A fell to Lieutenant Colonel Arthur D. "Bull" Simons, who would prove to be a paradox. As an officer assignment, Special Forces was a snag in the ticket-punching process. If officers remained in the unit too long, they were destined to go no higher than lieutenant colonel—if they made it that far. The Bull compounded this felony with remarks like, "I'd rather be a captain in a Ranger or SF unit than a general in a conventional unit." Before it was over, his career would bear out his statement.

Short, squat, and muscular, Bull was often called No Neck by the admiring NCOs who served with him. He was a soldier's soldier and a hero to the enlisted ranks of Special Forces. In reality, that's probably what he wanted to be. The Bull would die only after becoming a legend not only to Special Forces but to an ungrateful nation as well.

Sergeant Major Denton turned the formation over to Bull one sunny morning. "It's simply a night jump, assembly problem, and a hike back to base. Don't screw it up."

Officers were jumpmasters and kicked out the flashlight-adorned door bundles before we exited. Detachment A-4 landed near the tree line of the Sicily Drop Zone assembly point.

Searching for a beam from flashlights that had probably been extinguished on impact proved to be a formidable problem. Noise, normally a no-no on SF maneuvers, soon dominated the dark North Carolina night. An hour later, Bull Simons was far beyond the furious stage. Heading the column that flanked the road, he mumbled to himself as the company strolled thirteen miles back to home base. A home where we awaited an ass-chewing that was postponed until the dawn.

Sergeant Major Ed Denton, lanky and thin at six foot two inches and 180 pounds, again took the morning report and turned the sleepy crew over to Simons. The Bull started slowly but gained momentum rather quickly. He then dismissed the officers and ordered all team sergeants, and whoever they wanted to bring, into his office. The crowded structure grew quiet when Captain Rye, the officer who had been in charge of the previous night's fiasco, walked in uninvited. My team sergeant and I observed from a seated position.

Bull told off the captain, then ended Captain Rye's unauthorized visit—and violated Army policy—with a remark that lives enshrined in the memories of the fortunate NCOs who heard it. "The last thing, Captain. If you ever fuck up like that again, I'm gonna reach my arm down your throat and grab you by the asshole and turn you inside out. Dismissed!"

The C-130 aircraft approached Sicily Drop Zone again that very night. Insuring that the transmitter was turned on before its departure, Team Sergeant Stan Reed kicked the bundle out on the first pass and the green light. On the next pass, the steel-helmeted paratroopers of Company A, 7th SFG, exited the aircraft into the warm prop blast. My chute rudely jolted me when it finally opened. I checked it and only then looked down at the black sandy pits below. Approximately 150 yards from terra firma, I let my load-bearing rucksack, a forty-pound pack that was secured to the waistband of my chute by a release strap, swing free. Approaching the sandy loam, I looked straight ahead, feet and slightly bent knees together in a controlled but relaxed manner as I smacked home.

Fully releasing my ruck, I removed my harness and rolled up the canopy in a figure-eight roll and secured it to the backpack of the parachute. After removing a transistor radio from the rucksack, I hoisted the load to my shoulders. A weapon in one hand and the radio in the other, I headed toward the assembly point. The radio's beeping noise became louder so I continued on course. When the signal faded, I simply adjusted my direction. I met my teamy, Craig Wofford, but we didn't break noise discipline. Company A concluded the assembly in total darkness in only fifteen minutes.

Quietly, Det A-4 lined up behind its control team and the Bull led his warriors for another thirteen miles. It was the best night assembly Wofford and I had ever seen. Wofford, a redheaded veteran of Korea and the famous 8th Ranger Company, was an airborne warrior of some renown. Despite being jumpmaster-qualified, I was still new at the profession and valued his opinion in the matter. Detachment A-4 concluded the thirteen-mile march and was trucking in the back of an uncomfortable Army vehicle before I initiated the conversation.

"How can we look like dummies one night and so brilliant the next, Wofford?"

"Easy, Bill. Any leader worth his salt could have done the same thing. The Bull simply called the experienced people together and presented the problem, then he selected the logical solution and we executed. Makes him look good, makes us happy and keeps the bureaucracy off our ass. Slick! You and I have done the same thing on a lower level in conventional units."

"I think he's great, at least for a field grade. He sure brought smoke on Captain Rye's ass."

"Yeah, and he'll bring smoke on anyone else that ever screws up or that misses a field problem, too. Sergeant Major Denton told me he's a bitch on missing field training."

The field problem scheduled for A Company would be of five days' duration. The unit would, by detachments, war-game immediate action drills (IADs) against every type of ambush. The proper reactions by the teams being ambushed had been perfected by the Infantry School at Fort Benning, Georgia, and would be the basis for a new field manual to be published by the Department of the Army. The field problem was preceded by one week of classes on ambushes that included theory and practical exercise. The immediate action drills were new to us but the ambushes served as a refresher for most personnel with a combat MOS.

An ambush is a surprise attack from a concealed position on a moving or temporarily halted target. Ambushes are classified by category—hasty or deliberate; type—point or area; and formation—linear or L-shaped. The leader uses a combination of category, type, and formation in developing his plan. The key planning considerations include: covering the entire kill zone by fire; using security elements or teams to isolate the kill zone; assaulting into the kill zone to search dead and wounded, and collect prisoners and equipment; timing the actions of all elements of the platoon to preclude loss of surprise; and rotating teams if the ambush is to be of a long duration.

The leader considers the linear or L-shaped formation in his planning. In an ambush using the linear formation, the assault and support elements deploy parallel to the enemy route. This positions both elements on the long axis of the kill zone and subjects the enemy to flanking fire. This formation can be used in close terrain that restricts the foe's ability to maneuver against the platoon, or in open terrain if a means of keeping the enemy in the kill zone can be effected.

In an L-shaped ambush, the assault element forms the long leg, parallel to the enemy's direction of movement along the kill zone. The support element forms the short leg at one end of and at right angles to the assault element. This provides both flanking (long leg) and enfilading fires (short leg) against the enemy.

A platoon or team conducts a hasty ambush when it makes visual contact with an enemy force and has time to establish an ambush without being detected. The action for a hasty ambush must be well rehearsed so that soldiers know what to do on the leader's signal. In planning and rehearsing a hasty ambush the leader should consider the following sequence of actions:

a. Using visual signals, any soldier can alert the platoon that an enemy force is in sight. He continues to monitor the enemy force until relieved by the team or leader.

b. The unit halts and remains motionless.

c. The leader determines the best location for the ambush. He uses hand and arm signals to direct soldiers to covered and concealed positions. He also designates the location and extent of the kill zone.

d. Security elements move out to cover each flank and the rear. The leader directs them to move a given distance, set up, and rejoin the team on order or when firing ceases.

e. Soldiers move quickly to covered and concealed positions, normally five to ten meters apart.

f. The leader initiates the ambush when the majority of the enemy enters the kill zone. If detected, a soldier initiates the ambush by firing his weapon.

g. Cease-fire is given when the force is destroyed or ceases to resist. The assault element moves into the kill zone and conducts a search of the enemy. All others remain in place.

Deliberate ambushes were discussed and rehearsed by the detachments. They are conducted against a specific target at a predetermined location. The two types of deliberate ambushes are the point and area ambush. In a point ambush, soldiers deploy to attack an enemy in a single kill zone. In

(Left) Corporal Roamey T. and Mrs. Craig around the year 1925 at Fort Sill, Oklahoma. Picture was passed on to the author by his mother. (Origin unknown)

(Below) Corporal Roamey T. Craig cradles his youngest, Jean, while the author, on left, and sister Pauline look on. Enlisted housing in the foreground speaks for itself. (Origin unknown, author's collection)

(Left) Sgt. Roamey T. Craig at retirement time at Fort Sill, Oklahoma, in 1946. (Author's collection)

(Below) Men of the Pioneer & Ammunition Platoon, 2d Battalion, 179th RCT, bid farewell in late October 1951. Left to right front row: Sgt. Edgemon and two unidentified; left to right top row: Walt Kubala, Richard Funk, Glendon, author, Jim Hill, and Vince Zuriga. (Author's collection)

(Left) On again, off again: Corporal Craig's stripes in Hokkaido, Japan, in 1951. (Author's collection)

(Above) T-birds Jim Hill and Clarence Avery enjoy RCT reserve in Korea in 1952.

(Left) SSG Buddy Ryan in a group picture with Company F, 179th RCT in 1951. (Courtesy of Louis Rivas)

(Left) Clarence Avery years after his knee operation, enjoying Korea's fall weather. (Courtesy of Clarence Avery)

(Below) Some of the Fighting Foxes enjoy a reunion in Oklahoma City in the late 1950s. Dan Blocker, star of *Bonanza*, enjoys civilian life once again. (Courtesy of Louis Rivas)

(Left) 77th SFG enjoy ski training at Camp Williams, Utah, in 1960. (Courtesy of Gerry Stamn)

Detachment Metcalf in Savannakhet, Laos. The civilians are, left to right front row: Reed, Largen, Metcalf, Craig; top row: Wolford, Bean, two interpreters and Jurens. (Author's collection)

The author presents a weapons class in the NCO Academy at Savannakhet, Laos in 1960. The students are the future police (civilian) of Vientiane, the administrative capital of Laos. (Author's collection)

A valley and gentle hills near Buon Mi Ga, SVN in 1965. (Courtesy of Gerald Naquin)

The Buon Mi Ga Laundromat is hard at it in 1964/65. (Author's collection)

The native ladies go about their chores in Buon Mi Ga, South Vietnam, in 1964. (Author's collection)

A leader of the refugees and a 7th Company soldier near Buon Mi Ga in 1965. (Author's collection)

The Seventh Darlac Company crosses a danger point near Buon Mi Ga in 1965. (Author's collection)

(Left) The 7th Company's first kill in 1965. The sniper was killed near Buon Chat, in Darlac Province. (Author's collection)

(Below) Viet Cong feeds her child before our move back to base camp in 1965. (Author's

(Left) SFC Pronier extracting ricochet round from Viet Cong' shoulder/arm. (Author's collection)

an area ambush, soldiers deploy in two or more point ambushes. A platoon, about forty soldiers, is the smallest unit to conduct an area ambush. Because of the time and planning involved, points stressed in deliberate ambushes varied from the hasty-type ambush. Actions of assault elements should include:

a. Emplacement of aiming stakes to identify sectors of fire as assigned by the team leader.

b. Emplacement of mines and other protective devices.

c. Camouflage of positions.

d. Take weapons off SAFE beforehand. This metallic click could otherwise compromise the ambush. This is the last action performed by all soldiers before waiting to initiate the ambush.

e. Team leader's initiation of the ambush.

f. Utilization of the two-man search technique in kill zone.

g. Identification and collection of equipment to be carried back (all captured weapons on SAFE).

h. Planned withdrawal, normally in reverse order than that in which they established their position.

Only after rehearsals and practical exercises in all phases of ambushes did we go into the immediate action drills that we would use the following week against an aggressor force.

The drills were simple and in a day or so could be perfected easily. If hit from a linear ambush, the team turns into the ambush and assaults the enemy in a skirmish line of marching fire. If the point of your patrol is hit, you form a skirmish line on the lead man and assault the enemy. When the point man receives fire, the second man lines up on his right, the third man on his left and so on until a skirmish line is formed. Then the assault on the target begins. The classroom and field practice behind us, we were ready for our final exams.

The night before boony time, me and Asa Ballard, my

ole Fort Campbell buddy, decided to visit the infamous Annex-8 bar and thrill.

Asa Ballard, the Louisville, Kentucky, boy, was a good-looking, twenty-five-year-old buck sergeant of medium build and short curly hair. Girls gushed at his good looks. To say the least, he and I were a contrast.

We drove my paid-for convertible to the World War II–era den of iniquity. Because the annex was known for its rowdy customers, Ballard cautioned me for the third time before we departed the billets. "Peace, tonight, Bill. Got it?"

The peace pact was broken around closing time outside Annex-8. When it was over, Ballard had to drive back to the billets. The fun and games were finished but I was not about to have my eye sutured at Bragg's Womack Hospital, because they would report it through channels and might even keep me overnight. I had also reminded myself of the Bull's policy about missing field problems, regardless of the reason. "Hope Doc Wofford is in the billets when we arrive."

Upon arrival, Ballard woke up the redhead and I went to the latrine to clean up my bloody eye.

The operation was over in thirty minutes and eighteen stitches. Craig Wofford stepped back and admired his surgical handiwork while I continued muttering obscenities at my spectator-sidekick, Ballard.

Wofford placed a piece of gauze over the eye and taped it in place before remarking, "There, Bill, you're ready for the boonies tomorrow. After a week in the field, I'll remove the sutures and you'll be as pretty as ever. Better than being a corporal E-4 again."

Sergeant Major Ed Denton took the report from the detachments, did an about face and reported to Lieutenant Colonel Simons. The Bull returned the salute and softly asked, "What the hell happened to Craig's eye?"

"Oh, he and Ballard were having a good time at Annex-Eight last night, sir!" Denton replied.

"Damned if they wasn't. Okay, Sergeant Major, load 'em up!"

Company A loaded into the two-and-a-half-ton trucks while I continued cursing Ballard. We would stay in the field until the immediate action drills were perfected. They would become the Bible for the U.S. Army's fight against the guerrilla ambushes that lay ahead in the jungles of Southeast Asia.

One of the instructors in the exercise, a bloke by the name of Moe Copeland from England's 22d Special Air Service (SAS), would become one of my closest allies. Not that I needed any more allies, as I was in enough trouble the way it was.

When A Company returned from the field, Wofford took his patient to the operation room and examined my eye. "You're going to have a permanent scar below the eye but your eyebrow'll cover the scar above it."

"Don't sweat it, Doc. It's too late for me to become a movie star. Thanks for your help. We only have a week before the Green Swamp exercise. Hell, I can stay outta Annex-Eight that long. What's this Green Swamp deal, anyhoo?"

CHAPTER 15

"**THE WAY** I hear it, it's just to test some survival rations the Army has come up with. Green Swamp hasn't been invaded by man in twenty years, so the snakes and the bears have had it all to themselves. The only thing I don't care for is that we have to take a physical training test upon our return; gotta pass it, too."

We strolled from the latrine and the conversation was moving as well. "I'm gonna eat some of them snakes," I said, "that'll keep up my strength."

"I'll stick with the conventional fish, Bill, but to each his own," said Wofford.

"One last thing, Doc. I'll be damn glad when you get another operating room. If you don't, I'm gonna forget what the hell the latrine is really for!"

"Just stay outta trouble, Bill. Speaking of trouble, there's Moe Copeland, your old SAS pal. He's waiting on you."

The 22d SAS is an elite unit of the British Army. Although their missions are not exactly the same, Special Forces and SAS are somewhat comparable. Both units require airborne capabilities; both units have exacting qualifications, and both have varied missions. So much so, that the two units exchange students in order to learn from each other.

In the time since the IAD exercises, the British NCO and I had become close friends and never missed a chance to rib each other. We enjoyed each other's company but wouldn't admit it. So when Moe was assigned to Det A-4

154

for the Green Swamp excursion, neither of us lost any sleep over it.

Company A fell out Monday morning dressed for the occasion. All troops, including the commander, wore standard fatigues, jump boots, olive drab baseball caps, and web gear. We toted the Garand M-1 semiautomatic rifle of World War II fame. After taking the head-count report from Denton, Bull Simons issued some specific instructions to his enlisted chief. "Group headquarters is spying on us to make sure we move out by 0800, our scheduled time, and I don't like snoops. Do not start the truck engines until 0750, and move out on my signal at 0800 on the dot. Okay, Top?"

"Yes, sir. It's 0730 now, though, so I'll talk to 'em. We'll load up when I'm finished. We'll be ready, sir."

The entire company knew Lieutenant Colonel Tate of Utah fame was the spy on the spot from group headquarters.

Bull kept one eye on his watch, one eye on the spy, and one arm in the sky. At 0800, he made a third-finger salute and dropped his arm. Much to the disgust of Snoopy Tate, the trip to Green Swamp got under way at precisely 0800 hours.

The convoy departed Fatalburg, North Carolina, on Highway 301 and arrived in Lumberton hours later. Field rations were gagged down while the vehicles hit Bolton, South Carolina, on Highway 211. We were unloaded just outside the ville of Maktoka. Green Swamp was bordered by Winnabow, Town Creek, Bolivia, and Wilmington. Having already been briefed on our area of operation (AO), the detachment commander talked to a tobacco farmer before entering Green Swamp proper.

"Can't help you much, Cap'n. I wouldn't go in there if you paid me. Ain't been no white man in there for twenty years or so. Even the niggers seem to have more sense, too."

"What's so dangerous about it, sir?" Perry asked.

"Bears, for one thing. Bigger'n a house, they are. Come

out once in a while and steal my corn, too, the bastards. Snakes are a dime a dozen in there also—water moccasins, bull snakes bigger 'n pythons, and them poisonous little copperheads. Thought ya had better sense, though."

"When the bears and snakes see these ugly bastards, mister, they'll probably move out," Perry said. "Copeland, take point, Craig take slack man. Let's move out!"

Copeland tried to stay on solid ground but for the most part, it was hard to come by. "Wait-a-minute vines" and water plants made the going slow and wetter'n water. Water and mud soon filled our boots and clung to our legs up to the knee. The vines blocked the approaches to the objective and Copeland soon wished he was back in the British Isles.

Continuously checking his wrist compass, Copeland almost missed a large water moccasin that blocked his path. He halted the single-file formation and motioned me up from slack. I complied and stood next to the SAS soldier and also eyed the snake, who was suddenly outnumbered.

"What's the problem, bloke?"

Red-faced, Copeland answered, "That's the problem, Yank!"

Now, I normally don't like to be called a Yank, but I took no offense. I retrieved a limb and swung at the blockade. The water moccasin snapped at the stick and slithered off. Perry suddenly was at our sides, and after a brief explanation of the delay made a decision.

"Craig, take the point on the same heading. Find a night location within the next hour, one where we can build a fire and sling our jungle hammocks, if possible. Due to the terrain and snakes, we'll change point men every hour." Copeland was ecstatic. The detachment moved uneventfully to its first night location.

Detachment A-4 learned to live in the swamps, sleep in jungle hammocks, build up the terrain for fire-making, and lead a peaceful coexistence with the bears and snakes of South Carolina.

Diarrhea was prevalent for the first few days, but Doc Wofford's excellent medical treatment kept the effects to a minimum. Moe Copeland survived me and the snakes and the other creepy companions.

On the last day, the unit assembled in the morning and the Bull led his survivors back to the confines of Fort Bragg. A good night's sleep separated the Green Swamp warriors from a physical training test.

Moe and I were doing well on the PT test, and by the time the unit arrived at the last exercise, Copeland I were tied at 300 points out of a possible 500, the minimum to pass a Special Forces PT test in that day and age. I wanted to beat Copeland but the aftereffects from the rations and snake diet just wouldn't allow it. At the pullup bar, I did the minimum and scored a 355. Copeland managed to pull his chin above the bar eight times for a 400-point total.

But current events were about to present the 7th Special Forces and Det A-4 with more survival training and on-the-job training. In August 1960, I bid farewell to Moe Copeland, while my detachment and I were being discussed in other quarters. Moreover, that month the word spread throughout the 7th Special Forces Group that a task force was being formed to facilitate a classified mission. Twelve eight-man detachments would train for several months before departure to an undisclosed destination.

Detachment A-4 was notified of its selection and its single soldiers moved into the designated task force billets. But there weren't many of us due to the predominance of married personnel in Special Forces. A briefing by a group operations officer came Monday morning, and Detachment A-4 had a few changes before its initial appearance at the briefing. Captain Metcalf, Lieutenant Perry, Master Sergeant Stanley Reed, Sergeant First Class Craig Wofford, Staff Sergeant Dick Largen, Sergeant First Class George Bean, Sergeant John Stafford, and myself would be sitting on the front row.

CHAPTER 16

"THE KINGDOM of Laos is situated across the Mekong River from neighboring Thailand and borders North and South Vietnam. The kingdom is now a factor in the North Vietnamese rush to enlighten Southeast Asia about poverty and, worst of all, Communism." The briefer paused and allowed the audience to view the large map of the area.

Detachment A-4, two officers and six NCOs, occupied the first row in the Smoke Bomb Hill Theater. We were told that the situation in Laos would be completely covered in our area-assessment training. The task force (TF) would depart Fort Bragg and arrive in Laos in civilian clothes in November 1960. There, we would work for the Program and Evaluation Office situated in Vientiane, the administrative capital of Laos.

Upon completion of training, and before departure, we would be issued civilian ID cards and a civilian clothing allowance; for all practical purposes, we would be civilians. Some SF troopers didn't really like the arrangements and left the briefing in disagreement. The rest of the day, the task force's twelve detachments worked out the kinks of a very detailed training schedule. The next day physical exams were administered. Because we were to be in an area with limited health facilities, the exams were stringent and a few of the TF were disqualified for medical reasons. Replacements moved in immediately. Team Metcalf remained intact, but we were reminded that we could be dropped for many valid reasons during the training phase.

The force would be commanded by my Utah buddy Lieutenant Colonel Garbage Gut Tate. Training consisted of a 0500 chow call, 0630 language class, 0800 area assessment, with the rest of the day dedicated to methods of military instruction, weapons, and tactics—all that accompanied by the usual night jumps. The prolonged, very tiring course would cause some dropouts and replacements.

The majority of us civilians-to-be took well to the language training. Laotian is akin to Thai and in a few short months the personnel would know enough to present classes. The area-study presentations gave the group a feel for Laos and its situation.

Under the Geneva Accords of 1954, Laos was given complete independence. Its national defense remained under control of the French military forces, who were permitted to remain as advisers. Beginning January 1, 1955, the United States paid for the majority of the Laotian army salaries, food, clothing, and equipment. This was to support the U.S. attempt to keep Laos as a buffer between communist North Vietnam and friendly Thailand. The Geneva agreement prohibited the presence of American military personnel in Laos, so the United States had to work around this technical blockade. In December 1950, the Americans established the Programs Evaluation Office (PEO) in the administrative capital of Vientiane. The PEO was manned by "civilians," retired military officers who monitored how the furnished material was being used.

Brigadier General Rothwell H. Brown (Ret.) took over the reins in 1957 and was surprised at the condition of the equipment of the French-trained army—most of it was rusting away in storage sheds. Brigadier General John A. Heintges, an active duty officer, took over in November 1958. Heintges found Laos to be a political cesspool. Prince Souvanna Phoumi's efforts to maintain a unified nation had failed, and the North Vietnamese–sponsored Pathet Lao forces led by his half-brother, Prince Souphanouvong, controlled the northeastern portion of the country. The *Armée Nationale de Laos* lacked leadership and was poorly organized. Worse, the French officers and NCOs appeared unconcerned.

Because of Heintges's report, a meeting between the United States and France was held in Paris during May 1959. A military training plan for Laos was agreed upon. The French insisted that all tactical training remain theirs, and the United States agreed to provide only technical training, using eight-man U.S. technical field-training teams and French tactical advisory teams of identical size.

The mission called for military training on an infantry battalion level in a conventional environment. Naturally, many Pentagon officers thought the tasks should go to Regular Army and Marine units, but since the Special Forces were already organized along team lines, Heintges opted for and received—us.

Special Forces was ordered to form twelve initial teams that would be sent to Laos for six months on temporary duty (TDY). Their pay, records, and administration were provided by the 902d Counterintelligence Corps Group at Fort Myer, Virginia. The first twelve teams and a support team arrived in Laos in July 1959. The control team and three reduced A detachments were stationed in Vientiane, and the other teams evenly distributed to Luang Prabang, Savannakhet, and Pakse. The Laotian Training Advisory Groups, PEO, were named instead of numbered, many of them after their team leader (as with our Team Metcalf). The teams wore civilian clothes and carried civilian ID cards. (I couldn't speak for my teamies, but the program briefing to this point was fascinating to me.)

Bickering and disputes over authority soon had the French and the U.S. "civilians" working independently. The Laotians avoided both groups when possible. Recruits were becoming harder and harder to come by. The rest of the story, we were told, would come from our area briefing and Lao language classes.

Our day would begin in the area study and Lao language classrooms, enabling us to keep abreast of the situation in

Southeast Asia. My barracks companions and I had a lot to study every night in order to be prepared for the next day.

Unfortunately, the coexistence of the nice guy and Lieutenant Colonel Tate erupted into open warfare again. "Hats will not be worn to and from the messhall," said the sergeant major. "I'm sick and tired of the complaints about thievery of jump wings [worn on front of the caps]. Leave your headgear in the barracks during chow."

I walked bareheaded to the messhall Monday morning at 0515. Stationed outside the entrance was the infamous and overweight lieutenant colonel. I saluted him and almost made it to the door of the facility.

"Come back here, soldier," Tate shouted.

Despite the fact that the colonel was in his cups that chilly morning, I complied. Standing at attention, I said "Sergeant Craig reporting as directed."

"Where's your headgear, soldier?" Tate said, slurring his words.

"It's in the barracks, where it's supposed to be at chow time, sir."

Tate failed to understand the explanation. "Oh? You don't wear your hat outdoors, Sergeant?"

"That's what the sergeant major explained to us."

"Oh, I see," Tate said. "Colonels have to wear their hats outside but sergeants don't. You guys have a good deal. I'll see about this and you'll hear about it before this day is out, soldier."

I ambled to the messhall, mumbling to myself once again.

Mess Sergeant Norman Racibor met me inside the dining facility after observing the incident. "Are you and him at it again, Bill?"

"Yeah," I said, laying my tray on the metal serving line. "He never gives up. One of us has got to go. I'll not take that shit from him, nor is the officer's corps gonna do me that way."

"Go get him, Bill. You have enough witnesses, God knows."

In one week, the World War II veteran was no longer in charge of the task force. Lieutenant Colonel John Little relieved him and things went much smoother for the entire group. True to my word, I did more than my share on Tate's behalf. Word of mouth to the sergeant major and my team leader did more than just place the on-duty drunk at the scene of the crime. Colonel Yarborough, commander of Special Forces, could not condone his type of behavior. The Craig-Tate Saga was over except for one more incident.

Back at the ranch, the training was intensifying; even the 1600 physical training had become more than just routine. But it all served to bring the members of Team Metcalf closer. As a detachment we fired every weapon in the U.S. and Soviet arsenals and through hard work, each of us became much stronger in his weaker subjects. One of the task force's requirements was that every team member be able to send and receive a minimum of five words a minute in Morse code. With some night work by the detachment and the 05B radio/telephone operator supervising, the team reached that goal, also.

Old soldier and Team Sergeant Stan Reed was satisfied with the progress as well. My personal physician, Sergeant First Class Wofford, thrived on the language classes and his knowledge would enhance the team's performance after deployment.

Weapons man George Bean took pains during his instruction to help the young radio operator, Dick Largen, through cross-training instruction by his teammates. Largen would mature from a young Special Forces radio operator to a young Special Forces operator. There *is* a difference.

The two officers, Lieutenant Perry and Captain Metcalf, received the instruction as well. They became well acquainted with their team members as well as with subjects that they had only given casual attention to in the past. In October our well-oiled machine moved into its final processing week. Administrative details and more briefings took up this period.

After we received our civilian clothing allowance, the

two officers attempted to advise the enlisted men on their purchases. The team was receptive to the advice and was soon decked out for inspection. In the final week, civilian clothes were the only uniforms we were allowed to wear, on or off post. Haircuts were taboo as well. For once, an airborne unit frowned on the infamous crew-cut jobby; too military, you know. Actually we NCOs enjoyed the week of civilian orientation much more than the officers did. A kitty was established, and anyone caught saluting or returning a salute had to contribute to the pot. My personal physician and I were more than willing to help the beer money grow by luring officers to return salutes we hadn't actually made. Beware the NCO, for he is cunning.

The final briefing for the classified mission included communication procedures to be used with family and friends. "Your mailing address will be the Psychological Warfare Headquarters. The envelopes you use will be removed. Notations of rank or serial numbers will not appear on the container. Your mail will be read from time to time, so watch for any disclosure of classified information, meaning your destination and/or location. We will relay your mail to your families in sanitized envelopes."

When the TF boarded the World War II–era C-124 at Pope AFB, only Special Forces people were allowed to attend the farewell. Lieutenant Colonel Tate headed the line of well-wishers. I stiffened at the sight of my old pal, and so did my team leader. Metcalf moved to my rear to cover any trouble.

The colonel smiled, shook hands and damn near started a riot. "Good luck, you motherfucker." Metcalf couldn't believe he said it, either. The remark did not go unnoticed by the other well-wishers and officials as well. I halted the loading line and said, "I don't have to take that shit from you, you sonofabitch, and I won't. I'm gonna—"

Metcalf moved me on down the line and gave me to Wofford. And so, decked out in our odd-looking attire, Detachment Metcalf left Pope Air Force Base in November

1960. A day-long flight in the C-124 found us at Travis AFB, California.

I was still mouthing off about Tate when the group checked into the base's bachelor officer's quarters. "It's not bad enough to be insulted by one of 'em, now I have to live with the bastards."

We were informed that we were required to eat in the officer's mess, but before I could begin again, Metcalf took charge. "You will sit at the table with Lieutenant Colonel Little, Major Lewis, Lieutenant Perry, and myself. I do not want to hear any more from you about Colonel Tate's poor choice of words."

I was now thirty-four years old and gray tinged my wavy brown hair. The waitress approached and made my day. She looked at me, clearly the most distinguished man in an otherwise motley crew, and said, "What will you have, Colonel?" The hushed crowd eyed me expectantly.

I beamed and grinned for the first time all day. "Chicken-fried steak with cream gravy and iced tea. Mighty fine place you have here, ma'am. Good-looking waitresses, too! Reckon my men will enjoy your fine service and food." Colonel Little was grinning, but Metcalf and Lewis cast threatening looks my way.

While the troops ate, light conversation went on. Only the happy "colonel" abstained. Finally Little brought me out of fantasy land. "Would you care to join us for drinks after dinner, Colonel?"

"No thanks, John. Too many responsibilities. I'm an early-to-bed sort—maybe next time." Metcalf shook his head.

The words of our dinner were the talk of the task force the next day. Unbeknownst to me, I had inadvertently earned a nickname that would follow me throughout my twelve years and two months of Special Forces service. Still, the "Colonel" took it all in stride.

The four-engine C-124 managed to land on three engines in Hawaii for another overnight stay. Hickam Field was prepared for the "senators," as one crew member called us.

Team Sergeant Stanley Reed asked me a very earnest question. "Wonder why they call us senators, Bill?"

I straightened my civilian tie before answering. "Don't rightly know, Top. I guess somebody from the task force stole something back at Travis."

We landed the next day in Bangkok, Thailand. There we were broken down by detachments and flown to our assignments in Laos. All field training teams (FTTs) were equipped with passports, civilian ID, and international driver's licenses before we reached our destinations. Our khaki shirts and pants had no unit patches or Army decorations.

The TF had watched the Laotian events closely and was prepared to replace the combat advisers then in place. But the TF would go into a situation completely different from the three groups it had followed. Thanks to Captain Kong Le. On August 9, 1960, Kong Le and his 2d *Battalion Parachutiste* staged a coup d'état on the flatlands just outside Vientiane.

The Ranger-qualified captain controlled the best troops in the Laotian army, such as it was, but had unwittingly become a puppet of the Soviet-backed Pathet Lao. He demanded a return to neutrality, and a Laos free of foreign influence. A very lofty goal indeed. We on the task force often wondered aloud why such a terrific U.S.-trained soldier-patriot had pulled such an idealistic stunt.

Only after our field training team settled into comfortable quarters in Savannakhet, two hundred miles downstream on the Mekong River from Vientiane, did we go to work. Association with Lao trainees and school cadre taught us some things that our briefings had not dwelled upon while training at Fort Bragg, and this knowledge cast a different light on the Kong Le defection.

Vientiane funneled U.S. money to the Lao army under the not-so-watchful eyes of the U.S. Embassy. At Luang Prabang, the royal capital of the kingdom, the royalty played the games that kings, queens, princes, and princesses play. Rumors said the funds were going to the French, unscrupulous administrators, and possibly even Americans.

Kong Le's battle-weary soldiers had not been paid for months. Familiar with the shady side of politics in our own country, the task force had no reason to disbelieve the rumors.

Regardless, it was left to General Phoumi Nosavan and a brigade of Laotian troops to rid Vientiane of the Pathet Lao and Kong Le. Major Parmley, the commanding officer of the task force, and the task force of civilians coached, begged, and led the counter-coup troops. Within twenty-five days of our arrival, the task force and its followers stormed the Ca Dinh river line. With the help of the 1st and 3rd Parachute Battalions, which had been dropped outside the capital, Vientiane was back in the hands of the good guys come December 17, 1960, and our FTT was happy to have contributed to the effort.

After a Laos Military Advisory and Assistance Group (MAAG) was formed in Savannakhet, FTT Metcalf virtually took over the training at the NCO academy located on the edge of the city. Here, Bean, Wofford, and I found ourselves training a new Vientiane police force. We wrote lesson plans, translated them—with the help of Thai interpreters—into Lao, and in five weeks the new cops departed to write speeding tickets in the newly recaptured capital.

I was returning from work one day with an interpreter, when I got a lesson on the French-trained Lao army. My Thai companion was doing the speed limit in the U.S. jeep when another jeep, driven by a Lao *tahan* (soldier), suddenly ran a stop sign and banged into us at the intersection. Neither vehicle was damaged badly but a Lao lieutenant and I surveyed the damage before I spoke.

"Ran the stop sign, didn't you, sir?"

"Yes, Sergeant. I ran it. Me officer, you civilian, so you are at fault."

Of all people to make that remark to, the lieutenant had really selected a winner. "Rank," I said slowly, "does not give you the right to disregard civil laws, dumbass. If it ever happens again, I'll kick your ass, sir!"

The officer left in a huff while the interpreter looked on admiringly at his civilian sidekick. Not so Team Chief Metcalf. "T-A-C-T," he spelled. "I should make you spell it one hundred times."

"Ain't having no trouble spelling, sir. It's the French system of thought that's bothering me," I said honestly.

"Don't let it throw you. The French officer is an elitist and doesn't even carry his own pack on operations. He has a dog-robbing private to do that. He knew, in his heart, that you were an NCO, so you're wrong. In his eyes at least."

"The assholes."

"T-A-C-T," the team leader spelled again.

The battle of Mahaxy erupted in January 1961, and the Lao army was at its usual worst. The town was not far from Seno, the French airfield near Savannakhet, and if it fell, the Pathet Lao could cut the kingdom in half again. MAAG and the task force had other plans. One dark night Team Metcalf helped a Thai artillery battalion bridge the Mekong River from Thailand. The 105-millimeter artillery unit quickly formed outside Savannahket, trucks, weapons, and all. With blackout lights on, they moved into position just outside the beleaguered city.

When daylight approached, the civilians of Team Metcalf helped the forward observers from Thailand find lucrative targets for the artillery. The Thai shooters proceeded to drop something on the poorly disguised North Vietnamese Army that lye soap wouldn't rub off. The battle for Mahaxy was over by dusk that night. Team Metcalf worked overtime helping the Thai cross the river and return to their homeland. It marked the first time that the FTT had been impressed since its arrival in Savannakhet. "Shades of Fort Sill," one wit remarked. "You can tell where they got their training. It damn sure wasn't France."

Our FTT pulled a multitude of assignments as the French all but hung it up. For a month or so, I found myself flying with Air America in a World War II–era C-46 aircraft. It was not the aircraft that I enjoyed, though, it was the civilian pilot who manned it.

Art "Shower Shoes" Wilson was a middle-aged pilot who flew for fun and money. A companion of the late "Earthquake" McGoon of Dien Bien Phu fame, he was no less a character himself. He flew wearing only shower shoes as footgear, and even shaved and took a bath from time to time. He and his new crew chief got along swimmingly, and neither of us kept secrets from the other. Art even explained why he kept a pair of combat boots in the rear of the pilot's cabin. "Got shot down about a year ago and had to walk out of the jungle north of here. Damn uncomfortable."

An outpost on the North Vietnamese–Laotian border sorely needed weapons and ammunition, and Shower Shoes et al. came to the rescue. When the C-46 made its first pass I shoved the pallet of supplies but it fell short of the landing zone and Art and I watched the two factions fight over the food bundle.

"Art, I can't do it unless you get down, dammit. It's just too small a drop zone."

To the dismay of the Chinese copilot, Art replied, "No problem, Bill, we're going in almost at treetop level this time." We went in so low that I could have got in on the firefight if I hadn't been so busy with the parachute-rigged supplies. As Art began the last pass, Soviet ammunition sought us out and I nervously kicked out my last door bundle before moving to the pilot's cabin in relief.

Art Wilson landed in Vientiane for refueling and, as it turned out, repairs to the aircraft. While the Chinese copilot was heading to the hangar to turn in his quit slip, Wilson and I inspected the skin of the aircraft. The two engines were untouched; the wings were a different matter.

Each wing had at least eight hits. Fortunately, the rounds had not touched the gas tanks that were tucked away in the wings, and Art was grinning when the Philippine technicians from the Program Evaluation Office arrived on the scene. They shook their heads while talking to the pilot.

"It'll take us up to two hours to repair the damage, Mr.

Wilson. Wait in the bar and grill and we'll come for you when we're finished."

We walked across the concrete apron to the small terminal below the control tower. I settled for a beer and a sandwich, which Wilson paid for. Activity around the terminal was frantic but seemed organized. It was a new world to me but bothered Art Wilson not in the least. While we were eating, a well-dressed young man entered the small establishment and headed straight for our booth, then spoke to me as Wilson continued to stare out the window. "Mister Wilson, I'm from the embassy."

I pointed to Wilson, but continued to look at the intruder.

"Mister Wilson, we're loading your aircraft at this time. You'll fly your cargo to Savannakhet, where you'll be unloaded."

Without waiting for a response, he deposited a receipt and flight plan in front of Wilson. The veteran merely glanced at the information before signing. The very official person handed Wilson his copies before exiting. Art stared at the papers while my anxiety grew.

"Well, dammit, what have the bums from the embassy got us into now, Art?"

Wilson looked around the busy terminal before he faced me and offered an explanation. "I'll tell you when we get on board. It's a very unusual cargo, however."

The Filipino from the PEO was our next visitor. "Your aircraft has been repaired and serviced, Mr. Wilson. You're free to take off at your convenience." We ground out our cigarettes and followed the airplane doctor out onto the apron of the runway.

The C-46 was ringed with armed military police of the Lao armed forces. That only served to heighten my curiosity. I followed Art as the pilot checked the repair job. When he was satisfied, we both had to climb over large bales to get to the cockpit. I still didn't know what the cargo was. "Hell, Art, it ain't cotton, at least I know that much."

From the copilot seat, I assisted Wilson with the preflight

check list. "Okay, okay, enough already. What the hell is in those bales, Art?"

"That," pointed Wilson, "is the payroll for the Third Military Region of Laos. It's Laotian kip. They haven't paid the boys for three months, so it's aplenty. I guess the embassy finally got the stealing stopped long enough to make the government pay the troops."

"How much kip, Art?"

"An even two million dollars' worth, Bill. Let's go pay the starving Marvins!"

When the aircraft taxied down the runway, I was not thinking about the starving Marvins. I was thinking of how to steal two million dollars in Laotian currency. Art Wilson, in the meantime, did his number on the capital city of the kingdom.

He banked at three hundred feet and flew down the busy main thoroughfare at treetop level. The control tower was screaming as people on the ground darted away from our path; only then did Wilson gain altitude and head for the objective.

"Let's steal the shit, Art. It may be my one and only chance to become a millionaire," I blurted. "On E-5's pay, it'll take me three thousand years to earn that much!" Art glanced at me momentarily.

"They would shoot us down before we reached Red China. That's about the only place we could exchange it. We'd be wanted men without a country. Do you want to be a millionaire in Red China, Bill?"

"No. But the lost opportunity breaks my heart anyway. On to Savannakhet, Art!"

Wilson approached the capital of the Third Military Region from Thailand, crossed the Mekong River, and landed. The Savannakhet airfield was a virtual fortress by the time the wheels touched the dirt airstrip. Tanks and armored personnel carriers ringed the small strip, and Lao military police cordoned off the parked C-46 as Wilson and I were escorted to the small terminal. There, Art Wilson signed over the two million dollars' worth of kip.

Back at the team house, Team Sergeant Reed had new assignment orders for me. "We're now recruiting four hundred men for a new Laotian battalion. It'll be the first American-trained and led Lao battalion. You and Wofford'll give them physicals, then move them to their training area. We have a campsite about six miles out of town, where you'll have five weeks to train and arm them for duty up north. A fat, political Lao colonel will be the commander. I want a copy of your training schedule before the week is out. Physicals will begin Monday morning. You don't have much time, so get with the program. Any questions?"

"No, Team Sergeant. I'll get with Wofford and we'll be ready Monday. All I ask is that you keep that fat bastard off our ass. I'll holler when the schedule is ready."

Wofford and I cussed and discussed the problems for several hours before an agreement was reached. The plan was a relatively simple one. I would draw up and type the five-week training program while Wofford would be in charge of physicals on Monday. He would also select and train the medics for the battalion. In his spare time he would teach communication procedures and assist the non-commissioned officer in charge (i.e., me) and hold sick call each day for the sick, lame, and lazy.

From each of the new companies in the battalion, my Thai interpreter would find men with prior military experience and instruct them each day so that they would instruct the troops the next. The subjects would range from weapons, mines, and booby traps to tactics, but before the last week's field exercise, I would also teach staff functions to the officers. Wofford and the trainees, in the meantime, taught me a few things I didn't want to know during the physical exams on Monday. The gracious Wofford informed me at the makeshift dispensary that I was to be the Pecker-Checker-in-Charge. I did not look forward to the assignment.

When the Lao *tahans* came by the last exam section, I told them in Lao to drop their robes and skin back their foreskins. The Lao were a modest group, but I finally devised a way to overcome their shyness. "The next son of a bitch that doesn't do what I say has the clap as far as I'm concerned. A shot by Doc Wofford will change his attitude." After four or five had received painful shots, the procedure shaped up and I moved on to the next problem.

As soon as the physicals were over, Wofford issued each man a half bar of lye soap and I took them in a GI vehicle to the Mekong River. There in front of God and everybody, they were forced to bathe. At least the new battalion was off to a clean start.

We had a problem teaching the use of the M-1 mortar sight to the cadre. Because only a few could count, I had to spend a day teaching them to count to one hundred before I could move on to mortar adjustments using the M-1 sight.

Much to the relief of both of us, the plump colonel in charge stayed away from the training. Most Special Forces people believe that a fat body is the sign of some disease; whether the disease is gluttony, alcoholism, or just plain laziness we weren't sure and really didn't give a damn.

I had omitted dismounted drill from the training schedule and explained to Wofford why I had chosen to do so. "With their cadre of ex-GIs who served under the French, they'll use French commands, so we'd be of little help. I've explained to the cadre to practice at formations and when moving from one training area to another. It's all they'll need. They'll march better than the basic trainees of the American army within five weeks. We don't have time to waste on the menial shit!"

On graduation day, the troops marched by in perfect unison. Wofford had also been aghast at the absence of physical training from the training schedule. But I took pains to explain that you get in shape for the jungle by living in the jungle, not by doing pushups. The Lao diet would not enable them to stand up to it. The men were in shape for what they had to do just then. If the cadre wanted them to do PT, they'd have to do it on their own time.

In five weeks of working twelve- to fourteen-hour days,

we two civilians produced a battalion that we could be proud of, and Wofford was heartbroken that the unit would be turned over to a FTT then located near Luang Prabang, the religious capital of Laos. Again, I differed with my partner. "No, Doc! We don't want to go with them. If we did, I'd have that fat bastard assassinated. I don't want his lardass on our hands, nor to upset the political mess they have here. I do think the cadre is great, though; they'll do okay."

Team Metcalf never went on rest and relaxation, nor did it really need to. Savannakhet was small by most standards; still, it contained entertainment for the troops stationed in or near there. Civilian dining facilities featured good food as well as plentiful drink in addition to the troops' favorite pastime, Osaki beer. The bar girls who worked the troops were petite and generally very pretty. Of Vietnamese extraction for the most part, they knew the way to a man's heart and his pocketbook. The FTT's pay was going to a bank account in the Hugh Hess Hay, so "living expenses," or per diem pay, paid the way. Thanks to Doc Wofford, venereal disease was unheard of.

In the center of town was a well used by the entire city, and next to it was an old building that housed an opium den. Both establishments were well attended by the natives but were off limits to the U.S. personnel. The FTT drank only treated water and Doc Wofford saw to that. The task force would often sit in a nearby beer garden and watch the old men float out of the den of iniquity. We were amazed at the peaceful daze they appeared to be in.

In May 1961, our replacement crews were in place so the task force bid farewell to Savannakhet and the Laotian kingdom. However, because of an incident in April 1961, four of the original TF would not be on the aircraft home.

In northeastern Laos, the 6th Lao Infantry Battalion and its four-man FTT had been exposed to a very heavy artillery barrage and a flanking maneuver by two Pathet Lao battalions. Sergeant First Class Bischoff and Sergeant Gerald M. Biber jumped aboard an armored personnel carrier and moved down Route 13 toward Vientiane. Both were killed in the ambush that followed. Sergeant Orville R. Ballenger escaped through the jungle but was captured seven days later. He would be released on August 15, 1962, as part of the peace talks. Captain Walter H. Moon was captured in the initial attack. After several months of torture at the hands of Ho Chi Minh's benevolent troops, he was summarily executed by the "no-slack" Pathet Lao.

Otherwise, the task force returned to Fort Bragg intact and much wiser for its "civilian" experiences. Back in uniform, most of us would be assigned to the newly established Special Forces Training Group. After the establishment of the Military Advisory and Assistance Group (MAAG) in Laos—code-named White Star—replacements would no longer wear civilian clothes.

Established April 19, 1961, White Star had FTTs composed of twelve members each. Before the cease-fire in July 1962, 432 SF personnel would be stationed inside the borders of Laos. These detachments were on temporary duty from the 7th SFG at Bragg and the 1st SFG on the coral-rock island of Okinawa. The Laotian experiences would affect the future of Special Forces more than anyone would have thought only a few years prior. They would also ease the movement to South Vietnam that was only a few months away.

CHAPTER 17

BACK AT Fort Bragg, Special Forces was finally receiving some positive reaction from the Pentagon for a change. Current events in Southeast Asia demanded no less.

The expansion of Special Forces was in full swing when FTT Metcalf arrived home in late April. A training committee had been established to train and qualify the newbies in their military specialties. In addition, a branch committee was established to broaden the students' skills in other SF subjects. All of the classroom training would be conducted in the old wooden classrooms in the Smoke Bomb Hill area of Bragg.

Reassignments quickly broke up FTT Metcalf. Sergeant Bean was assigned to the weapons committee; Wofford would teach medical subjects; Team Sergeant Reed was assigned to the operations and intelligence committee. A wiser, experienced Lieutenant Perry would lead me to an instructor position on the demolition committee.

The demo committee got busy doing what Special Forces does best. The instructors were all veterans of SF, and soldiers like Sergeant First Class Johnnie Miller thoroughly enjoyed their work. I had honed my professional skills to a fine edge by August, when I decided to go home on leave.

At my mother's insistence, I put in for a thirty-day leave but to my astonishment, the leave came back disapproved. Naturally, I wouldn't take it sitting on my backside and told Lieutenant Perry so. "Sir, I haven't been home since 1959. My mother isn't getting any younger, you know."

"I'm truly sorry, Sergeant Craig, but Colonel Yarborough

said fifteen days is the max. People in Training Group are all affected by the order. Do you want fifteen days?"

"Sir, I want thirty days or nothing, and if I don't get it, I'm gone!"

"We don't want to lose you, but there's nothing I can do about it," was his departing remark.

My first request for the 10th Special Forces Group in Bad Tölz, Germany, was turned down by the host unit. "The Tenth has no openings for your military occupational specialty," the personnel clerk said. "Like to try for the First Special Forces Group on Okinawa?"

The 1st SFG (Airborne) had slowly taken over the effort in Southeast Asia and was hurting for personnel, SF-qualified or not. They snapped at my request. Colonel Yarborough's policies had presented the 1st SF with a Special Forces–qualified demolition man and the training group with a vacancy hard to fill.

"How many days' delay en route would you like, Sarge?"

"Well, the colonel says I can't have but fifteen and I want thirty, so make it forty-five," I laughed.

"You got it, Sarge. Have a good time on the Rock!"

I loaded my life's possessions in the 1956 Ford only after many fond farewells and a few beers. In September 1961, Lawton, Oklahoma, had not changed much since my last visit in my opinion. My brother, sister, and mother all welcomed me home while shying away from asking questions about my absence during the stint in Laos. I certainly wasn't going to volunteer classified information.

Before departure and among the bars and pool halls of Lawton, I never revealed where I had been in Asia, but, besides girls, I was interested in civilian attitudes about the conflict heating up in Indochina. My findings were not surprising—nor encouraging. The few deaths such as Biber, Moon, and Bischoff were ignored, their losses thought to be the hazards of the profession. "It's the chances you take for the money you make."

I was drawing top dollar for an E-5 at that time. The

$240 a month plus $55 jump pay helped me conclude my attitude about the civilian population of the United States. "They don't value the lives of professional soldiers as a top-dollar item."

While in Laos, I had saved $1,200. I placed $800 of that in my mother's account and bid farewell to my family. Me and the Ford headed for Oakland, California, and on to the headquarters of the 1st Special Forces Group (Airborne) on Okinawa. Located approximately 1,000 miles south of Tokyo, the island is also the site of World War II's bloodiest struggle. The battle of Okinawa cost 12,000 American and 110,000 Japanese lives in the last major Pacific campaign.

Leaving the Ford at the Oakland Terminal for shipment, I reported to the replacement depot for transportation and was soon flying high above the Pacific Ocean. I had just left my last stateside assignment for ten years. The trip and the destination would, before my return, change my life in ways I had never imagined possible. I would not return permanently until October of 1971, and upon my return, I would be an entirely different entity.

After I landed at Kadena AFB, the second largest airbase in the Far East, I was bussed to Hizagawa, the fenced-in compound and headquarters of the 1st SFG. Processed quickly, I was a proud member of Company A by nightfall.

After the unpacking of amenities in Hizagawa's stone-and-stucco barracks, I reported to Sergeant Major John Tryon at Site 3A at Yara. The small compound just outside Kadena Circle found the sergeant major stuttering through a briefing that left no doubt as to where the newbie stood. The unit was up to its proverbial neck in Laos and other places. Other places meaning resident teams in Thailand, Korea, Taiwan, and South Vietnam; TDY teams in White Star (Laos) had almost depleted the unit. Tryon concluded the stilted speech, "Do not plan on a long stay on Oki—we need people desperately in other places. You may last until your car gets here, but don't bank on it."

Assigned to an A Detachment, I knew many of the soldiers from Fort Bragg and Laos assignments. Willie Card, Bill Patience, Jim Tryon, Lou Woefel, and Pat Cotter were some of the old hands who greeted me.

The messhall at Hizagawa was a dining delight compared to the stateside facilities. Individual tables and no bread lines, in addition to the beautiful, short, almond-eyed Okinawan waitresses. I, for one, was very impressed with the entire lashup. I knew from my two-year stint in Special Forces that I was in the best all-around unit I had ever served in, and probably ever would serve in.

The 1st SF Group immediately filled a void in my SF training: infiltration by sea—at night, of course. After I had experienced my first submarine ride ever, washed down with a small-boat landing, my car arrived from Oakland. I had time to drive it to the storage compound before I was handed my first off-island assignment. The TDY assignment came as a shock, even to an old soldier.

In November 1961, I and two other replacements fresh out of the 503rd Airborne Infantry Battalion, also stationed on Okinawa, were airborne high above Thailand. They were part of the attempt by the Army to bring each Special Forces group up to its new authorized strength—1,500. Aboard the C-130 aircraft, I briefed the two on their destination, a destination that was not unfamiliar to me. A destination that I had in fact left only six months prior. The three of us TDY soldiers from Company A would land at Seno and be trucked to Savannakhet, Laos.

Sergeants Garry Stamn and James Lewis were astounded at their good fortune. The B-control detachment's mission and our possible assignments were explained from experience and I even included the names of the local bars and the movie stars who manned them. We were prepared for Laos when we landed at Seno at 1000 hours.

The old French air force base had changed in only six months. An efficient U.S. presence had made the transition a smooth one, and in an hour we deposited our gear in the two-story team building in Savannakhet. When we walked into the restaurant leased by the U.S. only two blocks away, people bustling around the busy establishment froze.

Dressed in the standard fatiques and jump boots, I didn't look like the civilian of only months before. But the help laughed, then mobbed me. B detachment personnel present were stunned at my reception; even the owner, Mrs Thu, came out of the kitchen and welcomed me home. I was having a tough time downing the cuisine because of the attention I was receiving. Team leader Major Warren Stevens and Operations Sergeant Jack Manley eyed the goings-on from a few tables away.

The control detachment had set up shop in the heart of the small city that bordered the Mekong River. An office building complex had been converted into a military headquarters that included a radio room and operations shop on the second floor. I reported to the boss, Sergeant First Class Jack Manley, who spent only thirty minutes briefing me because I knew almost as much about the mission as he did. The operations sergeant escorted me to the local airfield and I was again astounded by the improvement of the 1,800-foot runway and facilities since my departure.

"You'll be the air operations sergeant and will spend your time here or in the air as appropriate. We use Air America aircraft exclusively. That part hasn't changed since you left."

The unmarked H-34 helicopters and C-46 and C-47 fixed-wing aircraft were based in Thailand and worked the entire breadth of Laos for the White Star MAAG. The B detachment in Savannakhet used those aircraft to resupply FTT assets. The pilots were still civilians. I knew that Art Wilson—Shower Shoes—was a bona-fide civilian and my wearing a fatigue uniform didn't change our relationship in the least. The helicopter pilots were a different matter; I could tell that the rotary-wing crews were not civilians. In fact, most were captains or above, or warrant officers from the U.S. Army.

As the air operations sergeant, I had a squad of soldiers from the small Laotian air force assigned for assistance. We built a refueling dock to pump the JP-4 fuel for the choppers and we loaded and unloaded the aircraft that supplied the units in the boondocks.

The majority of the "civilian" pilots were very affable and I had no problems with them. Some, because of their Army caste-system training, were not; this minority refused to play the role of civilians. They not only talked down to me but acted like I should move to the back of the bus. Naturally this situation would come to a head before the TDY tour was over. The Lao crew on the other hand had nothing but good things to say about me as their American honcho. I treated them fairly and became interested in their personal lives and knew enough of the language to laugh and joke with them.

One day into the new year of 1962, I met a helicopter from an A site. The Lao unloaded it and then loaded equipment for the return trip while I conversed with the FTT team member. I looked into the sergeant's eyes and could only gasp at what I saw.

"Sergeant Mantooth, you have hepatitis or yellow jaundice, whatever. You ain't going back to the plains, you're going to our team medic. Your eyes are as yellow as ripe lemons!"

Sitting on the equipment during the H-34 flight to the A site, I knew what I was going to find even before I reached my destination. I chatted with the FTT troops after landing. None were much better off than Mantooth. On the flight back, I made my decision and reported to Manley that the entire FTT had yellow jaundice. Jack Manley told me that I had diagnosed Mantooth correctly and that he had been evacuated. A new detachment had to come all the way from Fort Bragg to replace the team. The grapevine that often strangles the U.S. Army had it that the team-leader captain was court-martialed for negligence. For once, most of the NCO corps sided with the officer-in-charge. Some, in fact, sided with him in a very verbal manner.

"That's bullshit, Jack. The team medic knew they shouldn't use untreated water over here, and he's the one that should be jailed." Manley was quick to agree but regardless of who was to blame, the episode had cost the United States a ton of money besides damaging the livers of the victims and shortening their lives.

In February 1962, I was notified that I would be a jumpmaster on a combat jump near Vang Vieng in northern Laos. I was dispatched to Seno in order to observe the jump training presented by French Red Berets to the replacements for the 1st Lao Parachute Battalion. I liked what I saw until the fifth and qualifying jump.

"Why are they all pulling their reserves after their main chutes have opened, Sergeant?"

"We teach that," Frenchie said, "to get them used to opening their reserve parachute in case of an emergency."

The second planeload did the same thing as the first jumpers. Some reserves wrapped around the main chutes and caused both chutes to collapse and I could contain myself no longer. Upon hearing the injured cry out for a medic, I began again.

"That is very dangerous and very stupid. You dumb Frogs should know that you may never have to pull or use your reserve. You're injuring people for no reason at all. I highly disapprove!"

"We French have been at it longer than you."

"*Wrong!* We've been at it longer than you, and you're using our equipment. That T-10 personnel chute will, nine hundred and ninety-nine times out of a thousand, open in some manner, provided that the soldier has hooked up his static line. You may have a Mae West or a streamer but not a complete malfunction. Opening the reserve chute is a mistake and you should tell the dumbasses that."

"You Americans are new at this war business, and we don't take advice from beginners."

I fumed while ending the conversation. "Amateurs or no, at least we have something in common. You have never won a war and we have never lost one. Fuck you!"

The French NCO reported the incident through White Star channels. Fortunately, the Americans knew I was not a diplomat, and didn't take the incident too seriously, for at least a week anyway.

A day before I was to jumpmaster an aircraft at Vang Vieng, I was told by Manley to report to Major Warren Stevens. The good-looking black soldier rose from his desk and returned my salute, then shook hands before inviting me to be seated.

The major was the first black officer I had ever served under and I was expecting the worst. But the smiling field-grade officer used diplomacy, something that I was sadly lacking, for the ass-chewing chore.

"Sergeant Craig, I'm happy to have a man with your experience in the control detachment. But a report has come down from higher headquarters that you've insulted our French allies. Do you confirm or deny that part of the report, Sergeant?"

I was taken aback by the precise, correct English used by Stevens. "Sir, I don't like to see people hurt for no reason at all. So I blew my stack. Insulting? It's a bad habit of mine, I guess. Yes, I did insult them. But our allies they're not."

Stevens smiled, proving that he wasn't too wrought up about it. "I agree, but technically they still are. What was it that provoked you?"

I told the entire story and topped it off succinctly. "I can forgive mistakes. I even made one once myself, but people who refuse to admit and/or change are committing a mortal sin. At least to my way of thinking, sir."

"I agree with you, but not your verbal solution. The next time—and I will try to see that there isn't a next time—use some tact, please!"

"Yes, sir," I lied.

"Okay, Sergeant Craig, I'll answer the correspondence and tell my superiors that you've been verbally reprimanded. Please don't let this upset you, however; it'll not go in your 201 records file. You are dismissed."

I saluted, did an about-face, and walked to the operations

shack and was still smiling when Manley asked the obvious. "How do you like your commander, Bill?"

"He's cool, Sergeant Manley. A very level-headed field-grade officer. How did the Army come up with him? A very pleasant surprise."

"You'll fly with Art Wilson tomorrow in the old reliable C-47. You'll jumpmaster a forty-man platoon of the 1st Parachute Battalion at Vang Vieng. Good luck, Bill. Have all your equipment ready to jump also, including a basic load of ammunition, just in case. You can't tell what'll happen in this screwed-up place."

"I've learned that much, Sarge. I'll leave at 0800 by jeep and be in Seno before nine. See you when I get back, if I get back."

"Good luck!" Manley shouted in dismissal.

I arrived at Seno at 0900 and waved at Shower Shoes Wilson, who was seated in the shade of the Gooney Bird. The other Air America aircraft were lined up on the apron of the airstrip awaiting their load-bearing personnel. Art Wilson informed me that we had a side mission after the drop. I chose to ignore the side issue.

"What altitude will we drop the troops, Art?"

"They tole me a thousand feet, Bill. Seems kinda high for a combat jump, at least to me. Any comments?"

"About five hundred feet would be right, especially if you're taking fire. That low, you wouldn't even need a reserve chute. Don't sound any combat jump I ever heard of, Art. Are you sure the French didn't plan this damn thing?"

Art laughed in response. "Don't think so, Bill. Want me to find out?"

"Shit no! I'm in enough trouble now." Regardless of my criticism, the paratroopers would exit the aircraft at a thousand feet actual.

As jumpmaster, I rigger-checked my planeload of paratroopers and loaded the aircraft by 1100 hours. Some of the men were wearing suitcases under their reserves and I inquired of the oversight to their Lao platoon leader.

"We did not have enough combat packs, Sergeant. It will be okay."

"Damn, Lieutenant, don't tell me the French stole the combat packs, too?" When the Lao refused to comment, I continued my rigger-checking.

We were airborne and all Air America fixed-wing aircraft were in a diamond formation at 1130. Wilson gave the ten-minute signal and I moved to the back of the aircraft near the door. In two minutes, I stood the jumpers up, using hand and arm signals to overcome the noise of the two props. When the green light came on, I shouted "go" in Lao. The airborne troops of *Groupe Mobile* 15 moved rapidly until the end of the stick. I gave them a boost with my right foot and the aircraft was empty in good time. I glanced out of the open door and saw the troops and noted that they did not appear to be under fire of any type.

I moved back to the cockpit and was briefed on the next mission as the C-47 moved out of the formation. "We'll pick up some of Bull Simon's Kha tribesmen and move them to Site Twenty. Maybe you'll get to see the Bull, even."

"Big deal! He's the best commander I've ever had in the U.S. Army, Art. Hope he's okay. Have these refugees ever flown before?"

"No, William. They've never even been in a wheeled vehicle, much less in an aircraft. Please have burp bags ready for 'em."

"I'll strap 'em in, Art, and look out for 'em. Can I change the subject a tad?"

"Sure, Bill. What's up?"

"These goddam Air America pilots are getting on my nerves. Are they really civilians, Art?"

"Come on, Bill, you know better than that. Were you a civilian a few months back? Gimme a break, old soldier, they're commissioned officers or warrant officers in the same Army you're in."

"I thought so, the sonofabitches treat me like a slave, their slave. I'm fed up with it. The bastards!" I said.

"Tell 'em to get screwed. Ain't nothing they can do 'bout it. I've had a few run-ins with 'em, my own damn self."

"You're a smooth-talking bastard, you've talked me into it."

"We're going down, watch this landing. It'll be as smooth as silk," Wilson said.

"I'll bet," I answered, sarcastically.

After the very smooth landing, I put the aircraft ladder in place and chattered with the mobile training team SF soldiers that met the aircraft. "That's as scroungy a bunch of people as I ever saw, Lou."

"They're the best allies and fighters we have over here, Bill. Treat 'em nice," Sergeant First Class Lou Woelfel said.

"Will do, Lou. Tell everyone hello for me. See ya around." I placed the ladder back in the aircraft and gave Wilson thumbs up. Moving from place to place, I made sure my charges were strapped in. The men were attired in loincloths, the females in skirts only. I attempted not to look at the breasts of the young ladies.

I also noted the cooking pots, goats, and cloth bundles. In only seconds, Wilson was heading for Site 20 at seven thousand feet. I moved up to the cockpit after distributing plastic burp bags to the highlanders, knowing damn well that they didn't know what the hell they were for.

The twenty-minute ride to Site 20 was not without its moments, however. The Montagnards were preparing to cook rice and build a fire in the floor of the C-47, but Wilson and I quickly smelled the smoke. I extinguished the fire as soon as possible while shouting derogatory comments in Lao, French, and Thai. Still, the Kha probably never knew why their benefactor was out of sorts. I strapped them back into their seats as Wilson prepared to land the modified cooking stove. Even the old pilot had his cage rattled by the turn of events, and the rough landing proved it. I sat next to him in the cockpit and commented on his landing ability before the aircraft came to a complete halt.

"Speaking of ugly bastards, there's Bull Simons waiting on the airstrip for us. Get to work, you lazy bastard," said Wilson, in retaliation.

I untied the captives and placed the ladder on the opened door and stood by the door to insure none of the elite firemakers broke an arm or leg unloading. A beret cockily posed on his balding head, the Bull walked to my side of the plane. "Have a nice trip, Sergeant Craig?" When I told him of the fire-building incident, Colonel Simons roared and shook with laughter. When he recovered, he graciously offered us a cup of coffee. The pilot said no, and I started another conversation in its stead.

"Sir, we could have all been killed, dammit!"

"Craig," said Simons, "you should have been killed at Annex-Eight so don't sweat the small manure. You guys come see us when you can, we get lonesome up here."

The C-47 was airborne and we waved farewell to the Bull and the most effective program of the Laotian struggle against the evil empire to the North. In fact, I was heading for my first tennis match of my eleven-year Army career. Tennis match?

Brigadier General John A. Heintges escorted the VIPs to Savannakhet, the headquarters of the 5th Military region of Laos. The prince and princess wasted no time issuing a challenge to the White Star lashup. "They want to play someone in tennis, Major Stevens. They're good at it, so naturally they're hooked on the sport. Do you have anyone that can play a lick?"

"I don't know, sir, but I sure can find out." The distress signal echoed throughout the control team area. It reached me at lunch time in the small café that fed our team.

"I'm serious Bill, dammit," said Manley. "Can you play tennis?"

I leaned over my food toward the question and whispered the reply. "Yes, Sergeant. I haven't played at all since college, but I can play a bunch. Me and a guy I was with in Korea were high school doubles champions of Oklahoma in 1945. Why?"

Manley laid it on the line for the Champ, finished his meal, and departed. I spent thirty minutes trying to eat and grumble to myself simultaneously. It wasn't easy.

I finally finished the meal and reported to Manley before going to the airfield. Manley had a few more surprises for me. "Yep, Bill, the match of the century is on. Sergeant First Class John Manthey can play a tad, too. Rackets and ball will be furnished by the Military Advisory and Assistance Group. It's all laid on for tomorrow at 1000 hours on the courts by the local school, bordering the Mekong River."

"Jack," I said, as my mind raced for a loophole, "I don't have clothes to play tennis in, dammit. I think I'll pass up this good deal."

"You had better not, soldier. The general, in addition to Major Stevens, would be so disappointed. So much so, that you might go back to Okinawa in handcuffs. Besides, that princess is a living doll. Wish it was me."

Manley, who had never been accused of being dumb, had finally won me over. "You smooth-talking bastard, see ya at ten. John and I'll do okay."

The two courts were parallel to the Mekong River facing north and south. Manthey and I noted that someone had maintained them very well. We were dressed in civilian slacks and sport shirts while our two hosts were in white shorts and T-shirts.

The doubles teams warmed up using both courts. I had to admit that I had never played using such an expensive tennis racket. I slammed a drive at Manthey and was pleasantly surprised when my well-constructed partner returned it. "We might do okay," I thought. Manthey was just as surprised at my reflexes and playing ability. In fifteen minutes, the warmups were over.

Manthey and I and two nervous MAAG officers conferred before the match began. "It's best two out of three sets, guys. Just do the best you can."

"Are we supposed to win, lose, or draw, sir?" asked Manthey.

At first the MAAG officers were stumped, but one young captain finally sputtered, "They're good at this, so I don't think you really have to worry about that part of it. Just try to do your best. You guys couldn't beat them in a month."

If the captain had wanted to get our juices flowing, he did a helluva job. We walked to the net for the toss of the coin. Manthey won the toss and selected the north portion of the court; the royal pair would serve first.

The first set surprised everyone but Manthey and me. It was close and we were still smiling after our 6–4 loss. Manthey was somewhat taken aback by my outlandish behavior. If the prince was at the net, I tried to take his head off with a forehand smash. When the doll was at the net, I played away from her. After a drink of water and wiping the sweat away, we were ready for the second set.

While the MAAG officers were smiling, Manthey said, "Bill, if you would quit staring at the lady and give her a chance to screw up a few shots, we might have won that set, dammit."

In the second set I was the proverbial ball of fire and even brought some smoke on the prince's better half. Manthey was his steady self, and it was a 6–4 reversal. The match now hinged on the last set and the MAAG officers were visibly nervous during the intermission.

The last set was hard-fought, but my long layoff and the lack of practice began to show. The Kingdom of Laos was apparently in good hands at the 6–3 finish, and the MAAG officers were happy. The Lao couple quickly erased the agony of defeat from our faces as the smiling prince shook our hands and the princess hugged and kissed us on the cheek. Two dazed paratroopers wandered by the MAAG officers muttering happily. "We want a rematch, we want a rematch."

It took Jack Manley a week to erase the dazed look from my face. Finally, an Air America pilot received my complete attention one Saturday morning. The silver H-34 helicopter was parked next to the makeshift refueling station. Short of help, I helped the Lao *tahan* push the fifty-five-gallon drum of JP aviation fuel up the ramp while an agitated middle-aged "civilian" pilot watched the procedure.

"We're in a hurry, Sergeant," he shouted. "Move it!"

"If you're in such a hurry, sir, get off your ass and give us a hand."

The red-faced pilot said, "I don't have to take that shit from you, Sergeant." He added, "I'll have you court-martialed, soldier."

I stopped the operation and glanced at the cockpit; tempers were now on overload. "If you do, asshole, you'll be the first civilian that ever got the job done. I've taken my final remark from a smart-mouth civilian. Fill up your own gas tank, asshole."

Later, Manley and I sat together in the corner of the restaurant over dinner. I expected the worst and just wanted it to be over with. Manley looked at me in sympathy before he began his dissertation. "You know you're wrong, Bill. Why couldn't you control your temper? Christ, we only have five days to go before a three-day R and R in Hong Kong and back to Okinawa."

"I like you, Jack, and I'm sorry I placed a burden on you, but you're wrong, not me. I won't take that shit from 'em when they're in uniform, much less in civilian clothes. He violated security, so not a damn thing is going to happen to me or I'll scream to high heaven about his indiscretion."

"Bill, you're relieved of all duties effective immediately. I'm passing that on from Major Warren Stevens. Enjoy the five-day vacation, but be ready for the return trip. Don't come to the control detachment headquarters, please!"

So I would return to Okinawa under the gun. But the U.S. Army had enough smarts to let bygones be bygones, just as I had predicted they would. Nevertheless, I learned from the experience.

And so I completed my second TDY tour in Savannakhet, Laos, in March 1962.

CHAPTER 18

WHEN THE control team from Savannakhet and some of their A detachments completed enriching the economy of Hong Kong, we flew to our home base. Many of us had spent little or no time on the Rock and were anxious to get acquainted with the unit. That proved to be a difficult task.

The 1st Special Forces Group (Airborne) had all but taken over the brushfires of Southeast Asia. Laos was beginning to wind down, just as South Vietnam began heating up. On April 8, 1962, just outside Da Nang at the training site of Hoa Cam came the first two combat casualties of the Vietnam War for the 1st Special Forces and Special Forces as a whole. Specialist 5th Class Gabriel and Sergeant First Class Marchand from Company C were killed when some of their indigenous charges unexpectedly changed sides. Sergeants Groom and Francis Quinn of Company A were captured in the action; they were released by the Viet Cong, unharmed, on May 1, 1962.

Sukiran Chapel, located in the heart of Okinawa, was overflowing on the day of the memorial services for the two soldiers. The Green Berets in attendance recognized the significance of the event and we mentally braced ourselves for our time in the barrel.

I was assigned to an A detachment once again and billeted in the barracks at Sukiran, just off Highway 1, opposite Buckner Bay. Our billets featured modern two-story barracks paralleling paved roads that ran from the gate to the Topper NCO Club and into the family housing area. Although of modern construction and more than adequate for the unaccompanied personnel, air-conditioned they weren't. For our comfort in the hot humid weather the tropical paradise afforded, we single soldiers bought fans. The barracks also housed an orderly room for administrative purposes. The actual training assignments for Company A originated from a training headquarters located near Kadena Air Force Base.

An event took place on April 30, 1962, that caused the living conditions to become inconsequential—to me anyway. After I had accrued eight and a half years in grade, Special Orders 57, 1st SFG (Airborne) promoted me from sergeant E-5 to staff sergeant E-6. I remained in shock for at least a week. I finally managed to stencil SSG CRAIG on my white T-shirts and got on with the program. The first day of June my pay deposit slip to the bank would read $255 base pay instead of the $240 I had received for lo those many years; if you're in the Army for the money, you're poor at math.

Off-duty entertainment at Sukiran could be found at the biggest NCO club on the island. The Topper Club, on the highest peak of the Sukiran military post, was available on a twenty-four-hour basis, but the Coral Hill Club, a stone's throw from the A-Company hootches, was favored by most.

Other units at Sukiran at the time were the U.S. Marine Corps and the 503d Airborne Battalion, which was fresh from duty at Fort Bragg, North Carolina. This unit would, shortly, be expanded into the 173d Airborne Brigade. Relationships between the Army units were very good but interservice rivalry with the Marine Corps would only worsen as time went by. This unhealthy relationship would carry over into the Vietnam conflict and even hamper the effectiveness of the units involved.

My new unit featured such stalward NCOs as Lou Woeffel, Pat Cotter, Frank Fowler, Bill Patience, Willie Card, Quinn, Grooms, Coble, and Eldon Payne. Payne, from Duke, Oklahoma, was a young, eager, good-looking soldier, and on the subject of our Stateside homes he and I always found something to argue or talk about.

Except for the obvious absence of cold-weather facilities, training at Site Yara was really not very different from the Stateside version. Each detachment presented cross-training classes in medical, weapons, demolitions, Morse code, and tactics. When things got boring, small boat training substituted for the lack of Korean-type weather. All parachute jumps were conducted at Yomitan Drop Zone, located just north of Kadena Circle. Because of its hard, rough surface this coral-rock World War II–era Japanese airstrip was a test of a man's desire to remain on jump status. The two runways ran the length of the drop zone. More often than not jumpers hit one of the strips. However, at that time quitters were unknown in Special Forces. But at least Yomitan offered you the excuse and the opportunity.

The months went by swiftly for the group's newbies, and we old hands managed to learn a few things along the way. The Topper Club didn't appear to be attuned to the funny hats nor to the unconventional antics of the Special Forces soldiers. Many of us were already barred for life by the staff, who were playing the same game with the slot machine money that was then being played by every NCO club the world over. Slot machines are a license to steal. One trick that most NCOs were aware of occurred when the machines were being emptied of their coins. The count had to be verified and that was no problem. Just select some customer who needed a beer, or better yet, one who had had one too many and have him verify the total. He just earned a beer while the club manager earned God knows what. Skimming gave the club managers a lot of money—a tool for leverage that they would not normally possess.

The Coral Hill Club was therefore quickly adopted by the serene troops of Company A, the newly returned soldiers from Laos being no exception. It was at this location that, with eight years in grade, I met the petite women who would forever change my life.

* * *

During World War II, the American bombings of Naha and Yomitan helped the woman make up her mind. She bundled up her two daughters and young son one morning and fled to the northern coral hills of Okinawa. Hatsuko, Tomiko, and Choei never knew—nor did Mrs. Ago—if they were fleeing from the hated Japanese army or the American bombings. Her husband, a merchant seaman for the Japanese, had died at sea years before, and World War II had become a struggle to survive. They moved by train just north of Nago near the village of Okuma. Here, a bamboo hut far into the mountains became their haven for the rest of the war. In addition to farming, Mrs. Ago often worked for food in the nearby village of Okuma.

In late 1945, the noises of war suddenly ceased completely. The outrageous tales of the cruel Americans were close to the surface as Mrs. Ago made yet another decision: her family must return to Naha if they were to do more than just exist. Packing their meager belongings wasn't a time-consuming task and the family was soon on a dirt road that terminated in Naha City. To the surprise of the small family, they met uniformed Japanese soldiers heading for the mountains they had just vacated. The soldiers stopped them and searched their belongings. The Japanese told them nothing of the concluded struggle but did manage to relieve them of any valuables and food they had in their possession.

When they heard the first Army vehicle to approach them, they fled to the side of the road. But the U.S. driver and his assistant had seen their desperation and stopped the vehicle and dismounted. The two uniformed Caucasians ordered the family back on the road. The three children began crying in earnest as Mrs. Ago held the two youngest and moved to the road with Hatsuko, her first-born, close behind. "How long do we have to live?" she thought. Despite their young ages, the children were thinking the same question. Using the universal hand and arm signals, the Americans ordered them onto the transport. Lowering the tailgate, the Americans assisted the family onto the truck. The grinning GIs closed the tailgate and the family sped off to their unknown destination and fate. The smiles and assistance of the strangers had quieted even the young children, so much so that the family leaned back in their wooden benches and enjoyed the ride to a refugee camp at Haneji.

The village of Haneji is a few miles south of Nago, in the northernmost part of the coral island. The truck stopped just inside the gate of the tent city and unloaded its cargo. The smiling GIs again assisted Mrs. Ago. The oldest girl, Hatsuko, was so impressed with their thoughtfulness that she smiled at the pair. The truck drove away followed by the waving of three children and their mother. Another American hired hand stepped forward and greeted the family.

The interpreter spoke in the Okinawan dialect rather than Japanese. "The Americans have built this camp for the war refugees of Okinawa. The tents have beds installed, therefore select a tent and move your family in. Food will be issued for one week at a time. We have rice and American field rations for your consumption. You are welcome to stay as long as you like."

Nodding at Mrs. Ago, the slight middle-aged male continued. "Employment can be found anywhere in Okinawa at this time. The southern cities and villages are being reconstructed and labor is at a premium. The victorious American forces are hiring natives for night clubs, motor pools, and such. If you want to return home, transportation will be provided. By order of General MacArthur, all unoccupied homes or houses are owned by no one; you can claim a house by simply moving in and living there. After signing in at the headquarters building, you have nothing but time to make your decision. Eat a hearty meal and welcome to Haneji from the victorious Americans."

Mrs. Ago worked locally while Hatsuko, Choei, and Tomiko attended a tent city school run by GIs. The English being taught there was enjoyed by the youngsters, especially the American songs. The young children picked up their third language in an outstanding fashion.

The summer of 1946 found Mrs. Ago wanting to return to her home in Naha City. Located far to the south of their present location, the largest city in Okinawa not only provided a permanent residence but a job with the American forces' very modern motor pool.

One day, Mrs. Ago was riding on the running board of a GI truck from point A to B. She jumped off the vehicle to the pavement before the truck came to a complete stop. In the resulting fall she lost one eye and her wrist was broken so severely that it would never again be normal. She was crippled to the extent that she could never hold another position, leaving her family unprotected in the free-enterprise system. Hatsuko, now twelve years old, had no choice but to quit the fifth grade and step into the breach. Her school days were forever over when she reported to the motor pool and answered "here" as her mother's name was called. The supervisor looked up, smiled, and ordered Mrs. Ago to report to the office. Hatsuko was mentally down as she reported to the motor pool office, glancing at the large GI buses as she entered. The supervisor soon arrived and listened to Miss Ago's explanation. Hatsuko tearfully explained her difficult position and the honcho nodded, finally saying, "We'll carry the matter as is until you reach your sixteenth birthday. At that time, report back here and we'll have an authentic identification card made for you and you alone. In the meantime, "Mrs. Ago," you had better get to work. Good luck, as the Americans say."

By her early twenties Miss Ago was employed by the Okinawan NCO club chain. At twenty-six she was still unmarried, but she had advanced to the position of cashier at the Coral Hill Club in Sukiran. By this time her English was very good. Her understanding and pronunciation were above reproach, and the Americans liked her good humor and upbeat manner. She liked the easy-going GIs as well, but Special Forces soldiers were another matter. She often remarked to her companions that "They are different, I think. They all act like they are crazy, for one thing, and drink and act like it's their last day on earth. I just don't understand them. They're complete animals."

That was her attitude when we first saw each other in 1962. My actions only reinforced her attitudes about the soldiers with the funny green hats; I never missed a chance to stop by her cashier's cage and harass the young lady, who was at least ten years my junior.

"It's eleven o'clock, Babysan. Does your mother know where you're at? This damn club is violating the child-labor laws. For shame!"

Admittedly, Miss Ago's baby face belied her age. The fact that she had been a breadwinner for thirteen years or more also served to rile her somewhat. "Papasan, I'm not a babysan. I am twenty-five years old and do not have to have my mamasan's permission to stay up past midnight, thank you." Facts never had been an important consideration when I harassed someone so I continued kidding her until she finally threw down the gauntlet one night. "Papasan, if you're so worried about my safety, you should give me a ride home. That way you will know if I arrive home safely." I did, but my first trip to South Vietnam interrupted the budding relationship for a time.

A twenty-three-man control detachment, called B-120, was ordered to Da Nang, in Vietnam's I Corps area, in September 1962. The detachment was formed and trained for only a few weeks before departure. If nothing else, the training enabled the men of the B team from Company A to get acquainted with each other. The mission briefing also prepared the team to study the area they were to control. Detachment B-120 would replace B-110, which was then operating out of Hoa Cam Training Center on the outskirts of Da Nang. B-120 would hand over the training center to a twelve-man A detachment and would control its camps from Da Nang proper. Funds for the task force would come from the Central Intelligence Agency.

When the list of B-120's personnel was released, not

many complaints were heard from the selectees. We all knew that 180 days of temporary duty was better than a one-year permanent change of station move. Besides, we would be reimbursed an extra six dollars a day for our troubles. It wasn't much money, but it would buy a lot of beer if and when we returned to our home station.

Commanded by Major Edwin Wilson and Sergeant Major Taylor, the detachment did well in the selection process, picking men like James Lewis, Clarence Counts, Pat Cottor, Lieutenant Slaten, and Captain Short. Camps that would be serviced by B-120 were all located in the northern province of South Vietnam: Try My, Phu Hoa, Mang Buk, Ba To, Tra Bong, and Khe Sanh. The camp at Khe Sanh was opened by Special Forces in July 1962. Years later that camp would provide one of the pivotal battles of the war. It was a camp that would directly affect many of the men of B-120. At this time the Tet Offensive was six years away.

In September 1962, the hastily formed control team flew from Kadena AFB to Bangkok and on to Da Nang. Everyone in the detachment had his assignment locked in before arrival. For the second time in my career, I was an air operations sergeant for a B detachment. I complained but no one paid me any heed.

A large, well-equipped air base at Da Nang welcomed the troops before we moved to new quarters furnished by the CIA. The spacious mansion was on the same street as the detachment HQ building. Both were adjacent to the bay of Da Nang. The detachment was hard at it in less than a week, and I spent my time at I Corps HQ trying to scrounge aircraft from the Army, Air Force, and the U.S. Marine Corps. The Army NCOIC of the air operations section, Staff Sergeant Graham, was sympathetic to Special Forces and helped us at every turn, but the USMC helicopter unit was another matter. A few weeks into a very frustrating situation, Graham and I discussed the truth of the matter as we saw it.

"Graham, I've flown with them twice now to A camps. They resent me and the A detachments and the U.S. Army as a whole. The pilots are commissioned officers and leery of the dangers of their profession. Send us some Air America choppers, or better yet, some U.S. Army choppers flown by warrant officers. Let's get on with the war."

"Amen, Bill. In the meantime we'll have to use the Army Caribous to the fullest. How do you like those guys, William?"

"I can't tell a lie, Graham, they're the greatest. If it wasn't for the 1st Aviation Company and those Caribou aircraft, we would have to shut down A camps like Mang Buk. I hate kicking bundles to them though, when we could use choppers. We have a lot of material losses when chutes don't open, or the winds take the load into Viet Cong country. The Marines ought to get off their butts and just worry about getting the job done. Hell, I don't like them either, but I fly with 'em."

The battle between the two services didn't abate in the six months that B-120 spent in the country.

One assignment that I was given by a CIA official spawned many questions that I would ponder for the next ten years of my life. I reported to my boss one morning and was given my orders.

"In the morning report to Mr. Jordan at his residence located just behind our HQ building. He has some work for you, Bill. Wear khakis, no uniform, please," the sergeant major said.

"Okay, Top, but I don't take to this spook shit. If I don't like the line of work, I'll tell him to kiss off, just like Moe Copeland taught me to say."

"You don't have to do it if you don't want to; I'll get some officer to do it, in that case. They eat it up, Bill!"

"Yeah, I believe that—they're young and dumb but they'll learn better before this war is won, or lost, whatever. I'll be there, sergeant major."

At the very prim, two-story stucco house the next morning a beautiful Vietnamese girl of twenty-two or so answered my knock. "I'm Trung Si Craig, *Co*. Is Mr. Jordan in?"

"Come right in, Trung Si; the boss is waiting on you."

I entered the foyer and watched in admiration as she walked away. Jordan met me in his study and appeared to want the pleasantries to end quickly. I was still hoping for the *co*'s reappearance when Jordan spoke.

"My driver will take you to the Da Nang airfield," the CIA case officer said. "A Mr. Chang will fly you in an L-20 aircraft to Khe Sanh where some of your people are having an airstrip built. Give this ten thousand dollars to Captain Korcheck. It's the payroll and he'll be expecting it. Do you have any questions, Sergeant?"

I noted the brown cash envelope was not sealed and replied, "Do you want me to count it?"

"No," said the case officer. "It's all there, just trust me. Anything else?"

"Reckon not." I moved out of the residence to the waiting jeep and its diminutive Viet driver.

I did have a question for the driver, however. About halfway to the air base, I dropped it on him in English and broken Viet. "Who is that *co* who answered the door, Nguyen?"

"That," Nguyen said, "is Mr. Jordan's housemaid."

At Da Nang airfield, Mr. Chang shook my hand and invited me aboard the modern two-seater aircraft for the long flight to Khe Sanh and the lonely detachment that toiled there. The pilot attempted to point out the new features of the aircraft that he flew very well, but I really wasn't that interested. I was thinking of the money I had in my pocket, more money than I had ever had in my possession at one time, yet it was uncounted.

A hell of a way to do business, I thought. *He's the case officer, not me. Khe Sanh must be his responsibility, so why am I doing his work while he stays in Da Nang to work out with the* co. *They're buying Special Forces, lock, stock, and barrel, and we're going for it. He makes more money in a month than I make in a year but I'm taking the chances. I guess Art Wilson tried to warn me about them. Damn civilians!*

The men of the A detachment were with their Bru Montagnards and Vietnamese, working on the airstrip, when the L-20 landed. Captain Korcheck and a couple of NCOs met our aircraft. While one NCO took Chang for coffee, I completed the business transaction with the team leader.

"Want me to count it, Bill?" Korcheck asked.

"You can if you want to, sir. I asked Jordan that question and he told me it wasn't necessary, so I didn't."

"That's good enough for me, Sarge." Korcheck pocketed the envelope and moved on.

Sergeant Frank Fowler and I chatted while waiting for Chang and the return trip. "How do you like it up here, Frank?"

"I'm in a good outfit, Bill. Good team sergeant and team leader. But I get lonesome for the mud, the blood, and the beer. Otherwise it's okay. How are the rear-echelon troops doing in woman-infested Da Nang?"

"War is hell in Da Nang, Frank. If I ain't into it with the Marines, it's the CIA or the military police. I need some A team time or I'm gonna be a private again, or worse, a corporal for the fourth time."

"Don't do that, Bill. I've had some of that and it's just impossible to get the stripes back right now."

The flight back to Da Nang city was uneventful and again found me in deep thought. *What if the $10,000 was not all there? Who would the Army blame? As if I didn't know. I'll be damn particular before working for these spook bastards again.* The experiences that humid day formed impressions that are still with me. By nightfall, I was ready for some of that rear-echelon duty that Frank Fowler had inquired about.

In 1962 the B detachment in Da Nang had some of the finest radio operators in the Special Forces, Sergeant Clarence Counts, a tall blond soldier from the hills of Virginia, being no exception. After a day of CW (Morse code) negotiations, he was also ready for the quiet nightlife of Da Nang.

Counts and I quickly covered the mile of waterfront from

the team house to the city. I never missed an opportunity to harass Counts about his mode of transport. "You and that goddamn bicycle are enough to drive me to drink."

Topsy Counts continued pedaling slowly but would not let the remark go unanswered. "That's not a drive, Bill. That's a very short putt."

"Funny, funny. I never met a RTO that I liked. Are you going to the Lobster Bar to drink beer with me?"

"No, Bill, I'm in love and heading for Choi's. I like that movie star working the tables. I think she goes for me, too."

"Yeah, she goes for you. Keep both hands on your piastres, just in case though. Us single guys can't be too careful. I'm going to move a little deeper into town, but if I run into those CIA assholes, I'll be back. Watch those MACV [Military Advisory Command, Vietnam] assholes, too, there's thousands of 'em. I'll be back to get you around 1130. We do have a curfew, you know."

"Yes, daddy, I know. You worry about Bill; I'm a big boy, now. Stay outta fights too; you haven't won one lately."

Lean and easy-going, the naïve six-foot-two-inch, 200-pound hillbilly parked his bike and watched as I moved away toward the heart of Da Nang's nightlife. *You're in trouble when Bill's worried about you getting into trouble. He's trouble looking for a place to happen.*

Regardless, promptly at 2330 I walked in front of Choi's window and looked in. Topsy was trying to converse with one of the local stars. I pounded on the glass and motioned for Counts to move it. Then I moved back away from the front and stood by Counts's bike, near the curbing of the brick-paved street. Instead of Counts responding, a short, well-built youngster with an MACV patch on his fatigues appeared. I chose to ignore the intrusion but MACV insisted.

"What the hell are you beating on the glass for, GI?" the intruder asked. Again I ignored the remark. I flipped my

Pall Mall into the darkened street. "I asked you a question, Sergeant," said a persistent voice.

A left hand came seemingly from nowhere and ended the one-sided conversation. The unconscious GI lay at my feet as I moved back to the bar front and motioned to the blond lover. This time Topsy Counts came strolling onto the sidewalk and secured his two wheels.

"What's wrong with him?" asked Counts, glancing down at the prone GI.

"Hell, I don't know. Maybe he's tired. Let's get the hell outta here."

We moved away but Topsy was aware that the pace was brisk. The streetlights cornering the Take Ten NCO Club were only fifty yards away when the noise behind us became a roar. Both of us looked behind and witnessed about forty GIs moving our way screaming and shaking their fists in our direction.

"What the hell's their problem, Bill?"

"I don't know. Quit asking dumb questions and just move to the streetlight by the club. Park that damn bike there and we'll probably make out about like Custer did. You know I decked that dumb asshole back there. He asked for it, so quit acting dumb!"

Topsy parked his bike and we faced a raging mob of misguided soldiers employed by the Military Advisory and Assistance Command, Vietnam. I homed in on the ringleader and knew what I was going to do in order to survive this onslaught. "Good luck, Topsy," I said and decked the largest big mouth and the obvious leader. When he went down, I held on to him for dear life. Boots of all sizes pounded various parts of my body as I attempted to shield myself with the barely concious victim's body. A few minutes later a military police siren and flashing red lights shut down the one-sided mêlée. Only then did I release my protection and get to my feet. I faced an angry MP sergeant, who had probably saved my life and to hell with my career.

"The U.S. is the loser in this fiasco," started the sermon. "All of you are a disgrace to your country tonight."

I interrupted my saviour. "Would you excuse me a second, Sarge?"

"Certainly," said the MP NCO.

I took three steps and again decked the leader of the riot platoon. The MP began dispersing the GIs and in a few minutes only two of us remained. "Put both of 'em in the jeep and I'll see you at the station!" the sergeant ordered.

While Counts and I stood in front of his high-platformed desk, a very serious desk sergeant wrote out a report that took at least a half hour to complete. *It's hell to be popular,* I thought.

"How did I get mixed up with this guy?" Counts asked. "It won't get any better—five years in grade shot in the ass. Why me, Lord?"

"You're dismissed. Report to your sergeant major tomorrow morning. You're in a heap of trouble."

I readily agreed. "It's after curfew. We need a ride home, Sarge."

The desk sergeant colored some but also agreed. "Take them to their team house."

B Team's Sergeant Major Taylor read the report over twice. "I don't believe this shit," was his only comment. Then he knocked on Major Wilson's door.

"Come on in, Top!" the short, heavy-set major ordered. "What's up, Sergeant Major?"

"Read this delinquent report, sir. I have, and I still don't believe it," Taylor said as he shoved the booklet at the team leader.

"I can't believe two of our NCOs would do something like this," Wilson chuckled. Unlike Major Wilson, Taylor was still not moved to laughter.

"You don't know them, sir. Those bastards will do anything."

The major sobered and addressed the last statement. "Yes, I think I do know them, Sergeant Major, and I think they're great. However minute this breach of discipline, we must deal with it, so I'd like to see them both at 1600. What kind of shape are they in anyhow?"

"Well," drawled Taylor, "Craig has two broken ribs, but Counts is only bruised. They didn't miss any duty, so I can't fault them there, I guess. Not that I approve of their actions, of course."

"I would hate to have to replace either one of them. I'll check with the provost marshal before I talk to 'em at 1600. Got it, Top?"

I had flown to Mang Buk that morning and was greeted at the noon meal in Da Nang by Counts's very nervous Southern drawl. "Our shit is weak, Bill. The old man wants to see us at 1600, and the sergeant major hates us, too. Oh, why did I let you get me into this shit? I like being an E-5—don't you like being an E-6?"

"Slow down, Topsy. We'll do okay. Ain't nothing going to happen to us. But to answer your question, no, I was an E-5 for eight years and I became sick of it. Sergeant McDonald processed through here a week ago and he was an E-6. I put the little shit through training group as an E-5. There's something wrong with the Special Forces promotion system. The stripes ain't coming to Okinawa or Vietnam, that's for sure."

My answer appeared to perplex Counts. "What the hell has that got to do with our delinquent report and thirty years in jail?" he said, raising his voice.

I finished my rice and beans before replying. "After the major puts his two cents' worth in, I'm going to ask him about that bullshit. Where are the stripes? I can't afford to be an E-6 for a hundred years like I was an E-5. I'll join the Foreign Legion before I run in place as an E-6 forever. We're getting screwed somehow, someplace, and sometime."

I lit up and smiled at my pal's misplaced anxieties. Counts rose from the table and mumbled all the way out the door. "We're going to jail and he's worried about making sergeant first class. Why a good ole hillbilly like me, Lord? Is it the company I keep or don't you like mountain folk?"

* * *

Before we entered the office of the head enlisted man, I again cautioned the Topsy. "Leave all the talking to me, Topsy, and quit acting like you're in the later stages of malaria. Everything is going to be all right!"

Counts shook his head, looked down at his jump boots, and led the way to the small adjoining office of the detachment SGM. Taylor looked up from his desk and motioned us to be seated before he entered the major's office. In seconds, he opened the door and said, "Report to the commander!"

We did so in our best garrison manner and were given "At ease" before the question-and-answer period began.

"What caused this commotion, soldiers? We don't need this type of paperwork showing up in Okinawa, we'll all go to the stockade. I'm sure you have some explanation, right, Sergeant Craig?"

I was delighted to have an opportunity to lie. Counts would have been too nervous to be convincing.

"Sir," I drawled, "we have no idea why them leg sons a bitches jumped us good ole boys but it don't seem right, twenty-five or so of them jumping on two of your people like that. Then to make matters worse, the MPs only writing up the two innocent victims."

The major wanted to bust out laughing but decided to let me continue with my fairy tale instead.

"If I were you or the sergeant major, I'd sure find out what them legs have against your people, don't seem fair to us."

Counts was aghast.

"I have another subject I'd like to talk to you about if I might," I said. The major only nodded.

I went into a dissertation about the lack of stripes in the 1st Special Forces Group (Airborne). The island rewards could be counted on one hand in the year or so that I had been associated with it. At the conclusion of my spiel, the major turned to the slighted sergeant major.

Pissed off though he was, the sergeant major's back was against the wall. "I am unaware of any discrepancies in the enlisted promotion situation on Okinawa, sir. There just aren't any stripes available and haven't been for years." He threw me a dirty look.

"I'm getting conflicting stories, but I'll look into it, Sergeant Craig. But to get back to you two outlaws: I'll see you in my office again tomorrow at the same time. You are dismissed!"

Entering the sergeant major's adjoining office we both turned to eye the seated senior enlisted man. An ass-chewing was forthcoming. "Staff Sergeant Craig, why do you present the ole man with enlisted problems? I'm your representative, and you know I don't appreciate what you did."

I refused to back down. "No, Sergeant Major, and I don't appreciate seeing kids being promoted while we have to have up to eight years in grade to make it. Those stripes are being short-stopped at Fort Bragg, whether you know it or not. No one in this outfit gives a shit, or something would have been done a long time ago. Sorry if it upset you, but it's 'bout time someone let 'em know how we feel."

Taylor was shocked at my impudence and dismissed us. Counts could only shake his head as we walked to the radio shack. "You've made things worse, Bill. Why me, Lord?"

"Let's quit depending on the Lord to do everything for us, and do something for ourselves for a change. Don't sweat the small shit, Topsy. Tonight, you and I are going to drink a beer at the MACV Club across the street. I figure we owe them leg assholes something, don't you?" Counts refused to comment and went back to work in the radio shack while I headed for the detachment operations center.

In the meantime, Major Wilson called the provost marshal of Da Nang and preceded to chew ass and take names. "They were what, Captain? Wouldn't you be if twenty-five people jumped your ass? If it ever happens again, there won't be a leg walking and talking in Da Nang city. You got that, *sir*?" The phone took a beating as Wilson concluded the conversation.

We entered the small upstairs MACV Club that very

night, and I went straight from the bar to the table-seated ringleader of the miniriot. "If you assholes ever jump us again, I'll call out the bad guys from across the street and this place—and you for that matter—will cease to exist. You got that, Junior?"

The MACV GI remained seated, nor did his companions rise to the bait. "I'm sorry it ever happened, Sergeant. It won't happen again."

We moved away and into the lighted main street of Da Nang and a bar far removed from Topsy's former habitat. The beer and conversation flowed freely between us. Promptly at fifteen minutes prior to the 2300 closing hour, the petite Viet waitress approached our booth.

"You have time, one more beer, GI. I bring you two, no?"

"Yeah," said Counts, "you talked me into it. Two beers for two steers, *Co*."

A U.S. military policeman entered the establishment, followed by a diminutive Vietnamese MP. The enforcers approached our table. "Drink up, it's closing time, soldiers. Drink up!"

Counts looked at his watch while I took up the verbal counterattack. "We still have fifteen minutes, Officer. I just paid for the shit, and we're going to drink it. We'll be gone at 2300 hours."

The MP made it obvious that he didn't appreciate our remarks and the questioning of his authority. Who was right or who was wrong was not a factor to him. "I said *now*, Sergeant." The help scattered behind the safety of the bar as the talk became loud.

"Hey, *Co*," I said, "give us our money back. We can't drink our beer." Nevertheless, I took a large gulp of Asahi.

The MP was determined to have his way. "Let's go, outside!"

We both rose and visibly stared at the flatfoot as we exited the establishment while I grumbled away.

Out in the fresh air of the city, we moved toward the team house at a brisk pace. "We're going to fix that misguided troublemaker." I said. "You're going to come in handy for a change, hillbilly."

"Leave me outta your schemes, Bill. I'm in enough trouble now. And look who's calling who a troublemaker."

The long narrow bar with booths opposite set the identical scene the next night. At 2245, I sat alone and ordered beer from the pretty *co*. Two minutes later, the short, well-built American MP entered with his Viet counterpart. Again, the verbal orders were dispensed and I again protested as vehemently as before. I was interrupted by the racing of a jeep's engine. The engine noise got the two MPs' attention.

"What's that?" asked the startled American.

"It sounds like a jeep engine, Sarge," I said. "You didn't leave the motor running, did you?"

I sat back down and grinned as I drank my closing-time beer and winked at a scared *co* standing behind the bar. The two MPs dashed into the street, and shouted at the rear end of their transportation as it raced toward the Da Nang airfield. The two embarrassed cops returned to the side of a happy, beer-drinking soldier boy. I didn't even look up.

"You are under arrest, Sergeant," the disgusted policeman said, "for stealing a military vehicle."

"For what? I have dozens of witnesses," pointing to the Viets and GIs in the bar, "who will testify that I have not moved from this booth. Get serious, flatfoot."

Despite the protest, the MP called his desk sergeant and two more jeeps were forthcoming. "This is ridiculous," was my only comment.

The desk sergeant sighed as he spied a familiar face before him. "What's the charge this time, Murphy?"

"He stole my jeep, Top."

"How in the hell did he steal your jeep if he's standing here in front of me? You're looking like a fool, Officer. I can't charge him with that. Where's the stolen vehicle?"

"Hell, I don't know. Ask him, Sarge!" said a confused Murphy.

The Desk looked at me and told me to get lost, but I

wasn't falling for that one. "Oh no, I'm out past curfew, and being a law-abiding citizen, I want a ride home."

Again sighing deeply, the headman turned to Murphy. "Take him to his team house."

The misappropriation was not corrected for two weeks while Murphy fumed. The jeep was found in an abandoned shack at the Da Nang AFB, but how it got there, no one ever said.

Sergeant Major Taylor called in Counts and me the next day and questioned us on the incident, but of course we could not help him. We then reported to a not-so-amused Major Wilson. Deep down he was proud of his avengers, but he pronounced sentence for the miniriot, regardless.

"Both of you will write, in two hundred words or more, why I shouldn't jail you for your misconduct. I expect the bestsellers to be on my desk sometime tomorrow. Also, Sergeant Craig, you are going to the boonies for a while. You're bad news in certain local circles. Are there any questions?"

Counts spoke before coming to attention. "Sir, I can't write that much."

I elbowed my partner in crime as the major said, "It's that way, Sergeant Counts, or take an Article 15 for misconduct."

I berated Counts in the safety of the headquarters hallway. "Don't sweat it. I'll write enough for you, me, and the sergeant major. I'll have the old man giving us a Good Conduct Medal before it's over." Counts did not seem convinced.

After air-dropping rice to the A camp at Mang Buc from an Army Caribou, I retreated to my room at the team house to write, producing five pages for Counts and ten pages of my own damn views about the injustice of it all. When Major Wilson finished my novel he was in stitches. Not so Sergeant Major Taylor. "Craig lies a lot. Bullshits a tad, also."

The grinning major said, "Yes, but he fell right into my trap. I need someone who can write an area assessment report on five locations that the commander in Nha Trang wants checked out for A sites in I Corps; I've got my man. He and Captain Lawrence Trapp from Ho Cam training center will move out by aircraft shortly. They'll be gone for about three weeks. When they return, they'll write the report for the old man. Think Craig can stay outta trouble in the Ashau Valley, Top?"

"Don't bet on it, sir. That fucker ought to be locked up."

"You sound like a provost marshal I know, Top. While they're gone, maybe Counts will stay outta trouble, anyway. I'm gonna be gone too, so hold down the fort."

"Where are you going, sir, and who'll be in charge?"

"Captain Short will take over while I'm gone," Wilson said. "I'm going to check out the stripes situation that Craig brought up. He could be right, you know."

"I think he's leading you on a wild-goose chase, sir. He had eight years in grade cause he's a troublemaker."

"Still, Top, something ain't right. I won't be satisfied until I find out for sure. Hold down the fort while I'm gone."

Thus, Major Edwin Wilson became an instant hero to the stripe-hungry NCOs in Okinawa and Bad Tölz, Germany. Indeed, *all* SF stripes were being short-stopped at Fort Bragg. The newly suspicious major solved the problem while overpaid senior enlisted people sat on their laurels. Upon our return to the home base in Okinawa, newly promoted staff sergeants (E-6) Counts and Cotter were among the first rewarded from B-120. Thank you, *sir*, wherever you are.

Trips to five prospective Special Forces Camps would wind up the six-month TDY for B-120, or at least for four personnel selected for the survey. Ashau Valley proved to be the most interesting, as well as the most demanding. Captain Lawrence Trapp headed up the small crew comprising 1st Lieutenant Slaten, Spec-4 Pointon, and myself.

The Ashau Valley is located in the northwest I Corps bordering Laos. The camp was secluded—or maybe excluded would be a better word—in 1963, secured by a battalion of four hundred Army of the Republic of Vietnam

(ARVN) troops and serviced by an excellent runway adjacent to the dug-in fortress. The trip would originate in Da Nang on a twin-engine Army Caribou aircraft.

All four of us had jumped from the Caribou shortly after arriving in country. Jumping aft from the lowered ramp eliminated prop blast from the engines and helped the chutist hold an excellent body position, gentling the opening shock of the T-10 chute. All participants agreed it was akin to jumping from a helicopter. The Caribou was a definite improvement over the Air Force's C-123 and the Army carefully selected the skippers of the fixed-wing aircraft, so crashes due to pilot error were unheard of.

So, one Monday morning in March 1963, the four of us were greeted by the Vietnamese camp commander and his staff. Quickly escorted to dug-in quarters, we were soon seated in the briefing and staff room. The CO spoke no English and used one of our interpreters to facilitate the briefing. We had already enjoyed an aerial view of the surrounding mountains and the long, flat valley that the camp rested in. Therefore, we were not too alert in relation to the terrain briefing.

The commander vaulted into the strategic importance of the fortifications. At that time, no hardcore North Vietnamese Army or Viet Cong had harassed the site despite the fact that it blocked one path of the Ho Chi Minh trail. The few VC and Pathet Lao units—and damn if the GIs could see any difference between them—that were nearby avoided the camp.

The area assessment team spent the rest of the day inspecting the fortifications and preparing for the next day's one-day patrol to the mountains east of the camp. We were impressed with the professionalism shown by the isolated ARVN unit. As a group, we also agreed on another point: There was not enough population to recruit from in and around the Ashau Valley, and Captain Trapp put that in the correct format in his final statement that night.

"There isn't any civilian population here, so where would an A detachment recruit its Civilian Irregular Defense Group [CIDG] people? Let ARVN keep this hell-hole." No disagreement was forthcoming.

With us tagalongs, the platoon-size unit of forty men or so moved out the next day in a professional manner. The patrol was uniformly dressed in fatigues, soft jungle hats, bloused jungle boots, and web gear consisting of a harness, first aid packet, ammo pouches, and two canteens. The weapons were a different matter, however. The Americans carried M-2 selective-fire carbines; the ARVNs were equipped with an assortment of firearms—Garand M-1s, M-1 semiautomatic carbines, and the Browning Automatic Rifle predominated among the Vietnamese. The first mountain was steep and teak trees prevented a line of sight of over twenty yards. The sweat was running from our bodies when something other than the sultry weather got our attention. Shots were fired, and we hit the ground. The closeness of the rounds to the assessment team left no doubt in anyone's mind who the sniper's targets were. My head came up as I muttered the prayer reserved for such occasions. "Lord, distribute those rounds like the Army distributes the pay, let the officers get most of 'em."

The Viet platoon leader talked to the lead squad over his radio and had them moving toward the sniper in just seconds. He motioned for the visitors to stand fast. Five long minutes later, the patrol was given the all-clear signal and we resumed our climb through the second-growth brush. After reaching the top of the obstacle, the patrol leader called the noon break and we dipped into our field rations.

"The 'Sniper' is a legend in the Ashau Valley," he said. "He's an excellent shot. You're very fortunate to be alive, as he usually doesn't miss. Maybe he only wanted to scare you away. We've chased him for years but always come away empty-handed. We don't believe he's a Vietnamese or *moi*. He's a white man with very large feet, and he is very experienced with a rifle."

The last statement decreased our enjoyment of the field rations. Three of us were thinking of Mother Russia but I was not. No wonder the Montagnards don't like the lowland Viets. The Viet officers go around calling them *moi*, savages. A poor choice of words, Lieutenant, especially to Special Forces people.

The patrol was concluded without further incident and returned to camp in time for supper rations. Our team was very impressed with ARVN after the operation, but were steadfast on our original point regarding the lack of civilians.

In 1961, A detachments formed CIDG units from civilian population in the Central Highlands. They were civilian employees of the U.S. Army, recruited, fed, clothed, and led by Special Forces detachments. The Mike Force, on the other hand, was developed in 1964 as a reaction force for CIDG camps. By 1965, there was a battalion of Mike Force in each of the corps tactical zones (later "military regions") I, II, III, and IV. They were recruited from their corps area, and trained and led by an A team. Airborne-qualified, they came—in the main—from ethnic Chinese Nungs and Montagnard tribes of the highlands.

Three days was all the time allotted for the assessment so we boarded the Caribou after noon rations. As the Caribou's two engines lifted the craft off the dirt runway, the Sniper struck again and I was cursing again. "Those bastards didn't secure the high ground. I hope the sniper eats their lunch, the sons of bitches."

The aircraft was only a few hundred feet above the floor when the right engine was cut off by the pilot. The Caribou leveled off and the crew chief explained the situation to his rather anxious passengers.

"Keep your seat belts fastened. The Sniper hit that right engine and the captain cut it off rather than risk a fire. We can gain very little altitude with one engine, so we'll fly the valleys to get through the mountains to the coast. Don't worry, the captain is an old pro at this. Any questions?"

"Yeah, Chief, how do you get outta this chickenshit outfit?" Pointon said in an attempt to ease some of the tension.

The trip was low and slow at best and it seemed like days before the Da Nang runway was spotted. Permission to land was immediate and a cheer went up from the four of us when the wheels touched the paved strip. Toasts were drunk that night to the officers and men of the 1st Aviation Battalion.

It would take our small team three weeks to survey the other four sites, and one week to write up evaluations to the commander. We recommended only A Ro as a Special Forces camp. But a month of sweat and high risks proved to have been wasted very shortly after the recommendations were forwarded. An empire-building "command decision" came back rather quickly, "An A Detachment will be stationed in each location visited by the assessment crew." Naturally, that caused some discontent among the lower-ranking personnel.

The Ashau decision would prove to be a boo-boo of the first water. In three short years, the camp would be the scene of one of the fiercest battles ever fought, and lost, by a Special Forces unit in the Vietnam war. In fact, one member of the assessment team would never forget Ashau and the battle that ensued on March 9–10, 1966. On March 10, hit by small arms fire in both arms and chest, Staff Sergeant Pointon was medevaced from just outside the camp by a Marine helicopter. After taking heavy losses from the Mike Force, CIDG, and seventeen Special Forces members, the 95th NVA Regiment overran the camp before it was abandoned. Many of the brave defenders in 1966 paid the price for somebody's indiscretion in April 1963.

But the consciences of the assessment team were clear as the men readied for their return trip to Okinawa. In six short months, they had established procedures that would be emulated by the "permanent change of station" (meaning "reassigned") 5th Special Forces Group fresh from Fort Bragg and B-120 would be the role model for the C detachments that controlled SF operations in each of the four corps tactical zones that made up South Vietnam.

In April 1963, we loaded a C-123 aircraft at Da Nang and returned to Okinawa. While families greeted the married personnel, the single men were cheered by having a week off after in-processing. Me and my single sidekicks were just as happy to be back as the family men. Probably everyone in hearing distance heard me vow aloud that it would be my last trip with a B detachment to war-torn Vietnam.

CHAPTER 19

I WAS glad to be back on Okinawa drawing E-6 pay with over twelve years longevity. I passed the newly instituted proficiency test, and was paid $30 a month P1 pay along with my jump pay. Adding overseas pay into the total would stretch my total compensation to $371 a month. I could handle that.

In May 1963, I flew home on a thirty-five-day leave. After seeing my brother, Joe Bob, and sisters Pauline and Jean, I visited quietly with my mother and stepfather. On one occasion, I wore my khakis, jump boots, and beret to a local pub owned by my ole 187th Airborne pal, Carl T-bone Brooks. The attention the strange-looking headgear attracted turned me off—I passed up any repeat performance. My high school pal Fray Palmer was slaving away trying to raise a young family, but found time to visit. All in all, I enjoyed the hometown affair. But still, when the time came to return to my unit, I didn't hang back.

I was welcomed back to Company A in Sukiran, still assigned to B-120. The 1st SFG (Airborne) had changed since my trip to Da Nang and Lawton. Trying to bring the unit up to strength was a burden. The trainees were not only recruited from the island-based airborne unit, but from other units on Okinawa and in Korea. Many were not even Airborne-qualified. The 1st SF started a jump school near Camp Kue to correct this deficiency.

Many of my teammates and I were shuttled from Matsuda range to Camp Kue to assist in the training that included demolitions, survival, weapons, methods of instruction, and even the useless—in my opinion—small boat training. We returned to the billets every afternoon in time for the supper meal.

No private room being available, I lived in the bay of the two-story complex belonging to Company A at Sukiran. I didn't give a damn as I stayed there very little. My visits to the Coral Hill NCO Club were becoming a nightly affair.

Miss Hatsuko Ago, previously mentioned, did not seem enthralled at my return. I didn't take the hint too well and the charade continued. Miss Ago settled the affair one dark, stormy night in June 1963. "If you want to take me out, why don't you say so? If not, stop the harassment, please."

It shocked me to think that Miss Ago could read completely through me but I recovered quickly. "Will tonight when you get off work be soon enough, Hatsuko, and where will we go?"

She sighed in return. "I'm not taking you out, soldier, you're taking me out. No questions, please!"

The evening of dining and talking ended late in the morning to the satisfaction of both participants. I was amazed that I had finally met a female I could talk with and Hatsuko was relieved to discover that the so-called super-soldiers were just as human as anyone else. The platonic relationship went on for several months.

One weekend, we were celebrating nothing in particular and woke up Sunday morning in a cheap motel in the sin city of Koza. Over breakfast in a local café, we discussed the affair.

"Let's find a place and move in. Hell, I'm an E-6 now; I can afford it."

The young lady had seen the question coming for several days and nights. "I'm a Catholic, and we're living in sin as it is. I don't think my church would buy that sort of arrangement."

"I'm a Catholic also, so we can fix that deal where everyone will be happy. Let's get married!"

Both of us were stunned for several minutes. "My priest will have to approve of that," said Hatsuko.

"To hell with the priest. Do you approve, young lady?"

"Yes," she sighed.

I moved quickly after the matter had been settled and told only a few of my closest associates of my future plans. Although they nodded in understanding, none of them believed I was serious. I, in turn, wasn't too damn convinced myself. A rude awakening came when I went to the SF personnel officer (S-1) at Bishagawa and told him that Saturday, September 8, 1963, I would be married in the Catholic Church.

"You may be married in the eyes of the Church come Saturday, but in the eyes of the Army, you're just shacking up, soldier. You have to go through channels to make it official, or command sponsored, and that'll take months, at the very least."

"I'm thirty-six years old and have to ask someone's permission to get married? Tell me you're not serious, sir."

"I wish I could, Sergeant, but I'm only telling you what I know. The Army will not recognize the marriage unless you take the following steps. First, fill out an application to marry a foreign national; after a background investigation and approval, you must both be counseled by our chaplain. Second, you go to the consulate at Naha and have vows repeated in three different languages. Only then will they notify the U.S. Army that you're officially married. We will then so note on all of your records and the fiasco will be over. In the meantime, in the eyes of the Army and the U.S. Government, you're shacking up with a foreign national. You have a top secret clearance, so the Army may well frown upon your actions and could withdraw the clearance. Sorry about that."

My argument was not with the personnel officer, who was only doing his job and doing it very well. Nevertheless, I said, "For the first time in my life, I'm not so proud or sure that I'm from the home of the free and the brave, sir. We may be brave, but free, we're not. Thanks for the advice and your time. The Army won't approve my marriage on Saturday, then. That damn clearance you spoke of doesn't matter to me in the least. If they don't approve of my actions, they can take the clearance, put a light coat of oil on it, and shove it up their ass. See you around, sir."

Staff Sergeant William T. Craig and Hatsuko Ago were married on September 8, 1963, in a ceremony in the Catholic church at Awase, Okinawa, by an American priest. The witnesses to the unauthorized affair were Staff Sergeant Frank Fowler and his Okinawan bride, Shizue. It was the first marriage for either participant.

I had, a week previous, found an SF trooper who was leaving the island and had been living off-post. I paid the man $200 for household goods that included a TV set and living-room furniture. We moved into the small rented affair at Kadena Circle the very next day.

The sergeant major of A company was well aware of what was taking place in his unit, but he refused to counsel a man just because he had decided to get married outside the bureaucracy of the U.S. establishment. He stayed aloof from the affair and used the only alternative he had to take the heat off of one of his troops. I was transferred that very week to Detachment A-132, which was going to Vietnam in November. Although not a unit of my choosing, I was more than satisfied with the arrangements. My wife continued to work at the Coral Hill Club and appeared indifferent to affairs of the military.

Captain Victor J. Hugo, Jr., had asked for and received a senior demolition man. The arrangement would be an eye opener for both of us. The captain was not a young, eager-beaver officer out of ROTC or Officer Candidate School; he was a 1951 graduate of West Point and, like seven members of his twelve-man unit, an old soldier. I took to him like white on rice, as did the entire detachment. My respect for each and every member of the team grew as the pre-mission training progressed.

The team executive officer, Lieutenant Harold Guarino, was an Artillery branch officer like Hugo. Under the guidance of Master Sergeant John Voter, our team sergeant, this would not prove to be an obstacle.

Voter was no newcomer to Special Forces and the team members looked up to him for guidance and leadership. He was able to handle that chore with the ease that came from experiences of one TDY assignment to Laos and a tour in the Korean War with the 187th Regimental Combat Team.

Besides myself and Voter, other Korean veterans were Sergeant First Class Robert A. Pronier, the operations and intelligence NCO, and Gerald J. Howland, the senior medic. Staff Sergeant Hugh K. Sherron completed the old-soldier division of A-132.

Five young SF operators rounded out the detachment. After his six-month stint, each young soldier would go on to make impressive marks in the Army or in society. James D. Munson was the junior demo sergeant and Spec-4 Philip M. Dierks would team with Howland in his medical specialty. Both radio operators were young and would glean the most from the pre-mission training. Sergeant Donald A. Green and Spec-4 Mortimer J. Duggan were the eager, "Morse code and communication" directors of a well-balanced A detachment. Not one person on the detachment was disgruntled about the composition or the training that preceded our deployment to the mountains of the Central Highlands of South Vietnam.

The detachment made its first parachute jump as a team in the last week of September. The equipment jump unloaded over the Yomitan Drop Zone during daylight hours. The drop zone was dreaded by even the most seasoned paratroopers. A Japanese airstrip during World War II, the DZ was laced with asphalt and concrete runways. A senior jumper, I had numerous jumps on the DZ and sneered at the references to danger I heard from other SF and the 503d Airborne Battalion troops. The conventional Airborne soldiers had the injuries and deaths to prove it.

Still, I was smirking at their jump stories when my chute opened that September morning. After checking my canopy, I looked down at the runways below. "Dangerous my ass.

I'm tougher than hell. Ain't no damn concrete gonna hurt me. They're all candy-asses. I think I'll hit the damn thing on purpose just to prove my point." Despite knowing that soldiers normally lie to women but never to one another, I began guiding the T-10 personnel chute toward the pavement.

Fifty feet from the strip, I grinned before assuming the preparatory landing attitude, eyes straight ahead, feet and knees together, and my hands on the risers. The iron man was ready. Fifteen feet above the airstrip, a gust of wind caught me and oscillated me to such an extent that I came down headfirst on the taxiway. My steel helmet saved me from brain damage but did nothing for my right shoulder, which was slightly out of position as the still fully deployed chute dragged me along the ground. My right shoulder was then where my chest should have been and the pain was almost unbearable. I screamed and that helped some but not much. To make matters worse and to add insult to injury, a non-Airborne-qualified leg medic was now running alongside me as I was preparing for my second takeoff of the day. The leg doctor at least spoke English. "What can I do, Sarge, what can I do?"

As a dragging-load victim, I looked at the tagalong in a very disgusted manner. "You dumb shit," I screamed, "collapse my parachute!"

"I don't know how! I don't know how!"

Fortunately, two members of A-132 came to the rescue and quickly collapsed the chute of a dying man. The junior medic, Phil Dierks, tried to soothe me as he removed the scarred helmet. "You have a dislocated shoulder, Bill, but you're gonna be okay. Here comes the ambulance now."

"Phil, please get some morphine from that damn leg and give me a shot. I can't stand much more of this pain."

Dierks shot the young medic a glance but he already knew the answer. "He isn't allowed to carry morphine except in combat situations, Bill. In peacetime leg units, it takes an officer to give you a shot; you'll have to wait until you get to Camp Kue hospital. We're gonna place you on the stretcher now. It may hurt some, but hang in there."

After much moaning, a ton of profanity, and insulting every leg in the U.S. Army, I was loaded into the Army field ambulance. The rough-riding vehicle did nothing for this hurting man and I practiced my foul tongue the entire fifteen miles to the large armed forces medical facility at Camp Kue.

As luck often dictated, no medical doctor could be found in the emergency room but that didn't deter my calls for the painkiller. Transferred to a bed on wheels, I was moved to the seclusion of a room on the first floor of the six-story complex. There an orthopedic doctor and two female nurses were ready for business.

"Give me a shot of morphine, Doc!"

"No morphine just yet, Sergeant. I have to put your shoulder back into its socket and I need your cooperation. It's gonna hurt just a little, so hang on. Okay?"

I grinned for the first time. "Do whatever it takes, Doc. I'm ready."

The doctor took the right arm from the side of my body and began a circular motion on the side of my outstretched figure. A sudden backward motion and the shoulder was back where it belonged. The bone-popping noise could have been heard in Japan—and so could my scream. The nurse began to sob in sympathy. The surgeon placed the arm on my naked abdomen. "I'll help you sit up, Sarge, and the lieutenant will give you a shot of morphine for the pain, then you'll be off to X-ray. I need to look at that arm and shoulder a little closer. I'll give you some painkillers when you leave the hospital."

Captain Hugo met me when I left the operating room and he noticed his demo sergeant wasn't smiling. He opened the door to the aisle leading to the X-ray room for me, but a Marine stepped into the doorway and bumped into me. I had insulted every Marine from the Halls of Montezuma to Iwo Jima before Captain Hugo finally halted the tirade.

In the X-ray room we found out that the head of the

humerus—the long bone of the upper arm—had a closed fracture. The orthopedic surgeon and a pair of enlisted medics placed a body cast on this very disgruntled trooper. For the second time in a decade, I was immobilized by heavy plaster. Hugo drove me to Kadena Circle and my unauthorized abode. Hatsuko was astounded by the turn of events.

Hugo seated himself in the small, sparsely furnished apartment and stared at his senior engineer before speaking. "Take the pain pills to get you through the night and stay home tomorrow. I'll have Howland check you out in the morning. We'll see what he says and then go from there. After all, we still have six or seven weeks before deployment."

While my wife was busily admiring the handiwork of Camp Kue hospital, I popped a pill and eyed the officer before replying. "Come on, sir, give up the ghost, I ain't going nowhere for a long time. See the sergeant major and get a replacement; you're going to need every able body you can scrape up. Forget it!"

"I don't want a replacement, Sergeant. You're feeling sorry for yourself just now, and may well feel different tomorrow. All I'm asking you is to give it a try. I need you and your experience and I can keep you gainfuly employed until departure. Whatcha say?"

"Sir," I said, "I cannot even put on my clothes, much less my boots. Gimme a break."

"Your wife and I will help you through all this. All I'm asking is for you to give it a try. Okay?"

I was feeling sorry for myself. "It's hell what a man won't do for $55 a month—$110 in your case."

Hugo's teamies had tried to rile him about the rank system in the past. He didn't take my bait. "Money has nothing to do with being in the Airborne, Sergeant. I'm still waiting for a sincere answer. Let's see what Howland has to say in the morning, then make a decision. Okay?"

I tried to grin but the dull ache in my arm and shoulder just wouldn't let it happen. "It's a deal, sir, but you're a helluva lot more optimistic than I am. See ya in the morning, sir."

I spent a miserable night lying on my back with my right arm extended from my body cast. I ignored the obvious—my wife wasn't exactly overcome with joy by my moaning, grouchy disposition. After helping me dress the next morning, Hatsuko welcomed medic Sergeant First Class Howland to our humble abode.

Howland gave me some more pain pills and checked me out. Captain Hugo showed up an hour later, and Hatsuko served coffee at the small dining table. Hugo eyed Howland and waited for a situation report.

"Sir, he could be outta that cast in three weeks, then it will depend on him and the physical therapy. To answer your question—yes, I believe he can do it. How fast and how well he responds is a mental thing. One thing I recommend, however, is that he move back into the barracks and room with a medic until that cast comes off."

I became very alert at the last suggestion. "Why?"

"For two reasons, Bill. One, you can't drive to work with that cast on. Two, a medic will be at your beck and call, and three, your outdoor Okinawan privy is at floor level and that will be a real obstacle to your recovery; your wife will have to help you, and you could even injure yourself again."

Howland had the team leader's support in the matter, and Hatsuko approved as well.

Hugo not only ordered me back into the billets but helped me put on my clothes and jump boots when Howland departed for training. While dressing me, his mind drifted back to his days at West Point. "Why didn't they tell me there would be days like this. I must be nuts."

He and Hatsuko packed my belongings and loaded me into his vehicle while I fumed. When we arrived at the company, A-132 assisted me with the new arrangements, malcontent though I was.

Howland concluded the day with a trip to the doctor's. There, after further examination, I was placed on bed rest for the rest of the week. When I returned, Hugo and the administrative NCO, Sergeant First Class Richard Perkins, came to my room and attempted to cheer me somewhat.

Perkins, or Mr. Special Forces, as he was known around the 1st Group, had taken the job of administrative NCO because he wanted to stay on Okinawa for a while. In the sixties, this was no mean feat, but Mr. SF was having a go at it. Perkins was famous for his jokes, and some of his stories caused my stomach to ache from laughter. To cheer me up, he let me in on the secret of his latest escapade at the expense of the Marines. Disgusted with himself for spending too much of his paycheck on the NCO club slot machines, Perkins had left the Topper NCO club via the side door and then walked down the hillside to the sidewalk below. Turning west on the paved walk leading to the barracks, he saw two Marines approaching. He moved only a few steps before arriving at a drainage pipe at the bottom of the hill. There, he stopped, removed his beret, and looked into the fourteen-inch corrugated-steel tube. After a few seconds he put one hand over his ear. "Say again, I can't hear you," he shouted. Perkins nodded as he deciphered the silent message, then quickly replied, "Just hang in there, I'll go for help ASAP." He moved briskly away from the area. The two Marines took Perkins's place at the pipe, and after only seconds of observation, the taller Marine asked, "Do you hear it?"

The short gunnery sergeant straightened up before replying, "I think so, but how in the hell did he ever get in a pipe that small?"

"It's no time for theoretical bullshit, Gunny, it's time for action. Here comes the armed forces police. I'll flag 'em down."

A chain of events had started that would not finish until darkness. A situation that would find the United States Army Ryukyu Islands engineers tearing up half the coral-rock hillside to remove an empty drainage tube. A red-faced high commissioner went over the events with his operations officer time and time again. The hoax soon became as clear as mud. "If we only knew who the culprit was that cost us thousands of dollars and man hours, we could hang him before daylight," the boss said.

"We know he was in Special Forces, sir," replied the operations officer.

With just a short sentence, he had managed to raise the general's blood pressure to the danger point. "Yes," he spat, "and so are a thousand others. You haven't narrowed it down much. I'd give a million if I could only ship those bastards to Korea—or to hell for that matter. Hell, at least I can chew on the group commander's ass. Get him on the phone!"

I roared at the story, which did my body no good. Promising that I'd be back after a pain pill and a nap, I left Mr. SF in the orderly room.

After completing a week of rest and relaxation with Perkins, I was enrolled in a two-week intelligence school at the Machinato military complex. The short, informal course made for just a six-hour duty day but, considering my condition, the time was ample and helped me pass my convalescence. Three weeks later, I was summoned for my checkup and to my joy the cast was removed. The OD sling that held my right arm was a welcome relief from the fifteen-pound body armor. Without consultation, I decided to move back in with my bride.

After a few weeks without having a shower or bath, I had become almost fanatical about them. Despite welcoming me home, Hatsuko was determined to do something about cleaning me up also.

Physical therapy each day at Camp Kue was followed by training with A-132, after which I went back to my apartment. Each night, my wife accompanied me to the public bathhouse at Kadena Circle. That the public, segregated-by-sex, steaming facility was off limits to GIs never crossed my mind. The ninety-eight-degree water soothed and speeded the healing of the arm and shoulder, in addition to making me more pleasant to be around.

In 1963, NCO promotions in the Army had reached a

level that I hadn't seen since the Korean War ended in 1954, and Special Forces on Okinawa was now receiving their share. With only eighteen months in grade, and drawing proficiency pay, my chances were remote. However, on October 31, 1963, orders were handed to me by Captain Victor Hugo. I was, as of that date, a sergeant first class (SFC, E-7) in the U.S. Army. Time in the Army, time in grade, and proficiency testing were the basis for promotion at that time. Despite being an Army-wide endeavor today, the prerequisites have changed very little. It took me twenty-one days to get over it.

On November 21, 1963, orders were cut placing Det A-132 on TDY to Vietnam for 180 days or less. I was happy even though my shoulder wasn't completely healed.

CHAPTER 20

THE 5TH Special Forces Group (Airborne) head-quarters was quartered near the improving airfield located on the outskirts of the city of Nha Trang, South Vietnam. Although the buildings that housed the headquarter complex were permanent, in December 1963 A-132 would have to settle for squad tents nearby. We went to the temporary living quarters, selected a GI cot, dumped our rucksacks and duffel bags, and moved to the HQ building for our first briefing.

"You will replace A-131 at Buon Mi Ga." Pointing to a wall-mounted map of II Corps, the operations officer continued. "Buon Mi Ga is situated halfway between your present location and the city of Ban Me Thuot, the capital of Darlac Province. Your mission is to command, advise, and train the 7th Darlac Province Battalion. The battalion's mission is to root out and destroy any Viet Cong in their area of operation. This battalion is composed of a small headquarters and three rifle companies consisting, all together, of approximately six hundred Rhade and Jarai Montagnards. You will patrol an area of operations that consists of five smaller villages in addition to this mountainous region.

"Your secondary mission is to test and evaluate the Armalite 15 and M-79 grenade launcher. Your evaluations will be turned in prior to leaving country." The rest of the briefing was mundane and allowed the minds of the audience to drift.

The Armalite rifle was developed and produced by the Colt Patent Firearms Manufacturing Company of Hartford,

Connecticut. To Detachment A-132, the rifle looked like a weapon from outer space. It made extensive use of aluminum and formed plastics in its construction, and it chambered a caliber-.223 cartridge. After you inserted a twenty-round box magazine, the selective-fire lever was placed on safe, semiautomatic, or automatic, after which the charging handle was pulled all the way to the rear and released. You were now in business. With the loaded box magazine inserted, the weapon weighed only six pounds.

The M-79 grenade launcher was a shotgunlike weapon that fired a high-explosive grenade more accurately than a rifle-grenade launcher. The instructions were short and to the point: move barrel locking latch fully to the right, break open breech, place weapon on safe, and insert cartridge. Closing the breech and taking weapon off safe allowed you to fire the grenade. The weapon could be fired from the shoulder or by placing the cushioned buttplate on the ground and firing it like a mortar. Loaded, the 40-millimeter single-shot weapon weighed only six and a half pounds and was about twenty-nine inches long.

Our unit moved to the nearby firing range the next day and received classes on the weapons before firing. The afternoon was spent qualifying with both weapons. No one in the unit had any problems qualifying with the space gun, and after cleaning the weapon we discussed the piece. We all concluded that it was an improvement over the .45-caliber World War II–era M-3 submachine gun (the "grease gun") that was one of our basic weapons.

We also agreed with Team Sergeant Voter's assessment of the AR-15 as a basic rifle for the armed forces. "It just wouldn't take the punishment it would receive in combat with a rifle company. The M-14 we now use in infantry units has the same features as the AR-15 and packs more punch with the thirty-caliber round. The lighter weight just isn't that important."

The team concurred, but the politicians and greedy members of the armed forces would shoot down this argument. In a very short time, the AR-15 became the M-16 rifle and was adopted by the entire armed forces. We never understood why the Army had the peons evaluate equipment that it had already made up its mind about.

Detachment A-132 fired the M-79 for the rest of the afternoon before cleaning and turning in the device. Again, a bull session that would form opinions six months later was dominated by the weapons men of the unit.

"It's a great improvement over anything we or the Russians have. It would add a much-needed dimension for the foot soldier. Go for it!"

To the disbelief of the peons in the rear ranks, only a short time later the bureaucracy actually did just that. The M-79 became known as the "thumper" and received an extensive workout before the Vietnam War came to its horrible conclusion.

Wearing experimental jungle boots, soft boonie hats, and tropical fatigues, Detachment A-132 was ready to go to war. Buon Mi Ga was one of the two hundred villages controlled by the Montagnard program, which was administered and paid for by the funds allocated to Special Forces—and Special Forces alone. When the ten thousand Rhade tribesmen were paid on payday, an alert team leader would be present at the paybook. There was never any doubt in anyone's mind where the money came from or who was in charge.

As the C-130 landed on the dirt strip, each of our twelve-man detachment knew, in detail, the goals for our six-month tour of duty. As Detachment A-131 departed, Captain Hugo made his acceptance speech in French and the battle to remove the bamboo fence that surrounded the village went into its final stages. Village bamboo fences with watchtowers on each corner were, long ago, a factor in the intertribal conflicts in the highlands of Vietnam. At that time, crossbows and machetes were the lethal weapons at hand. Explosives, mortars, and rifles caused the old ways to become full of holes. Today, Captain Hugo explained to the elders why barbed-wire fences would be an improvement; the watchtowers would remain in place.

After the acceptance speech was interpreted into the tongue of the Frog, the partying and drinking began. The Rhade killed a young water buffalo slowly, to the disgust of the Americans; to the delight of Voter, Pronier, Hugo, Howland, Sherron, and me, the rice wine made up for the barbaric slaughter in our honor. We old drunks made the village elders proud as we sucked the jugs dry through the bamboo straws. The younger members—Green, Dierks, Webb, Dugan, Munson, and Guarino—made only a half-hearted attempt on the alcohol, but they made up for that by damn near eating the Rhade out of house, home, and water buffalo. The presentation of brass arm rings to all of us concluded the ceremony and made us pale faces part of the Rhade tribe. Upon our acceptance, the cheering of the natives must have awakened every Viet Cong in the area of operations of the 7th Darlac Province Battalion.

As the senior combat engineer, I spent the first few weeks with Sergeant Munson, my junior engineer, supervising the Rhade in the replacing and destruction of the bamboo fence that surrounded the village. Before the fence was destroyed, barbed wire arrived by cargo aircraft so that there'd be no gap in the camp's fortifications. With the help of the Rhade, who were not strangers to barbed wire, the double apron and rolls of concertina-wire fences went up quickly.

The village was typical for the location. The bamboo huts were elevated on stilts and had a ladder in the front and back for access to the longhouse porches. Here one had to enter an open door to the compartments of the structure. Several families lived in each forty-five-foot-long building.

A visit in the third week by the 5th Group executive officer broke up the party for Detachment A-132. The meeting was held in the dining facility of the one-story team house. The lieutenant colonel leaned against the serving line that separated the bench-filled room from the kitchen. The team leader looked to the galvanized-tin roof as the speaker began. "Because of the success of the Montagnard program, we're short of detachments. Your detachment will be split

down the middle to form two detachments, one half will stay
here and fulfill this mission while the second half will move
back to Nha Trang to recruit and train Mike Force people
for a reaction force that can be used to relieve detachment
sites that are under siege or threatened. I'm sorry to have to
be the one to bring you the sad news. You'll be reunited if
and when manpower becomes available or upon departure,
whichever comes first."

Hugo had to designate those who would stay and those
who would go to Nha Trang, but after consulting shortly
with Voter, he announced his decision. Hugo, Pronier,
Webb, Sherron, Green, Dierks, and myself would make up
the Buon Mi Ga end of the split. First Lieutenant Guarino
and Master Sergeant Voter would lead the other half back
to the wilds of Nha Trang. It was a sad moment for all concerned. The split detachment had been gone only a few
days when Captain Hugo and Webb took out the 6th Company on the first sweep of the AO (area of operations). Sergeant First Class Pronier was left in charge.

Despite not making contact, the patrol was not without
its moments. The company surrounded one village and
questioned the village chief about alleged consorting by locals with the Viet Cong. They were not satisfied with the
answers and Hugo explained the ticklish situation in his
night location/situation report to base camp. Pronier, RTO
Green, and myself listened in the commo shack located
next to the team house. I looked at Pronier and commented,
"Tell him to use sodium pentothal on the old bastard."

Pronier grinned and took the remark as it was intended;
young soldier Green took it at face value, however. "Your
demo man said to give the individual the truth serum. How
copy?"

The silence lasted only a few seconds. "Tell Darlac-five
that I roger his transmission. Darlac-seven over and out."
Information gleaned through the drug gave the detachment
enough intelligence to begin our cleanup of the AO. I
highly approved of my team leader's action and said so.

"The old man wants to get the job done. He's a Special Forces operator."

Christmas of 1963 and the New Year of 1964 went by quickly for the busy split detachment. It was my fourth holiday season in Southeast Asia and that was no big deal. A cooked meal of turkey and the usual holiday fare shipped from the 5th SF Group HQ eased some of the homesickness of the younger soldiers. By then Phil Dierks and I had recruited and trained the replacements for the 7th Company. The seven-day-a-week job produced outstanding results but brought about a disagreement between Captain Hugo and me: I wanted to operate with the same company all the time, but the captain wanted the advisers to rotate through the units. He won—he had the rank. I stomped off to indicate my disagreement.

Our meals were prepared by the Rhade's version of Porkchop Racibor, and with the assistance of the Rhade cook's two dark-haired daughters. I was uncommunicative the morning after our disagreement, chewing my ham and turkey eggs slowly, while staring straight ahead. My head turned quickly when Hugo spoke.

"I want to see you after chow, Sergeant Craig!"

"I don't want to see you, sir," I mumbled to no one in particular.

The sandbagged team house featured a galvanized-tin roof, four picnic tables, and a kitchen to the rear. A small radio shack adjacent to the messhall separated the wooden, screened living billets from the messing facilities. Here, in my quarters, the team leader squatted on my roommate's bunk and watched his uncommunicative demo man closely before beginning.

"Okay, Craig, quit pouting like some damn schoolboy."

"Okay, Hugo, say what you must. I have work to do even if you don't."

"You are not only pouting, you're stepping across the line, Sergeant, and being an Army brat, you know that better than I do. Why do you push me to the limit? I do have limits, you know!"

"Being an Army brat yourself, you already know the answer to your question. But let me ask you one, now. Why do you seek advice and then reject the responses you receive? Responses that have been thought out based on years of experiences. Sir!"

"I rejected the idea only momentarily, Sarge, to give me time to think it over. I have done just that, and I think it's a great idea. You will be the honcho of the 7th Company, and Dierks will help you when he isn't busy being a medic. You have a week to train for your first operation, so get with the program. I'll have the 6th Company and Pronier will have the 8th Company."

I rose as the captain was leaving. "Sir, I was wrong and insubordinate. It won't happen again, sir."

Hugo couldn't resist responding. He sounded very much like me. "Bullshit!"

"What a filthy mouth," I said, in admiration. "Sounded just like my old man."

Now an Adviser, Commander, and Honcho-in-Charge, I quickly wrote out a refresher training schedule and handed it in. A detailed conference, through an interpreter with Captain Y Lull, the Rhade commander, was a success that day. All three of us shook hands all around before the training began the next day. I reused my Laotian experience, training the cadre one day and allowing them to give the classes the next. Dierks joined me in the close-in training area every afternoon after his very well attended morning sick call for troops and villagers. I advised the CO of the 7th to allow all of his platoon medics except one to help Dierks in the morning. The Rhade captain consented and his medics clung to the big redhead.

The day of grenade training turned into a festive occasion for the entire battalion, and the village as well. The warriors stationed four men downstream of the small creek that ran parallel to the training area. After pulling the pins and tossing dummy hand grenades all morning, the trainees were moved into position for the live exercise. In pairs, they moved up to a hasty throwing position with me and an interpreter, a position overlooking the running water below. Downstream, detailed troops filled large baskets with dead or stunned fish. By the end of a long, humid day, the baskets were filled with enough fish to feed half the Rhade nation.

The 7th Company was, in my opinion, ready for its first operation under the guidance of A-132(-). If Dierks and I knew nothing else about our unit, we knew its state of training and we had established rapport with our charges. Bring on the Viet Cong.

The briefing was simple. "There are no occupied villages in your operational area," said Hugo to the 7th Company commander and platoon leaders. "You'll sweep the valley floor and both ridgelines. Anyone carrying a weapon is the enemy. Any structures that can house the VC will be destroyed or burned. Any personnel found unarmed in the area will be brought back here for relocation to one of our pacified villages. What is your plan, Captain Y Lull?" Hugo asked.

Y Lull deferred to me and I was quick to relate the plan we had agreed to the night prior.

"We'll sweep the north ridge on the way out and the south ridge on the way back, sir. All villages in the valley will be checked out thoroughly. We'll move out the gate at 0530 and wait a few hundred yards down the road for daylight, then proceed to search the ville at the mouth of the AO. We'll be in a night location about 1600 or so. We'll not radio base camp until that time, unless we make contact."

"There hasn't been any contact in this area for five months, Sarge, don't worry about making contact."

"If I believed that we weren't going to make contact, I'd stay home. Sorry, I refuse to go out the gate in that frame of mind, sir."

An officer and a gentleman, the captain apologized. "The *Trung Si* is right, you must go out the gate with the idea of making contact. I was only jesting."

"Once we're in our night location, we'll make contact with base camp. Commo will be kept to a minimum. Any questions, sir?" There were none.

Dierks followed me to our small quarters. While making small talk we began packing our rucksacks for the combat operation. But I had more on my mind than small talk.

"I take five meals—one meal a day—on operations. With the C-ration condiments included, that's enough for me."

Dierks, at 195 pounds, was astounded. "I would starve on that diet, Top. I'm going for fifteen meals, period."

"Okay, dumbass, but you'll bring back half of it, we're not on a five-day picnic. Try half of that. Hell, you're thirty-five pounds heavier than me. Watch the natives, they'll eat goodies they pick as they go. When I go on an operation, I'm dead to the outside world the entire time. That way, I have my mind on what I'm doing, not on chow, not on the girls, not on the Army, and sure as hell not on making base camp happy. In war, a soldier just survives. He doesn't, and can't, win."

Dierks discarded a few cans of weight. He also noted my omission of any soap, deodorants, and toothpaste, including shaving gear. He decided to follow my lead. Socks were packed, along with the last item. A toothbrush?

"Yes, Doctor. Brush your teeth once a day, but no toothpaste. There's no dentist out here."

Dierks even packed his jungle hammock. I grinned, but said nothing.

"What do we do with our billfolds, Top?" the redhead asked.

"A good question, young man, even for a rookie. Here's mine. Take them to the commo safe and have 'em locked up! You do have taped dog tags, don't you, rookie?"

"Yes, Sergeant Craig," Dierks said sarcastically. He left our hut and moved the few yards to the commo shack.

I knew in my heart that I had a winner in the young medic. "Me go on an operation without a medic with twenty-six weeks of medical training? Are you crazy? I don't give a damn if he's fourteen years old."

Notifying the American on watch of the 0430 wakeup, and Cookie of the 0500 coffee call, we collapsed into a deep, sound sleep.

CHAPTER 21

WE LEFT a darkened Buon Mi Ga with the one-hundred–man 7th Company at precisely 0530. Rain dampened our camouflaged fatigues before we were outside the wire. Dierks and I fingered the insect repellent when we halted; the leeches would seek our body heat as soon as we were on the ground. Dierks was happy that he had sprayed his bloused trousers and exposed skin before departure as he had been instructed.

The clouds blocked the moonlight and the stars. Dierks had never been on the march in such darkness. For a time, the teak tree we waited under protected us from the rain.

AR-15 cradled in my lap like a child, I leaned into the teak after removing my rucksack and harness. Taking the repellent from my pocket, I squirted it on the black leather, canvas-top jungle boots. Some of it found the small ventilation and drainage holes above the instep. I continually glanced at my luminous watch and finally breathed a sigh of relief at 0645. I was sure we had left Buon Mi Ga without being seen by the enemy and could now see well enough to move on.

Dierks became alert as I moved the few yards to Y Lull's position and nodded before returning. I carried my firearm despite the small distance involved.

Once I was seated again Dierks whispered, "What happens now, Top?" The commander's RTO was whispering into the hand-held HT-1 radio.

"The first platoon is moving toward Y Song, our first

objective. We'll give them a five- or ten-minute head start, so be ready to move shortly, Doc."

Dierks nodded. "Anything there?"

"Hell no, too close to Buon Mi Ga. It's good training for them, though. They will surround it, and then we will move in for the search. After that, we will deploy as a company again. Let's go, Rookie!"

I hoisted my harness and rucksack, then secured the rifle before watching the doctor do the same. I handed the youngster his heavy aid kit. "You dumb shit, those company aidmen are getting over on you. Make them carry that damn portable hospital. You're a sergeant, you know."

To my relief, the mist soon lifted. Dierks and I formed up on the road with the company and the small HQ detachment, while the two rifle platoons secured the point, the flanks, and rear of the march. I nodded at Y Lull, the RTO spoke into his HT-1 walkie-talkie, and the main body of the 7th Company moved down the dirt road and rice straw to Buon Song.

"Shit, Sarge," said Dierks, "this is easy." I managed a grin before replying.

"You wait, Rook, until we move out of Buon Song. There'll be no roads or trails to walk on. Things will get worse."

The flat terrain offered no resistance. The main body halted momentarily a few hundred yards from our objective. A relay—or contact—squad moved out with the rest of the body following up. When the troops came into the cordon set up by first platoon, many of the first platoon's men rose to greet the doctor, but they returned to their positions when I shot them a look of disgust. In response to the greetings, Dierks only grinned under his floppy jungle hat.

The headquarters detachment and a platoon moved into the abandoned ville. I was happy to note no surprises as we halted, and I gazed at the five longhouses and two shacks before issuing orders quickly. "Search all huts and cut the stilts that hold up the longhouses. Destroy those two shacks with machetes, and then let's move!" The open terrain around us made me nervous; Dierks watched in awe at the Rhades' quick reaction to commands.

Y Lull had the company moving out of the destroyed ville in ten minutes. The point platoon that had secured Buon Song now brought up the rear. Dierks and I began to sweat profusely as we fought the rotting vegetation.

The jungle of towering brown-black trees supported a canopy of green foliage. Dierks made a lot of noise while clearing a path through the gnarled wait-a-minute vines that dangled like limp tenacles from the branches overhead, and he flinched when the thorns of the vines held onto his fatigues and the freckled skin they clothed. I grinned but the Rhade GIs cast disparaging looks at him. He'd learn.

The air was full of the smells of mold, mildew, decaying vegetation, and the tangled vines, ferns, and moss, wet and dripping from the perpetual humidity, finally got a quip from the Doctor. "Everything sweats at dawn, I guess," he murmured.

One o'clock found us surveying our first danger point. The small stream also offered us our first break and an opportunity to fill our olive drab plastic canteens. While one platoon secured the far side, our small detachment flopped down in exhaustion. Dierks emptied both his canteens and started for the waterhole when I stopped him. "Give them to the company aidmen, Rookie, they'll fill 'em. Here's mine also. I don't need a dead medic to take back to camp. Make sure you use halazone tablets, and tell the troops to do the same."

Through an interpreter, Dierks gave his aidmen orders, which were relayed to each platoon. The next command I gave to the captain was to announce that it was chow time.

A can of beans and franks, a can of cookies, and a candy bar later, the big soldier leaned back on the damp jungle floor. While devouring a can of fruit from my meager food supply, I watched in awe. "I'm glad you can do something besides waking up the dead, Doc."

"I'll learn to move quietly, Bill. I wasn't born out here, you know."

The clouds again blocked out the sun while I glanced at my watch. "Move at 1430, Y Lull!" The misting rain fell again as the unit began to move to our night location.

Buon Chat was another abandoned ville in the valley floor. The first platoon again moved up and cordoned off the area. Metallic voices broke up the rest and the remainder of the company and the HQ contingent moved into their night location. The first platoon would secure the ville, really just a longhouse and a bamboo shack. The rest of the 7th was dispersed on the low surrounding hills.

Y Lull, his RTO, and a medic moved into the stilted building while Dierks and I, with our interpreter, sprawled underneath the shack. Dierks's curiosity got the best of him once again.

"Why don't we get inside, Sarge? To hell with this rain!"

I continued laying out my poncho liner and poncho before opening my first C-ration meal of the day. "Too high off the ground, Rook. The men of this unit apparently think they are on a Sunday outing. Mortars and/or small arms fire could ruin your whole day, being that high up. No thank you."

Dierks noted that I didn't tell him he couldn't move into the longhouse with the Rhade if he so desired. I nodded at the RTO and began calling base camp when the first rounds banged into the longhouse.

We rolled over on our bellies and watched the river. Y Lull and his alpine troops literally flew down the bamboo ladder and joined us. But before they could get comfortable, five or six more rounds sought out our small group.

For the moment, the Rhade captain was frozen. "Open the net, dumbass!" I shouted at his RTO. "Get your head off the ground, Doctor, and try to see where those rounds are coming from!"

I changed directions and spoke kindly to Captain Y Lull. "Order that roving squad that's across the river to get those bastards, sir."

Y Lull finally got it together and spoke to his squad leaders. The transmission took the unit off the defensive and we all stared at the riverbank hoping to spot the welcoming committee. Two more rounds went high but Dierks was sighting his AR-15 at the noise. Then an M-3 submachine gun sounded off and the fun and games were over for the Viet Cong.

We only listened as the RTO took the report. Y Lull spoke to the interpreter and smiled at us. "One Sedang tribesman with a French MAS-36 and some papers has joined his ancestors, *Trung Si.* Do you have any further orders?"

I understood without the aid of a translation. "Yes, Captain. Have them search the body then booby-trap it with a grenade and set up an ambush nearby. One last thing, no fires and no smoking unless it's hidden. I'd better not see any light after darkness or I'll kick someone's ass. Understand, sir?"

Y Lull relayed orders to his platoon leaders before moving his small group out of the sheltered area to a nearby teak tree. Dierks, our interpreter, and the RTO remained in place. I was more than delighted to make contact with base camp.

"Yes, Darlac-seven, you heard it right. One Sedang tribesman KIA [killed in action]. One MAS-36 and documents captured. Will fill you in on the details in the morning. Over!"

I answered Hugo's congratulations promptly. "Thanks, sir, but they did it, not us. There went five months shot in the ass, though. Darlac-five, over and out!" I smiled broadly and handed the phone back to Joe RTO. I began nibbling from my can of ham hocks and beans. "You're eating enough to feed a Chink regiment there, ole combat veteran."

"Damn, I ain't no rookie no more," Dierks said around a mouth full of cold rations. "Thank God! I'm tired of hearing that shit. I'll get the Combat Medical Badge."

"Yeah, Doc, you will if you live thirty days."

The body sweat dried and caused us to smell like rotting vegetation, just like the environment we had became a part of. I removed my jungle boots, massaged my feet and put on a pair of clean socks before lacing up. Dierks did the same. Both of us were feeling the exhilaration of being alive, a feeling I had enjoyed many times before but had never tired of.

"You know, Top," said Dierks, "that you just became a war criminal?"

I knew the road that Dierks was traveling all too well but went along with him. "Hell, I've been one since Korea. Killing's a crime, and I know that, but my country insists."

"No, no, Top. You violated the Geneva Convention by ordering the troops to booby-trap that body."

"Sergeant Dierks, I am only an adviser. Theoretically, I cannot order them to do anything. So why are you trying to jail me?" We were enjoying ourselves by this time.

"Okay then," Dierks said, "the Rhade are violating the accords."

"Doc, the Rhade didn't sign that useless piece of shit so they aren't violating anything. Why does the U.S. insist on us carrying these stupid cards? Hell, I don't know. Screw the Geneva Convention. That manure is for the REMFs in Saigon, not us."

"Regardless, I don't appreciate being hooked up with a war criminal in a combat situation," Dierks said.

I shook my head before striking at the bait. "Okay, okay. I'll get on the first available chopper and leave your ugly ass out here. How will that grab you?"

Dierks decided to change the subject. "Being's how we're having lessons-learned hour, I have a question, old soldier."

"Shoot, Doc."

"Why did Captain Y Lull and his crew move away from us, anyhow? Do you have some disease that I'm unaware of?" Dierks smiled weakly but I did not.

"For a combat vet you're dumber than homemade manure. We were too bunched up. Besides, the Viet Cong were shooting at the most valuable pieces of property in the Seventh Company, you and me. We pay, recruit, and train these people. We can call down the wrath of American air on the VCs' asses. You keep their foes in good health, so you're worth at least $1,500 to the lucky marksman. So get your mind on what you're doing and make them earn their blood money, rookie.

"I'm gonna smoke one more cancer stick before retiring. Wake me up in two hours and I'll take watch. No smoking, no lights, and no bullshitting after dark. One of us will be awake at all times and so will one of our pals here," I said pointing at the interpreter and the RTO. "Bury that trash, too. Protect the environment and leave nothing behind they can use. Night Doc. Be ready to move at dawn!"

After the morning amenities were dispensed with, I ate a piece of pound cake while Dierks ate everything that wasn't tied down. I watched in fascination and the Rhade were no less impressed. I was speaking to the interpreter when the Browning Automatic Rifle sounded off angrily. All four of us were on our bellies like reptiles in quick time. The RTO opened the company nets as we stared at a small hill just above the village. A few small-arms rounds joined the cacaphony of noise before it ceased as abruptly as it had begun. Excited voices on the company commo net had the RTO's attention while I waited patiently for an explanation. Then the interpreter filled me in.

"Two Viet Cong were coming down the trail that is below the hill, *Trung Si*. The CIDG opened fire and killed them both. They are standing by for orders."

"Any weapons, Y Cha?" I asked.

"Yes, *Trung Si*, two more MAS-36s. Also, the VC were once again Sedang, not Rhade."

Y Lull and his group joined us. They were excited as well. "Two more Viet Cong, *Trung Si*." The captain smiled. "What now?"

"We'll move down and inspect yesterday's kill, then assemble the company on that hill." I pointed. "After that, we'll move on the ridgeline until we find a night location."

The first kill was not a pretty sight. I looked at the black-pajama–clad Yard while my mind raced. "Where's the weapon, sir?" To answer my question a MAS-36 French rifle came seemingly out of nowhere. I plastered the stock with masking tape and wrote the date, time, and location of its capture. Then, in a single-file formation, with flank, rear, and point security out, our unit moved to the location of the "good morning" fire fight.

At the bottom of the small hill two Viet Cong had used the worn trail for the last time. A smiling Rhade NCO came forward and claimed the kills. The VC had been torn to pieces by the World War II Browning Automatic Rifle.

The M-1918A2 Browning Automatic Rifle (BAR) with its powerful .30-caliber cartridge was the ideal weapon for the jungle. Despite its fifteen-and-a-half-pound weight, the weapon was the standard squad automatic weapon of WW II and Korea. After the advent of the CIDG program, the men of the Central Highlands also learned to swear by the weapon, a piece that had been discarded by the U.S. Army.

The Rhade sergeant smiled and displayed two front teeth that had been capped with gold. He explained what had happened to his commander while we stood by watching the performance intensely. Goldtooth smiled throughout the lengthy explanation. I marked the weapons and moved away from his bloody mess with Dierks in tow.

"His BAR settled the issue quickly, didn't it, Doc?"

"Yeah, but did he have to go on and on with it? Those two poor bastards looked like Swiss cheese, for God's sake."

"Yes, that bastard likes his work. There's a few like him in every army in the world. They're just not people I care to associate with, Phil."

The captain joined us and waited for orders. "I'll notify base camp, Captain, then let's move. It's gonna be up and down all day. No unnecessary noise and keep Goldtooth's people bringing up the rear. He bugs me. Doc, you make contact with base camp and give 'em the situation report and tell 'em we'll get back with 'em from our new night location. You need on-the-job training on that damn radio, anyway."

The rest of the day was an up-and-down march that had everyone looking forward to our night location. I was not happy with the march discipline because the 7th acted like it had just won the war. The noise and the giggling had me frowning and bitching the entire time.

At our night location on a small knob of second growth and wait-a-minute vines, I laid down the law. "Sir, tomorrow we'll begin our march across the valley before taking the high ground back to base camp. Tell the troops that their noise discipline today pissed me off no end. If it doesn't improve on the third day, I'll take measures to make them wish they had joined the VC."

By then Dierks and I truly stank and our clothing clung to our sweaty bodies. Fortunately, from time to time a cool breeze eased our discomfort.

As the Rhade commander reamed out his subordinates, I finally commented, "At least he's trying. If they don't conform mañana, I'll put something on 'em that lye soap won't rub off. Considering their rice and lack of protein diet, they can ill afford to miss a meal."

"They seem to be able to stay up as well as we can, Top!" Dierks lamented.

"By the third day, we'll hurt no more than usual, Phil, but not so the Yards. From here on in, we'll march their bods in the dirt. Our diet gives us endurance. You just hide and watch, Doctor!"

During the morning meal, there was no improvement in noise discipline. While gulping down my peaches I eyed the young Rhade RTO for ten minutes. As he whispered over the unit radio, the RTO giggled from time to time. I finally reacted, even though his CO pretended nothing was taking place. The young man had stationed himself behind a large teak and was stooped over. A size 8½-EE jungle boot unexpectedly interrupted the unauthorized conversation. The HT-1 went skyward, the RTO was driven into the damp hilltop. When he rolled over on his backside, he found an angry, red-faced adviser staring down at him. That set the tone of the third day's operation. The commander finally got off his rice-eating duff and once again lectured the small headquarters detachment about noise discipline. At 0800 the unit moved across the valley into yet another ridgeline.

High noon found us reconnoitering a danger zone, a small stream that was finally cleared by the point platoon before I called a halt. Dierks and I handed our plastic OD canteens to the HQ crew for refilling as the sun won its battle with the rain clouds and dominated the soaked scene. The CO spoke to the interpreter but had eyes only for me. "We need to eat, *Trung Si*." Dierks nodded in assent, but I had a different notion. As perspiration rolled down my forehead into my blinking eyes and into my mustache, I said, "No, Captain, what we need is some noise discipline. We'll eat when I believe we have attained that goal. Be prepared to move in fifteen."

"Damn, Top, even I'm hungry. Maybe we ought to eat," Dierks said.

I didn't even glance at my companion. "You're always hungry, young man." I raised my voice to include the entire assembly. "We'll eat when they quit acting like we have won the war, and not until." I smiled as Y Lull proceeded to gnaw on the platoon leaders. It would be the only thing he would have to gnaw on for a while.

At 1630, the quiet tactical march halted as the radio reported to the command group. "They've discovered a newly constructed bamboo village, with longhouses and all. It's built on the side of the ridge and appears to be empty, *Trung Si*," Y Lull said.

"Have the point squad surround the ville and ambush all trails in and out of the place and remain in place until morning." After the orders were relayed, I continued.

"This is our night location. Eat, refill canteens, and keep down the noise, or else." The unit responded well, Dierks being no exception. Despite the time of day, he was whispering.

"You were right, Top. They can't keep up with us. I'm not sure I understand why, though. The first two days they brought smoke on me," said Dierks.

I washed down my corn beef and cabbage before replying. "It has to be their diet, Phil. Meat is a novelty to 'em, is all I can think of. Missing lunch hurt them but in the long run, it might have saved our ass. They'll be fine the rest of the way."

As I spoke, Dierks wolfed down enough rations for two people, concluding the small talk. "When we get back to base camp, I'm going to improve their diet. Man cannot live on rice, alone."

The next morning, we moved into the ville with one rifle squad. We were amazed at the newly built longhouses and equipment shacks. "This place can't be over a month old, Phil," I said, eyeing the green bamboo. The crying of an infant deterred any further conversation.

When the roundup was over and the sheep herded into a group, Doc Dierks counted eight women and four small children. Our groups eyed each other suspiciously. Dierks hushed the crying children with some candy from his aid kit, and I watched the prettiest of the women nonchalantly breastfeed her infant. Then the oldest woman of the refugees began jabbering to Y Lull, who quickly relayed her message to Dierks and me.

"She says they have done nothing and they are unarmed, so why do we bother them?"

"What did you tell her, Captain?" I asked, eyeing the gray-haired mamasan.

"She is right, *Trung Si*, so I don't know what to tell her," Y Lull admitted.

"Sir, they are giving aid and comfort to the enemy. That's a crime, especially if the enemy is trying to kill you

and to impose a foreign ideology on you. Enough already.
Burn the damn huts and let's move outta here!"

The commander and Dierks were shocked. Y Lull answered the betel-nut–stained hag, who was the leader of the
stay-behinds. Finally my impatience got the better of me.

"Move 'em out, I don't like standing out in the open.
This is VC country, move it, goddammit!"

The command group moved the refugees into a jungle
clump outside the village. Finally black smoke and the pop
of bamboo signaled the objective while the women wept
openly. Just as I knew it would, the pitiful scene affected
Dierks. The hag approached Y Lull and asked if they could
harvest a field of manioc and yams before leaving.

The captain, an apt pupil of the ways of the Army, con-
veniently passed the buck to me. "Secure the field, sir, and
have one platoon help them. Food will not be left for the
Viet Cong, either. Tell the unit it's chow time too. Hell, I'm
easy today."

Me and the medic moved to a large tree and Dierks began his war on the world's food supply anew. I watched the
country-fair contest for a moment before smiling and speaking to the doctor. "We hit the jackpot today, old soldier.
Took away their loving material, their children, their food,
and destroyed their shelter. You'll see some defections before this little drama is over. This is guerrilla warfare at its
best."

"We greased three of 'em already. That's not bad, Top."

"This is even better, Doc. We could win the hearts and
minds of a platoon of 'em with this little action today."

"Kinda like blackmail to me," Dierks said. "I hated to
see those new homes go up in smoke, Top. You're a cruel
bastard."

For the second time that morning, Dierks had tripped my
wire. "You dumb shit! At this moment, those people who
lived here are plotting to kill you and me, but you feel
sorry for 'em. Get your mind into this war or you'll go
back to Iowa in a body bag. That's the last time I'm gonna

warn you. You're a combat veteran now, so start acting like it, goddammit!"

Fifteen minutes later, Y Lull said, "We're ready to move, *Trung Si*. We have the yams and manioc harvested."

"Captain, let me confer with base camp and then we'll plan our next move. Please wait one," I said. Y Lull nodded and the RTO rushed the transmitter to my sitting position.

"Base camp, this is Darlac-five, need to talk to Darlac-seven, over."

Sergeant Green, the detachment's RTO, came up quickly. "Stand by, five, he'll be here ASAP."

"Five, this is seven, *go*!"

"Glad you could make it, seven. Are you ready for the situation report, over?"

"Ready to copy, five. Go ahead!" came the reply.

I proceeded in the clear and hoped that every North Vietnamese cadre in Darlac Province was monitoring the transmission. I also proved that NCOs could pass the buck. "We are strapped with women, kids, and foodstuff. What are your wishes pertaining to our next move, over?"

"Congratulations to your people, Darlac-five," Hugo blurted. "Select a night location and close base camp earliest, over and out!"

"Pay attention Doc, this is important! Captain Y Lull, ambush all trails and approaches to the burned-out ville. This will be our night location. The women and kids will stay with us. Inform the troops that cooking fires are authorized. We'll return to Buon Mi Ga tomorrow. Congratulate the troops on a fine performance, also. Any questions, sir?"

"Fires, *Trung Si*? I no understand," said the perplexed Captain.

"Yes, Captain, I want the Viet Cong to try and do something about their losses. We're defying them to jump our ass. They may go for it, but I doubt it. At least we're making it easy."

The CO and the 7th Darlac CIDG Company were delighted to comply with their latest orders, and Dierks seemed to revive somewhat also. With the interpreter, he moved among the refugees and catered to their every whim. Bribing the children with his never-ending candy supply, the big redhead became a hero to the VC dependents. He also furnished the evening's entertainment for them and the fired-up headquarters section.

While Dierks was preparing to mount the jungle hammock hanging between two trees, he asked me about manioc.

Christ, now he's gonna start eating like 'em, I thought. Despite the interruption of my smoke break, I dutifully answered the question.

"Manioc is a brownish-red, long fat root. It resembles an Irish spud and tastes like warmed-over vomit. You'll probably like it."

Since Dierks wanted to try out his jungle hammock, I graciously offered to give him a few pointers based on my experiences in Panama. But he seemed unteachable. No matter what I did, he could only fall out—much to the amusement of the 7th Company and its captives. We finally broke up the three-act comedy by removing the device from its suspension.

We enjoyed our first cup of hot C-ration coffee the next morning. Dierks acted like he was going to his first day of school, his mouth never taking a break. I was, frankly, happy when he moved to the refugees to check on his children.

I spoke briefly to Y Lull before following Dierks to the refugee campsite. "We'll move into the valley quickly, pause, then place out all security on the flanks, front, and rear. Only then will the main body move forward. One last warning, sir—the troops know they're going home to mama, so slow them down. We want no unnecessary casualties before we get to the front gate. It's now or never for the Viet Cong to get their revenge."

"We will do fine, *Trung Si*. The refugees and soldiers carrying bamboo baskets of yams and manioc will march down the trail with us," Y Lull said. "We'll receive a hero's welcome from our people."

"Yeah, you will, but slow 'em down, I want 'em to be live heroes." To facilitate the movement, I moved to the refugees' encampment with my interpreter.

Dierks was still examining the children when I approached the circle of humanity. The hag greeted me with a pomegranate grin of betel-nut gums, lips, and toothy snags. As was expected of me, I eyed the sitting beauty with the nursing child. After flashing her brown eyes at me, she released a pointed breast from her blouse. The eager child fastened on quickly. Only Dierks heard me mumble to myself. "She really knows how to hurt a guy."

Speaking to the hag in an authoritative tone, the interpreter finished our business with the refugees. "Be ready to move in fifteen minutes. We'll move into Buon Mi Ga today. You will march with our group."

The company reached the flat valley floor quickly and paused only long enough for the tactical deployment of the unit. The trail to the Rhade ville was easily walked by the women, kids, and command group. The flank, rear, and front security's only obstacle was the six-foot-high elephant grass. That time of the year, the grass was razor sharp and unsparing of bare skin it encountered. As I had predicted, the march gradually became a foot race. Finally I stopped the unit. Me, Dierks, and the group of stragglers were sweating profusely by that time. We moved off the trail and drank our fill and refills. Dierks took pains to make sure everyone used halazone tablets.

I took the opportunity to speak angrily with Y Lull. "If they promise to slow down, we'll take a chow break, if not we're moving on like right now."

Y Lull knew the ploy would work. He had only to remind the platoons of the consequences in order to obtain compliance. When he nodded, the men chowed down. Dierks, Y Lull, and I divided our meager rations among the refugees and abstained completely.

Dierks looked at his deflated stomach and dreamed of

Cookie and the feast that would await us, while I killed my appetite with water and products of the North Carolina tobacco fields. I also filled the communication void with small talk while leaning against my damp rucksack.

"Yeah, Phil, you got rid of the baby fat, you're a lean, mean Special Forces operator now. In the next five months you'll treat more patients than a Stateside medical doctor will treat in five years. You'll be among the best medics the armed forces has ever produced. Ain't you proud of yourself?"

"Naw, Top, just hungry," Dierks said.

The 7th Company closed the ville at 1430 and the greeting at the gates of Buon Mi Ga was indeed a sight to behold. The remainder of the split A detachment had come out to greet us, and the entire village lined the streets, creating utter chaos. Captain Y Lull finally managed to form his unit and announced a reward of the next day off; but only after I nudged him with a reminder of an in-ranks inspection of weapons and gear the following day, were the troops dismissed.

A grinning Captain Hugo shook our hands and patted us on the back. Before dismissing us, he reminded me of the afteraction report that was due. Cookie was hiding behind the serving line in anticipation of Dierks's assault on the banquet he and his daughters had painstakingly prepared.

Dierks and I deposited rucksacks and gear in our abode and headed for the creek and a bath. Upon A-132's arrival, Howland and Dierks had marked the stream near the ville into three sections with white engineer's tape. One section was for bathing, one for washing clothes, and the upstream section for drinking water. We waded in, then came out and lathered down with GI soap. Dierks doused me with a pan of water to wash off the suds, and I returned the favor. Drying, we put on clean cammies and moved to the wash rack. A quick shave, and Cookie began quaking in fear of the Bear's appetite.

Pronier, Hugo, Sherron, Green, and I ate the fried chicken and mashed potatoes delicately while watching

Dierks in awe. When the medic finished without leaving toothmarks on the picnic table, Cookie was delighted.

A few beers and some good-natured banter followed. Hugo came in for some backhanded remarks from me. "No contact, my ass, sir." Regardless, I couldn't arouse the happy team leader on that day.

"You wait," said Bob Pronier, "the Eighth Company will tear them a new one, too."

"Correct," said Hugo. "We have the Viet Cong's attention now, he's got to squat or get off the pot. At the end of our stint, we should have our area of operations pacified, don't you think so, Ho Chi Minh?"

I did not particularly like the nickname, but went along with the good times. "I think you're right for a change, sir. If we stay after their ass, they may not last five more months."

All five men in the team house and the radio operator on watch would pull their load in the endeavor. Yet, an all-knowing and very political Military Advisory and Assistance Command and the often-overthrown government of South Vietnam would not only upset hard-won progress in the Central Highlands but get the war within a war out in the open as well. To the older hands in Special Forces, the problem was an extension of two wars that had been going on for some time.

MACV wanted to control Special Forces, period. The Vietnamese wanted to control "the savages"—the *moi*—of the highlands. In a very short time, the Mnong-Rhade 7th Battalion of 614 men and Detachment A-132(-) would play a part in this diversion.

CHAPTER 22

AFTER THE assassination of President Ngo Dinh Diem on November 1, 1963, the South Vietnamese special forces were integrated back into the regular forces of the army of South Vietnam. After years of being palace guards for Diem and other malassignments, the elite politician-soldiers had to be retrained.

In January 1964, in the second month of A-132's TDY, we were informed that two Viet special forces (LLDB) officers would arrive our location. This attempt to integrate lowland Vietnamese into a *moi* Montagnard program flabbergasted not only the Mnong-Rhade tribesmen but us, their paymasters and guardians, as well. The team house of Detachment A-132 was the scene of a team meeting to discuss and cuss the ill-advised actions of MACV and the government of South Vietnam, then led by General Khanh.

The team house was situated in the middle of the village, adjacent to the dirt road that ran from gate to barbed-wire gate. The one-story structure was composed of board siding and a screen that stretched from the siding to the galvanized slanted roof. The serving line divided the eighty-foot building in the center, separating four picnic benches the soldiers and their team leader occupied. The electricity for the team house was furnished by a lone ten-kilowatt generator and a five-kilowatt backup. The generator also supplied power to the commo shack and our billets. The small backup generator sat beside the big one, and both were up and off the ground in a sandbagged position behind the messhall.

Hugo briefed our small unit while standing in front of

the benches with his back to the serving line. It was times like these that most NCOs were happy with not being a commissioned officer. As one wag put it, "How can you persuade your people to accept Viet special forces, a group that's protected a corrupt leader such as Diem. Those troops look down on the Yards and call them savages, or worse. *Those* troops are supposed to take our place and persuade the mountain folk to their way of thinking? This elite, pompous group that has actually helped the Communist effort by creating an active dislike for the South Vietnamese government?"

Captain Hugo's briefing proved he wasn't sold on the idea either, but we all agreed with his commonsense approach. "Therefore, we cannot deal with the countrywide reaction to the move. What we must deal with is the local reaction and convince the Mnong-Rhade of the 7th Battalion that the move is in their best interest. A negative approach would only heighten the difficulty and encourage events that could get out of control."

Eyeing each individual in his detachment, he proceeded to empty the can of worms sent to him by MACV. The NCOs knew—but the Captain would not confirm it—that our leaders in Saigon—whether General Harkins or Westmoreland—couldn't tell a Montagnard from the fawning U.S. ambassador. Then, knowing that he was addressing the best-educated, best-trained NCOs ever to serve in the U.S. Army, Hugo nevertheless asked, "Do we have any sensible questions, gentlemen?"

Bob Pronier glanced at me and I passed it along by glancing at Hugh Sherron. Sherron, in turn, looked at RTO Green, who turned to newly promoted Sergeant (E-5) Dierks. As was expected of him, Pronier finally rose from the picnic table. The team house/messhall of A-132 became very still. "Buon Mi Ga, sir, is a model of efficiency and self-sufficiency in the Civilian Irregular Defense Group program of the Highlands. I was always taught that if an engine is running smoothly, you don't try to fix it. MACV seems to be going against that premise." Pronier quickly regained his seat.

Hugo remained standing and again made eye contact with each of us before answering. "Again, Sergeant Pronier, such decisions are far beyond our jurisdiction. They are also far beyond the jurisdiction of the 1st Special Forces Group on Okinawa, or the 5th Special Forces Group in Nha Trang. That decision was made at the highest level of command; our job is to make it work. Anything else?"

Phil Dierks treated the sick, lame, and lazy at sick call every morning. After diagnosis, he administered not only to the 614-man CIDG battalion and their dependents but to the civilians of the five Yard villages that the battalion had wrested from the VC. The Yards had won over the medicine-man farm boy from Iowa. Anything or anyone that would injure his patients, or potential patients, was an affront to the Doctor himself. So he now rose to ask, "Will they send medics to give me a hand, and what ethnic group will the LLDB contingent be?"

"A very good question, young man, one that I can answer, anyway. The first two officers, who will arrive shortly, are of lowland Viet extraction and they'll bring their families as well. That'll present yet another problem. The LLDB were politically involved with the Diem regime. In other words, they are political outcasts as far as General Khanh's people are concerned. The 31st LLDB Group under a Major Tat is preparing for jump school in February at Camp Dong Ba Thin, south of Nha Trang. When these forces are trained, the U.S. Special Forces' job will be to support them in their mountain and border missions. At that time, our job will be to work ourselves out of a job. Sergeant Dierks, you'll not see any LLDB medics in the short time we have left at Buon Mi Ga. We're leaving in May 1964 for Okinawa. Have I answered your questions, young man?"

"Yes, Captain, and thanks for the good news. I'll continue to train my Yard nurses—they are getting better and better, sir."

Sergeant Don Green, barely in his twenties, would some-day rid himself of the body fat and his naïve ways and stay in the Army to join the field-grade rank of major and above. The personable, likeable, very proficient RTO spoke to our commander. "I am not that familiar with the CIDG because I'm practically confined to the radio shack. I'd appreciate any help I could get on that damn CW radio net. I'd like to go on operations like anyone else, and rest and relaxation wouldn't be bad either. Any relief in sight, sir?"

"I wish I could say yes, Don, but I don't lie as well as I should. We'll relieve you at times so you can go on an operation or two. The rest of us can handle only five words a minute, which would cause havoc on that damn Special Forces net, which runs at twenty-one words or more. Right, Ho?"

"I'm slow at Morse code, sir, but no slower than you, or the rest of you for that matter. CW is like anything else, you don't get any worse at it, so I'll take my turn like everyone else. Getting back to the LLDB, if you don't mind, sir! Two Viets of lowland extraction and their wives? They'll be very lucky to leave this place alive. The Yards hate 'em, and I'm not sure that I don't either." I took a swig of Cookie's worst-yet coffee before continuing.

"The only way a program that MACV has outlined would work is to train Montagnards as Special Forces operators and that would take years and years, sir. As you said, we have no choice but to go along with their idiotic plan.

"My question? Who's in charge, us or them? I need to know that before I go out that gate with any of those assholes."

"A very good question, Ho. I'm glad you finally got there. We're still administering the pay, so that should partially answer your question. My directive says they're here to observe and learn from the indigenous unit as well as the USSF. We're in charge, and I wish it would end right there, but it won't."

Every noncommissioned officer in the room knew the direction the briefing/discussion was about to take. We only smiled when Hugo finally arrived at the same place he had left me.

"They're officers, you know, and are no different in that respect from officers in any army in the world. They'll resent enlisted people telling them what to do and what not to do. How to get around that two-thousand-year-old tradition will be your problem, as I certainly won't experience it. How will you work around that when you're on operation, Staff Sergeant Sherron?"

"If it comes to that, and it damn well might, sir, I'd just pass my orders on through the Montagnard commander. That way the caste system will not come into play. Technically, the Yard CO is the ranking man on the operation anyhoo!"

"Very good, Sergeant Sherron," Hugo exclaimed. "Have we answered your questions, Ho?"

"Yes, Captain. Sherron got to the crux of the matter and I'll go for it. If any other problems arise, I'll come to you with them and let you take the heat. If those Viets act up out there in the boonies surrounded by a hundred armed, mean Rhade troops, there'll be a lot of sad singing and slow walking in Saigon City."

At that point the briefing and discussion ended for Detachment A-132(-). A voice from the radio shack hastened our departure. "Radio talk, *Trung Si*! Radio talk, *Trung Si*!" Green went back to his labor of love, as did the remainder.

Days and nights between the company-size operations were not idly spent. I helped Dierks with sick call each morning. I enjoyed working with the medic and I was expanding my meager medical knowledge. Dierks appeared to enjoy my help but didn't overlook his on-the-job-training nurses. They were progressing at a fast pace and would be a great asset to their people once the Americans had departed.

In the afternoons, I worked with my beloved 7th Company on camp defenses and security. When and if I detected a weak link in their military knowledge, I scheduled classes on the subject in question. The fact that I had to teach through an interpreter bothered me somewhat. However, I did grasp enough of the dialect to dispense with the interpreter during weapons classes.

The misty, dark nights when we weren't on radio watch, we would drink Vietnamese and French beer. After downing two of those jewels, famed for their formaldehyde aftertaste, we needed a night's rest to recover. I was downing a Ba Mui Ba ("33") beer the night that Buon Mi Ga received its very first mortar attack. I only glanced at the 2230 reading on my watch and ran from the team house to my alert position.

The 81-millimeter mortar pit was already occupied by my indigenous assistant, Sergeant Y Chum. Just as I leaped into the pit, Chum released a mortar round down the tube. Fortunately, the round missed my head as it soared to its destination, but it did nothing positive for my left eardrum, turning me into a deaf-mute for several minutes. Even so, I removed the bore-riding safety pin from the rounds and handed them to my friend. I believe Y Chum knew he was being chastised with some of the best American profanity west of St. Louis, Missouri. At one point a close-in blast from an incoming 82-millimeter round knocked both of us to the ground. Though dazed, we managed to rise just as the attack ended. I forgot my injured pride and my ear as well when answering the sputtering HT-1. "Yes sir, we have no casualties, no thanks to my dumbass Yard pal. Over and out."

Nor did the ville of Buon Mi Ga take any casualties. The brief attack did serve to illustrate a few facts of life to the Yards and us. First: A war was going on in the Highlands and not everyone was pleased with the CIDG program. Second: The Viet Cong were no respecters of women and children.

The 7th company was preparing for its next operation when bad news came from the 5th SFG headquarters in Nha Trang. In 1964, according to Department of the Army regulations, people on jump status had to jump at least once every three months to receive parachute pay. Being in a war zone notwithstanding. The timing gave me three days' lead time to try to wiggle out of it.

Finishing my Ba Mui Ba, I turned off the lights of the team house and walked the several feet to the stairs of the logged, sand-bagged radio shack. I spoke briefly to Sherron before leaving but Sherron was not fooled by the cordiality of his teammate. He knew what was on my mind and said it aloud to himself. "If I broke my arm and dislocated my shoulder on my last jump, I'd be scared shitless, too!"

I walked slowly to my wooden, sandbagged home where Dierks was snoring away. I was careful not to wake him; conversation was not my cup of tea that night. I sat on my GI cot and stared past Dierks into the solemn, lonely darkness and, very worried about the forthcoming jump, began a one-sided mental discussion with myself; an exercise that I had practiced so often over the years that it was now an exacting science.

Two H-34 helicopters with ten T-10 parachutes aboard came to Buon Mi Ga on Tuesday, piloted by a major and a warrant officer. The two were welcomed to Buon Mi Ga by Cookie and the detachment. Happy to see strangers, everyone attempted to talk at once with our visitors. Cookie watched the chaotic situation for only a few minutes before speaking to Hugo in French. I cast the old spoon a few dirty looks and winked at his grinning daughters before addressing Hugo my own damn self. "What's wrong with that old bastard, sir?"

"He wants us to drink our coffee and get outta here. He says the morning hours are his busy time. I think he's right. Let's get on with the pay jump. Listen up!"

My guts churning again, I suddenly quieted.

"Three jumpers to an aircraft. I'll jumpmaster Major Butz's ship and Sergeant First Class Pronier will jumpmaster the warrant officer's. There's a small clearing three miles down the road that has been secured by the Fifth Company and marked with orange paneling. After turning in our parachutes, we will be trucked back here. Your AR-15 and webbing is all the equipment you'll need, wearing your steel helmets, natch. If you want to jump in jungle boots, that's up to you, but I'm not. I need the ankle support offered by the jump boots."

I was very quiet, even when the group moved to the airstrip to suit up, and never uttered a word when Pronier rigger-checked me before we loaded. Pronier patted me on the butt, indicating my chute was on correctly, and whispered, "Relax, Bill. It'll be okay. No prop blast from the chopper and there's no ground wind to speak of. R-E-L-A-X."

I smiled weakly and hated myself for the display of fear; I had thought no one could tell how I felt. My mental harangue began again and I chastised myself brutally.

When Pronier finished his jump commands with "Stand in the door," he told me I could sit or stand in the door. I was not feeling strong enough to stand, so I seated myself in the door; legs outside the aircraft, jump boots resting on the landing strut.

We both peered groundward in order to spot the panels and were both rewarded with their sight at the same time. When my left foot was over the paneled T, Pronier needlessly shouted, "Go," and to my relief, I was able to do so. When I finished counting one thousand, two thousand, three thousand, four thousand, I felt the gentle tug of the opened chute. I looked up and checked for a full canopy before looking down. Now for the hard part, I thought.

The small clearing was visible through the teak tree. The trees offering no alternative, I was suddenly busy trying to steer the nylon canopy to the clearing. An anxious Rhade interpreter was watching the six men heading for his location, and he noted that his boss—and friend—would be the first to land. I missed the panels by only a few feet, taking the majority of the shock on the balls of my feet before executing a perfect parachute landing fall and bounding up again. I collapsed the forty-two-pound chute before rolling it up for turning in.

Two weeks later, the sins of ex-President Diem descended upon Buon Mi Ga and the Montagnard battalion. The two LLDB lieutenants were welcomed into the hostile environment by Captain Hugo, who tried to look upon the bright side: Both Viets could speak a tad of English. Only one, Lieutenant Nugent, had brought his wife; Lieutenant Soy had declined. The two appeared to have a grasp on the situation in the Highlands and neither was thrilled by events. The remainder of the Americans observed the goings-on from a distance. The soldiers with a few trips to South Vietnam received more from the casual observations of protocol than might be suspected. These pooled observations would be remembered for their accuracy:

"Nugent is a Saigon wimp," started it off. "His old lady is a living doll who'll look down her nose at the Yards and expect them to wait on her hand and foot. She might well get 'em both killed in a month," came another observation.

"Nugent's slender and tender with a good education. He comes from a well-to-do family and has no common sense to speak of. A typical asshole who was taught by the French to look down his nose at enlisted people and treat 'em like shit. Expect the worst!"

"Soy is a little older than Nugent and not as brash. He's a very worried individual, fearful of the environment he finds himself in. Probably left his family in war-torn Saigon; a good move on his part, but it bothers him. We won't have any trouble with Soy, only that young dumb shitass and his movie-star wife. He's trouble looking for a place to happen."

Like most armies of the world, the 7th Darlac Province Battalion was paid on February 1, 1964. The only change the payday made for the American advisers was to take a few hours out of our schedule for monitoring our units when they crossed the official documents. The advisers studied the rates of pay long and hard before their units were assembled by platoons. Although we trusted the unit commanders, we still tried to insure a no-graft situation.

The bamboo headquarters building served as the finance center that rainy afternoon. I seated myself next to Y Lull and Hugo was seated to the Yard's right. LLDB Lieutenant Soy sat next to Hugo and appeared bored by it all. The mumbling and complaining from the rain-soaked troops outside spurred me into action.

"Let's go, Captain Y Lull. The troops are wringing wet," I said. Hugo and Y Lull dispensed with their double-checking and nodded at the armed payroll guards stationed at the entrance. A happy line began to move.

The procedure went smoothly and quickly, and I was especially proud that my troops were able to sign the payroll voucher. Even Hugo complimented me and my unit for our assault on illiteracy. At the end of the day, the men of the battalion had their pockets full of useless Vietnamese piastres and nowhere to spend them. Except for rice, there was little to purchase in Buon Mi Ga, or anywhere else in our area of operation.

Sunday was fishing day for the battalion. As the senior demolition man, I prepared the charges that Sunday morn and Hugh Sherron helped issue the modern rods and reels to each platoon of the battalion. I prepared the quarter-pound blocks of TNT, priming them with a nonelectric blasting cap and a foot and a half of time fuse. Sherron was to issue two blocks to each platoon-size unit. The catch of dead or stunned fish would, hopefully, supply a forty-man platoon and its dependents with a fish dinner Sunday afternoon. Before I was finished, I heard the noise from the line of procurers outside the ammunition shack and cautioned Sherron one last time.

"Hugh, make sure you don't give more explosives to one platoon than you do the next. Any show of favoritism will cause more problems than we can handle. Got it?"

"Yes, Sergeant Craig, I get the idea. Bring on the sportsmen."

After a light Sunday meal at Cookie's place of labor, we remained in place to settle any problems that might arise from the fishing expedition. Each platoon would dutifully bring its catch for the suppliers and game wardens to review and admire. After the amenities, we would politely decline offers of selection from the catches. "They need all the calories they can get," said Sherron. "Right, Bill?"

"Yes, Hugh," I said. "You cannot live on starch alone. I'll never forget the first time my ole pal Johnnie Miller brought a couple Bahnar elders from Mang Buk to Da Nang in 1962. That camp is like way out in the boonies of I Corps. When he escorted them to the bay of Da Nang, they saw the China Sea for the first time.

"They tasted the water and wanted to know who the dummies were that dumped the salt in the water. Salt is like gold out here in the sticks. The diet suffers from its lack. My point is that we're teaching much more to the Yards than just how to grease the Viet Cong, but you'd never get MACV or the people in the States to believe that. To them, we're killers who teach killing, period."

Pronier's unit came back from its company-size operation without any contact to speak of. The NCOIC was very disappointed. A veteran of the 3d Airborne Ranger Company of Korean War days, to the men of the detachment he was one of the most combat-qualified people in Special Forces. Over a beer or two, we tried to rebuild his morale.

"Hell, you ain't gonna flush 'em out every time, Bob," Sherron said. "We're keeping the pressure on 'em. Compared to the VC, the people in our villages have it good. The VC have to do something soon. If they don't, their indigenous troops and support are going to dry up. Just you wait and see."

"The area you covered might have something to do with it, Robert," I said. "Your unit's luck will get better. Next week, the Seventh might not see a soul on our operation. It wouldn't piss me off in the least."

Y Lull, the commander of the 7th Company, broke up the after-dinner speeches by entering the team house. He nodded at me but spoke to the officer-in-charge in French. I was annoyed at the company CO for going over my head. When the conversation ended and Y Lull exited without even a nod at his adviser, my face was flushed as I stared at my team leader. "What's the problem, sir?"

"Lieutenant Nugent's wife has your unit's families very upset, Ho. We have to do something, like right now, or face up to a revolt."

"Mash it on me, sir. I didn't like Y Lull going to you with his problems and skipping command channels. You should have referred him to me, dammit. I'll remember that."

Hugo choose to ignore the last remark. "Nugent's wife is treating your unit's wives as if she owns them. She picks and chooses whoever she wants and they do her menial chores for her without pay. The Yard wives are up in arms about it. Y Lull is very unhappy with the situation. What's the peaceful solution there, Adviser?"

Hugo knew he was fanning the flames that had been lit thirty-seven years earlier on the prairies of Oklahoma. "Regardless of what army we are speaking of, officers' wives have a knack for causing hardships and ill feelings to the enlisted swine's families. They use their husband's rank to obtain privileged status they don't deserve. Many of them are on an ego kick; in fact, that's the only reason some of 'em marry officers. I went to school with a bunch of girls who did just that. The bitches!"

Hugo took the remarks in stride, resting his chin on his hands and acting as though he knew what I was going to say before I said it. "You're bringing your childhood into the damn thing, Ho. I want the solution; I understand the problem, dammit. Y Lull asked Nugent to put a halt to it, but Nugent locked his heels, and told him that the Highlands belonged to the Vietnamese, not the Montagnards or CIDG. In other words, they would do as they damn well please around here. The Yards and the Americans be damned!"

I looked down at my coffee cup for a few seconds and when my head came up, I offered a solution. "The CIDG rank means nothing to that dumb elitist, huh? Sooo, sir, your rank will settle the caste-system problem. Let's get the two LLDB in here and you explain that part of their training to be special forces operators is to learn to abide by the customs of the host people. If they give you a ration of shit, let 'em know what might transpire on a dark, lonely night while out on an operation. It's blackmail, and life-threatening, but it's good advice. If that doesn't work, put her and Nugent on report through Special Forces, MACV, and LLDB channels. Whatcha say, sir?"

"It'll work, Sergeant Craig, I'll see to that. In addition, I'm sending the spoiled bastard to the field with you and the Severe Seventh next week. I'm holding you responsible for his safety. You do understand what I'm saying, don't you, Sarge?"

"You really know how to hurt a guy, sir. But yes, I understand and can do easy, but if the VC greases him, don't hold me responsible." As an afterthought I said, "If the VC are dumb enough to do that, we oughta win this war quicker than I thought."

Captain Y Lull, Nugent, and I sat side by side at the briefing. Hugo droned out our areas and routes of our one-week outing. Using his pointer, he slammed the map in conclusion and turned it over to the warriors of the CIDG unit. "Are there any questions, gentlemen?"

Y Lull had nothing and Lieutenant Nugent acted bored by it all. Although I definitely wasn't a gentleman, I held up my hand and was recognized. "I would like to go over procedures and the state of training of the Seventh Company. The unit is well trained in tactics and movement; they know the AO better than the Viet Cong. Only when the advisers, Lieutenant Nugent or myself, can offer advice that will improve the effort should we interfere. To avoid confusion, until the LLDB take over, Lieutenant Nugent should work through me. I want that spelled out before we go out the gate. It's best for all concerned. Okay, sir?"

"That point has been made previously, Sergeant. Have you anything else to add?"

For one of the few times since serving with Hugo, I didn't believe my Team Leader, but did not make an issue of it. In addition to getting Nugent's attention, I had accomplished what I wanted to. My final remarks were like a high school pep talk. "We hurt the Viet Cong on our last operation and we're gonna make him and his North Vietnamese cadre wish they had stayed home before we come back from this one."

When the interpreter emulated my speech, tone, and facial expressions, the Rhade-Mnong Cadre came up shouting—"Kill VC, Kill VC, Kill the VC!" I smiled smugly; Nugent looked scared out of his wits. The Severe Seventh was ready and able for its next operation.

Medical NCO Dierks missed the briefing due to a sickcall appointment at an outlying village. While we were packing our rucks, I quickly filled him in. "I don't care where I'm at, or what I'm doing, that young puke will not tell the unit what to do. If I'm gone, you take over, not him. Got that, Doc?"

"I'm no tactician, Bill. I'm a medic!"

"Good, but don't apologize, there's nothing to it. Ask for solutions from Y Lull and that snot-nosed lieutenant, and then make the best choice and see that the decisions are carried out in a military manner. We're in charge—we furnish the money, the air support and the supplies. Until the LLDB can do the same, screw 'em. I'm counting on you, Junior!"

"Yes, Daddy. I'll take over, dammit! I do have a question, however," said Dierks, as he continued packing. "Can I take my jungle hammock, again, Top?"

"Yeah," I drawled, "we need the laughs."

CHAPTER 23

WE WERE both thoughtful and quiet in the darkened mess hall the next morning, where Cookie used canvas to black out the light to outsiders. I spoke first as I arose from the picnic table. "One more cup of Cookie's tar juice and I'll be ready, Doc."

Dierks did not respond but Cookie did. "You no like, *Trung Si?*"

"No, Cookie, it's too strong again. Can't you learn to make it a little weaker?"

"No, *Trung Si*. I make it for men, not babysans." He scooted out of harm's way and the messhall but heard my retort.

"You old sonofabitch, I'm gonna choke you one of these days. If I ever meet the SOB that taught you English, I *will* choke him for damn sure!"

Dierks watched me grimace as I downed Cookie's eye opener, then he grinned. "We've got about five minutes, Top. Any changes that I should know about?"

"No, we move out the gate before daylight—in about twenty minutes to be exact. Once outside, the company will deploy off the road and out of sight. We'll move from there at daylight and secure and clear our first ville by 0800, then move onto the ridges and the high ground. The terrain will be tough from there on out until our night location is reached. Remember what I said about Nugent."

"Okay, Bill. It's still misting rain. I just can't wait to get wringing wet. Let's go!"

We met Y Lull, Nugent, and the support group in the

center of the darkened village. A whispered conference between myself and Y Lull was short and decisive. The first
platoon moved to secure the road outside the gate and the
unit followed suit. In twenty minutes, Dierks and the HQ
crew were in a tight circle seated under towering black
trees and the canopy they supported. Dierks was chilled to
the bone and was amazed at the pre-deployment orientation
that had stressed the complete lack of cold weather in Vietnam. When the hint of daylight arrived, he was more than
ready to move. The HQ sauntered down the road while the
point platoon surrounded the first objective. The point platoon had leapfrogged ahead and secured the forward approaches and flanks. When the last platoon was in place
and had secured the rear, the soggy command group entered
the abandoned village. A hyper rifle squad searched all
shacks and the area around them. When they finished, everyone took a break. The Asian sun was beginning its ha-
bitual battle with the rainy-season clouds. As the NCOIC, I
went over the routes once again for Nugent's benefit, but
the baby-faced lieutenant just wasn't interested.

Dierks had noted other aspects of the LLDB officer's
performance. "He moves in the jungle about like I did a
month ago. He can't believe there's a damn thing out here,
and he has never heard a shot fired in anger."

Y Lull spoke softly into the company radio and the
group moved into the green foliage. In the single-file formation, I followed Y Lull and the RTO. Dierks tagged
along behind Nugent and the company medic. The smell of
mildew, tangled vines, vegetation, and moss, wet and dripping from the humidity, no longer fazed the redhead.

The march was leisurely but we slowed, or stopped, only
to check out unexplained noises or danger spots. At the
short noon break, Nugent managed to ruin my appetite. He
looked directly at me and asked, "Who brought my rations,
Trung Si?"

When I recovered from my choking fit, I managed, "I
hope you did, *Trung Uy*, everyone else brought their own.
You're in a strain, if you didn't."

"I am an officer, I should not even be carrying my pack, no less my food," Nugent said.

"Trung Uy," I said, slowly, "you were issued indigenous rations for the operation. Where are they?"

"I brought only the bare necessities. I thought the *moi* would feed me." Even my interpreter choked on *moi*.

"Dierks, give him a can of C rations. Sir, from here on out, you'll have to subsist from your 'bare necessities' and the jungle. If I were you, I'd delete that word 'savage' from my limited vocabulary. These people don't need much reason to kill you, the way it is. I hope they overlook it this time."

Dierks grudgingly passed a can of ham hocks to the Starving Marvin as ordered. I looked at the Yards to ascertain if they had overheard the lieutenant's indiscretion. They had gone back to their meal but still cast looks of hatred at their future adviser.

"He's a dead man looking for a place to be buried," Dierks said.

The unit moved down from the crest and ambushed the prominent trails in the valleys while selecting a night location. The command group was on a hill above the trail when I radioed base camp to give my no-contact situation report. Preparation for a night's sleep took only minutes to complete. Because Dierks chose the ground to sleep on and not his hammock, the night passed without incident.

The next morning, the unit moved high once again and avoided trails. At the noon break, I noted the jungle vegetation that had been passed back for Nugent's use as a ration supplement, as did Dierks. "Damn, Top, they really like him," he said, glancing at the pile of greens.

"Yeah, if he eats that shit, he's a dead man. It's poison ivy and other less desirable cuisine. Get rid of it and let him die on someone's else's operation. The old man would eat me alive if I allowed that to happen."

On the fourth day of the ordeal, we marauders were high above the valley floor. The occupied peak was virgin territory for the CIDG and they were alert and cautious. When the intermittent rain ceased, I called a halt on the north–south ridge. An entire day had been spent traversing the jungle and I had never been in any terrain of its equal.

The trees supported a canopy of gnarled vines that dangled from the branches overhead, and Dierks and I were bleeding proof of the efficiency of the local wait-a-minute vines. A stand of bamboo with broad leaves and palm fronds was selected as the command party's night location. After the situation report, we observed our command group while eating our way back to health. I was eating my first can of C rations of the twenty-four-hour period, Dierks was on his third. I noticed that after the first day Nugent had managed to uncover hidden ration reserves. Dierks and I were secretly pleased the LLDB commando was taking a worse whipping from the vegetation than we were. Nugent's delicate features and effeminate ways made him stand out like a cherry on top of a heap of whipped cream.

"From the tough palace guard duty to a common foot soldier in only a month or so. My heart pumps piss for him. Can't wait to see how he handles the crucibles of war."

Dierks readily agreed with me. Our conversation was discreet and could not have been heard by the Vietnamese lieutenant, who was sitting on a stump six yards away. Regardless, he began mouthing in Vietnamese. The interpreter was busy passing along the remarks, which were critical of the operation, its methods, and its U.S. advisers. In seconds the entire command group turned on Nugent. Four days in the jungle had apparently upset the officer's thinking process, not just his physical routine.

I started my rebuttal very slowly and restrained myself for a change. "I don't agree, sir. We know what we're doing. We haven't made contact because the Viet Cong obviously knew we were coming. How? Hell, I don't know. This is the first time the effort in the Highlands has penetrated so far into their sanctuaries. They'll take the bait before we get back to camp. Bet on it! We're open to sensible suggestions that would improve our lot, however. Hell, anyone can critcize, but we'd like solutions, not just a restating of the problems."

"We're not making contact because you and the commander are too cautious," Nugent said. "Throw caution to the wind and let's see what happens. Are you afraid to die?"

At that point Y Lull chose to withdraw to preserve Nugent's health.

"You are the first person who ever questioned our courage, sir. But you are correct. We don't want to die for our cause, we want the other bastard to die for his. We refuse to break our tactical discipline to make some air-conditioned asshole in Saigon happy. By tomorrow, if it's a body count you want, you'll have it, but we'll do it by the book, thank you."

The LLDB shook his head and prepared for the night. If he didn't know he had just shortened his life span, he was dumber than he acted; no mean feat, even for a lieutenant.

Much to my relief, Dierks again passed up his hammock act in favor of the damp earth. I was aching from the all-day struggle with the terrain and just didn't need the laughs that dark night. I dozed off, leaving Dierks to pull the first four-hour watch.

The fifth day, the Sad Seventh moved down into the valley amid well-worn trails that appeared to have been recently traveled. The unit paused for refills and refreshments around noon. Dierks and I had exhausted our water and welcomed the pause. Small talk began only after Nugent and I checked all unit ambushes and security. Satisfied the outfit was doing all it could do, we returned to the group's location above the well-worn trail.

In hushed tones, Dierks greeted me with the usual GI complaints. "I swear, Top, this humidity and up-and-down walk in the sun and rain has me beat."

"Yeah," I answered, "this ain't my first rodeo but I swear I've lost ten pounds, like lately."

"If you lost ten pounds, you'd be down to zilch, Top.

I've lost twenty," said Dierks, stuffing his mouth with corned-beef hash.

Eyeing Nugent while I filled my face, I changed the subject. "After the first day, Nugent came up with his own rations. My, my, I wish we'd make contact and ruin his know-it-all attitude."

A Browning Automatic Rifle from *Trung Si* Goldtooth's area answered my prayers. The short burst was followed by a few carbine rounds.

Everyone was on their bellies staring toward the noise as the RTO was relaying information to Y Lull. Suddenly I was enjoying myself. "Get your head up, *Trung Uy*."

A fearful face lifted up from the jungle floor and glared at me. I couldn't hide the obvious; I was enjoying Nugent's discomfort. "Give me the sitrep, interpreter!" I demanded.

"Three Viet Cong, *Trung Si*, coming down the trail in the third platoon's area. Two are *fini*, one is wounded and has been taken prisoner. They are awaiting orders from headquarters."

Before I answered the request for orders, my mind drifted back to the last operation. The Rhade platoon sergeant with the gold teeth had killed a few in that escapade as well. What bothered me and Dierks was that we knew the man enjoyed his work. That worried me no end. In the absence of instructions from Y Lull, I responded.

"Tell Goldtooth we'll be there shortly. Secure the area and don't grease that prisoner of war or I'll knock out those damn teeth."

The interpreter somehow tip-toed around the slang in order to relay the instructions. I rose to a standing position, strapping on web gear and securing my AR-15, but I paused when I noticed Dierks enjoying the comfort of his jungle Lazee Boy. "Come on, Doc, get your indig medic and aid kit, we have a wounded soldier boy down there, you know."

Y Lull had not been idle. In just minutes he had a rifle squad ready to escort our group to the scene of the action.

Nugent didn't look so eager to join the fun, but the fact that he was being ignored seemed to motivate him somewhat.

The reinforced rifle squad approached the scene of the action and Goldtooth, grinning as usual, greeted us. We viewed the gore and mutilations caused by the BAR. "Does that bastard know you can fire that damn weapon on semi-automatic? There's twenty rounds in each one of these bastards. It's overkill, pure and simple," I said, turning to the interpreter.

Goldtooth sobered and his morale tumbled a tad when my mouthpiece was finished. "Poor fire discipline! It doesn't take a ton of lead to grease a soldier. Tell that grinning bastard to work on it; this is unnecessary, goddammit!"

The wounded Yard VC had been moved from the trail and Dierks was now administering to him. I moved away from the gore to the side of the medic. Dierks pressed the needle into the POW's buttocks and relayed instructions to his native assistant before standing to address his boss. "His shinbone is broken by a round from that BAR, otherwise, he's okay. He'll have to be supported, though, in order to travel. What else?"

I eyed the enemy and the wounded soldier returned my stare. "He's Rhade, so I guess his companions were too."

The interpreter confirmed my suspicions and Dierks asked what the plans were for the rest of the day. Y Lull and I conferred while Nugent listened resentfully. I passed on our solutions to the medical NCO. "I'll have to notify base camp of the contact, then we'll move our command post a few yards from Goldtooth's butchers and await orders.

"The wounded soldier stays with us, not Goldtooth, because I hate the way he gets his jollies. Have your medics watch the POW, Doc. I've got to call base camp." It was 1415 when I roused the green radio operator from his slumber.

I smiled as I admonished the young sergeant. "*Pak* time's over, Junior. Listen up! We had contact at LZ460570 at 1345 with the following results: Two VC KIA, one POW WIA, three MAS-36 rifles recovered. Need transportation for wounded POW. I'm standing by for instructions from Darlac-seven. Over."

Y Lull and the interpreter were seriously discussing a subject when they approached me. I handed the transmitter back to the RTO and held up my hands in feigned disgust. I espied Nugent in an alert tree-leaning position before I spoke. "Gentlemen, what's the problem?"

"Trung Si," said the interpreter, "you have instructed us many times not to bury the VC dead, to let the Viet Cong use their own manpower for that purpose. We agree; however, we have a problem with that proposition at this time. You see, one of the dead is the brother of Y Kant, a rifleman in the third platoon, and he wants to bury his brother in an appropriate manner."

I was stunned, but only for a few seconds. For the first time, I noticed the Rhade rifleman who stood behind Y Lull was sobbing softly.

"That throws a different light on things, Captain. Of course he can bury his brother and his platoon should assist him in the ceremony. We're not *moi*," I said, casting Nugent a smirk. "I'm sorry, Y Kant, that this had to happen. I will attend the burial also."

I nodded at Y Lull, and the CO got on the horn with the third platoon. Goldtooth would now be in charge of the funeral arrangements. I thought he'd probably enjoy the job.

Minutes after Dierks and I paid our last respects to an individual who had, only hours before, been our foe, the PRC-10 radio sounded off. The metallic voice of the team leader came up. "Congrads again, Darlac-five. We're at your service. Go!"

"Darlac-seven, this is Five, I need a medical evacuation helicopter for a POW, ASAP. Can you help? Over!"

"Not today, Five, but will try again in the morning. Anything else? Over!"

"No, Darlac-seven, but in that case, we will be standing

by at LZ460570, our night location. This is Five, over and out!"

The medical specialist was apparently not satisfied with the day's excitement, and therefore requested he be again allowed to use his hammock for sleeping purposes. It had been a trying day for everyone so I said, "Sure, Doc, go ahead, we're safe up here and security is out far enough. We need the laughs, anyway."

Dierks mumbled to himself as he tied the device to two large teak trees, which served to alert the small contingent of the coming comedy. Nugent was unaware of what happened on the last operation and paid no heed to the preliminaries. But the Yards remembered the numerous brutal encounters and were grinning from ear to ear.

This evening's entertainment was no less side-splitting than the last, because Doc had obviously been practicing new routines in secret. The capper was one in which he managed to zip himself inside the hammock before turning over. We all fell asleep with sore sides.

The 7th Company reported in at first light. "Darlac, this is Five, any luck with that chopper request? Over!"

"Darlac-five, this is base camp. None thus far. We'll let you know ASAP. Base camp, standing by, over and out!"

The unit stayed on the high ground and the going didn't improve much. Four men were alternating on the POW stretcher detail and were grateful for the noon break. I tried my hand again with base camp while Dierks checked out the wounded prisoner. He returned just as I received the closing message.

"No luck yet, Five, but we're trying. Darlac over and out!"

Y Lull and Dierks hurriedly approached as I dejectedly handed the transmitter back to the RTO. Before I could figure out for myself what the excitement was all about, Dierks blurted out, "They want to kill him, Top. Do something!"

The pair kneeled next to me and we all noted that Nugent was monitoring the action from a few yards away.

"Calm down, Junior, everything's gonna be all right. What's going on, Captain Y Lull?"

"The troops are weary of carrying the prisoner and want to kill him, *Trung Si*. I really can't blame them."

Dierks stared long and hard at me and I knew what was bouncing from brain cell to brain cell in that red head of his: *Here's my chance to become a war criminal; it just ain't gonna happen,* I thought. "Sir, I'm trying to get the POW outta here. There's just no chopper available right now."

The smirk on Nugent's face was doing nothing positive for my anxious disposition.

"We still have five hours or so of daylight; we'll make it. We need that POW for intelligence purposes so talk to 'em, dammit. I cannot condone such an act. It's up to you. But if they do kill him, they do so without my permission."

As I stated previously, it wasn't my first rodeo; I could pass the buck as well as anyone else.

Y Lull withdrew to converse with his stretcher bearers and security squad while Dierks followed the commander along with his Rhade OJT medic. I watched them leave before remarking, "Damn, Doc don't care who they are, VC or CIDG; if they're his patients, he's concerned. Good soldier!"

After a light lunch, the march began anew. The unit was approaching a slight incline when the PRC-10 sounded off. I signaled Y Lull to halt the advance before taking the call from base camp. It was Green's time to rile a very weary demolition man.

"Darlac-five, this is base camp," Green said. "U.S. technology inbound your location ASAP. Secure landing zone and have POW ready to load. Over!"

"Knock off the cute shit, RTO. We'll be ready in ten. Five, standing by, over."

Y Lull and I selected a small clearing on a nearby hill and the unit had it secured in exactly ten minutes. I heard the H-34 rotary-wing aircraft before I saw it. "Unknown aircraft, this is Darlac-five. Come back, over!"

Major Swartz came right back as instructed. "Five, this is Chop-two. Gimme your location. Over!"

"Roger, Chop-two, we're at LZ590460, have smoke. Let me know when you're ready for it. Five, standing by."

Our crew saw the helicopter at the same time we received our orders. "Five, this Chop-two, pop and identify smoke. Over!"

I nodded, Dierks pulled the retainer pin and cast the cannister into the clearing. Thick, hot-purple smoke jetted from the metal container, waterfalling, splashing, and cascading into the ravines. Captain Hugo's old West Point buddy hovered momentarily before the olive drab H-34 landed.

Dierks supervised the stretcher crew in the loading of his VC patient while the command crew waited in the wings. Grinning broadly, Hugo assisted the chopper crew. When the medic was finished, I nodded at two indigenous soldiers and they threw the captured weapons onto the aircraft. I handed the still-grinning Hugo the captured documents and stepped away from the whirlybird. He gave Swartz thumbs up and the aircraft went almost straight up. Everyone breathed a sigh of relief as the helicopter cleared the treeline and contoured to base camp.

Y Lull insisted on a conference before moving, but I cut the discussion short. "Thanks to that damn helicopter, every Viet Cong in Darlac Province knows our location. Move, goddammit, move!"

The unit marched for two hours before selecting a night location and reporting same. For all practical purposes, the operation was over. I informed Dierks of the fact while aiding him with his jungle hammock.

"They not only know where we're at but in what strength. They won't jump a whole damn company; the operation is over. The only danger we face now is a clumsy redhead trying to sleep in a hostile jungle hammock."

"Funny, funny. I've got it cold now, Top, I'll rock myself to sleep in no time." Much to the relief of the entire unit, he did just that.

"Darlac-five, this is Darlac-seven. Roger your night location. Close soonest. Your POW helped us some. He's in the hospital at Ban Me Thuot at this time. You now have a price on your head and so does Darlac-four. How copy? Over!"

"Darlac, this is Five. 'Bout time somebody recognized our talents. How much are we worth to the VC? Over!"

"You're worth $1,500 and your medic is worth $1,000. Not bad, huh? Over!"

"Not too shabby, Darlac-seven. Tell 'em not to get it much higher or we'll both defect. This is Five, over and out."

When the villagers, families, and split A team saw the column of ducks approaching the home base, they sounded off. The cheering, hugging, and back-slapping embarrassed Dierks and me but we smiled. Despite the noisy confusion, once we were inside the village, Y Lull got his unit into a semblance of a formation. Nugent spoke to him and he saluted the Viet and dismissed his troops, then walked with his interpreter on a straight line to the hootch of his U.S. advisers. We were stripped to the waist by then and were surprised by the visit.

"Lieutenant Nugent says we must have a weapons inspection in one hour, *Trung Si*!" said Y Lull, excitedly. "We've always conducted it the next day. What shall I do?"

I ceased the striptease and answered the sincere question. "We'll have weapons inspection and equipment layout tomorrow, just like we always have, *Dai Uy*. Screw Nugent."

Y Lull and his interpreter exited the hootch, smiling broadly.

Soon Dierks and I were both stripped naked, and the lower portions of our bodies were a bloody sight. The leeches had done a number on us during the trip back to base camp.

Dierks used medical gauze and bug juice to rid me of my passengers. When he finished, I returned the favor. We walked slowly to the bathing hole in the creek that ran by the village. After a while Cookie sent word to us beachcombers that a hot meal was awaiting. Dierks almost broke both legs getting back to the hootch to put on a clean uniform. Shaking my head and wondering if Cookie had learned to make coffee yet, I tagged along. When we finally found the teamhouse, Dierks did not disappoint Cookie and his crew. Hugo waited patiently throughout the exhibition. When I finished my meal, Cookie surprised me by personally serving my coffee. I was wary because Hugo and the Doc had not been served.

"Babysan coffee, just for you, *Trung Si*," said Cookie, smiling. I immediately drank the best cup of java I had ever had at Buon Mi Ga, South Vietnam.

Cookie and his daughters exited the messhall while Dierks and I debriefed our team leader, omitting no details, including the actions and reactions of the native commanders and the LLDB. "Wanna talk about Nugent, Captain?"

Despite knowing damn well I was preparing to enjoy myself, Hugo agreed. "He's an elitist with no practical experience in his profession. He'll never accept the Yards as his equals—military, social, or otherwise. He's a French-trained asshole. The Yards want to grease him, like five days ago. I kinda side with them, don't you, Phil?"

Dierks nodded. "Hell, sir, he won't accept *us* as his equals, much less the Rhade. I just hope they don't kill him—I don't need any more dead patients."

"All we can do is hope that he changes," Hugo said. "If he doesn't, it probably won't matter anyway, since he'll be dead. Lieutenant Soy is another matter, however. He has been working with the Rhade commanders and seems to get along very well with them, and with the troops as well. I'm gonna send him out with you the next time you take out the Seventh."

"Thanks, sir. You're all heart, but after Nugent we can stand anybody; bring 'em on. Anything else, sir?" I asked.

"Yes," said Hugo. "That POW gave us an earful. He said, in essence, that you and the Severe Seventh were bad news to them and they want you dead, ASAP. The North Vietnamese Army cadre has been preaching hatred of everyone in this detachment. He said that if and when they get their numbers up, they're going to hit our operations, but not until. He also said that the NVA officer, cadre, whatever, is also of Vietnamese extraction and the VC unit likes him about the way the Mnong-Rhade like Nugent. Sooo, we do have some advantages. But I want the detachment to be alert at all times." There was a loud knock on the team house screen door.

"Come on in, Captain Y Lull," Hugo said loudly.

Hugo and Y Lull conversed in French. When it was over, Y Lull saluted, did an about-face and departed. "What's the problem now, sir?" Dierks asked.

Cookie and his small crew came back into their kitchen. The banging of pots and pans made Hugo raise his volume. Nodding at me, Hugo blurted over Cookie's disruptions.

"It's your Lieutenant Nugent's wife, Bill. She's stirring up the local population again."

"Damn funny how she's suddenly become mine? What's she doing now, sir?"

"Remember how we passed out vegetable seeds and encouraged the families to plant their own gardens? Well, Mrs. Nugent liked the idea also. In fact, she's been picking vegetables from everyone's damn garden. An officer's wife, you know."

"They're all alike," I said. My mother's trials and tribulations again passed before my eyes. Hugo was waiting for me at the pass this time.

"No, Sergeant Craig, they're not all alike! Some of them do wear their husband's rank, but only if the officer allows it. You're prejudiced because you were raised in the Army and only remember the Mrs. Nugents, not the others." Hugo presented a plan to prevent me from going off on my favorite tangent. "Here's what I have done, Sergeant, and I hope you approve. Nugent's wife will be issued seeds and the battalion commander will give her a garden plot. The rest is up to her. If Nugent comes crying to me, I'll remind him of his mission, again."

"Which is what, sir?" Dierks asked.

"To win the hearts and minds of the populace to the side

of the government of South Vietnam," Hugo said. While answering Dierks, Hugo had not removed his eyes from a very senior enlisted man. I finally responded.

"Okay, okay. I like it, sir. It might even work but don't bet on it. She's a bitch. Pretty, too."

"Let's not get horny, either. You're a married man, you know. We could make arrangements for a trip to the sin city of Saigon. It may take a week or two but I could arrange it," Hugo said.

"Glad you reminded me, sir. I'd damn near forgot I was married, it's been so long since we left Oki." For some reason, Dierks was now paying attention to the give-and-take.

"By God, I'm not married and I've never been to Saigon. I'm ready whenever you can lay it on!"

"From this detachment we go in pairs only, Sergeant. Start breaking in someone to take your place on sick call and I'll try to get you and Ho Chi Minh a ride in a week or so."

"How did I get involved in your fun and games, sir?"

"You've been to Saigon and know the ropes, Sarge. I think you could be talked into it," Hugo said.

"Yes," I said, sincerely. "I could show red-on-the-head the places all men of good breeding and culture should review—the temples, churches, museums, and a few of the better art galleries. Not a bad idea, sir."

"What the hell are you talking about, Top?" Dierks exclaimed. "I wanna see eating and drinking joints and women. Lots of women. The hell with that educational bullshit!"

"Don't let Ho kid you, Phil, he was over here long before he got married. I'm sure his knowledge of Saigon will fit in with what you have in mind. He told me once that the Oriental philosophy preaches that soldiers drink and chase women. That's their lot. If that be the case, believe me, he's up on soldiering."

We would be three more weeks into our tour before being allowed to practice the philosophy of the Far East.

CHAPTER 24

DIERKS AND I had our ditty bags packed and were sitting in the team house on a Thursday morning. Major Swartz and his whirlybird would arrive shortly with some supplies and to pick up would-be sinners. Eagerly awaiting our ride to Saigon, we were dressed in our cleanest camouflage fatigues, green berets, and jump boots. Hugo came from the radio shack and joined us.

I knew that Cookie would be displeased at our happy dispositions and therefore the coffee would be strong as rain for my benefit. Hugo seated himself opposite us as Cookie rushed to give the CO his morning coffee. He then spoke to the officer, ignoring us enlisted peons.

But I didn't ignore Cookie. "You old suck-ass! Why didn't you bring me and Doc some coffee?"

Cookie ticked me off even more by speaking to Hugo in French and again ignoring us completely. "Are supplies coming, *mon Capitain*?"

Hugo replied in kind. "Yes, Cookie. One C-123 cargo aircraft and one helicopter will be here shortly. *Beaucoup* rice for the troops. *Trung Si* Dierks and Craig will leave with the helicopter for Saigon for three days. What else?"

A head-shaking chef walked off mumbling in three different languages. We all heard his last remark, however. "Saigon, number ten."

"Screw you, Cookie," I shouted.

"Let's get down to business, men!" directed Hugo. "The major will let you off at Ton Son Nhut airfield. Let him know where you'll be staying, just in case. Okay?"

I also got serious upon hearing the last statement. "Just in case of what, sir?"

"Just in case," emphasized Hugo, "that he has to look you up on Sunday, the day you're supposed to return here, Sergeant. You and your company will go on operation come Monday. Soooo, try to sober up by Sunday morning! Dig it?"

"Sir, we'll be in perfect shape by Sunday morning. I'll let the major know our boarding-house location. Hell, we'll be thinking about the operation the entire time. Right, Phil?"

Sergeant Phil Dierks refused to be drawn into the big lie.

Major Swartz gave Dierks an example of contour flying on our flight to sin city. I was rather bored, but Dierks was taking in all the sights, in addition to a stray tree limb from time to time. In 1964, Ton Son Nhut Air Base was beginning to become one of the busiest international airports in the world. Although it had been a year since I had been there, I was simultaneously impressed and amazed. New aprons and aircraft-parking areas had easily doubled, as had the traffic. Swartz taxied to his unit's allotted space, and parked. A jeep and maintenance mechanics awaited the aircraft's arrival.

While Swartz conferred with the maintenance supervisor, we loaded our ditty bags and bodies into the back of his jeep and waited. After relaying instructions to the crew, pilot and copilot approached their two giggling visitors. Swartz attempted to keep a straight face when addressing the soon-to-be-drunks.

"Do you have a place to stay in mind, Sergeant Craig?"

"Not really, sir. We're open to suggestions, though."

"I did promise Hugo I'd have you back sometime Sunday. Can you find this place, Sarge?" asked Swartz, pointing at the unit designator.

"Sure, sir, no problem. What's the closest hotel from here?" I asked.

"The Dragon is just off the main drag of Tu Do. We'll

drop you off there. Try to sober up in time to meet us here at 1000 Sunday. Okay?"

Sunday morning, after drinking our breakfast at the Dragon's bar and thrill, we were at a Tu Do street intersection. The traffic cop spied us two accidents looking for a place to happen. He showed his admiration by halting the four-way traffic and allowing us to cross. The Vietnamese philosophy about soldiering affected the onlookers' point of view about us, and they admired us as well. They all knew by our very condition that we had been soldiering hard for the past several days.

After we'd cleared the obstacle and reeled safely up onto the sidewalk, a jeep with two U.S. officers stopped and got our attention. Through the haze and human fog, we recognized Major Swartz and his copilot.

"Get your asses in the back," Swartz ordered.

We had enough presence of mind to obey and were still giggling when the copilot stated the obvious. "Sir, those soldiers are still drunk."

The major now turned his wrath on his copilot. "What the hell do you think they came to Saigon for?"

Knowing his people would be sick, sober, and sorry, Hugo met the helicopter. Wrong! Dierks and I were still giggling, trying to talk French and otherwise act the fool when we fell off the whirlybird. "Get your asses in the messhall and eat, then to bed. You do have an operation early tomorrow morning, you know."

We moved to the teamhouse and Cookie wasn't over-joyed with his employers either, but he got us onto solid food. In addition, he served me the strongest coffee he had ever brewed. But I acted as though I enjoyed it and drank it all, ruining Cookie's whole day. The next morning at 0500 hours was another matter, however.

We two somber warriors gagged down water-buffalo steak and turkey eggs with our French bread and Cookie's coffee. While exiting the messhall, I gave the chef the third-finger salute. Cookie apparently knew he had done something right, and smiled in satisfaction.

The meeting with Y Lull and Lieutenant Soy lasted only minutes. Despite the darkness, the natives knew that Dierks and I were not up to snuff, but that changed nothing as far as the operation was concerned. The company would move outside the confines of the ville, deploy tactically before daylight, and remain in place. At first light, we would move to our first objective. While moving to our first objective and up our first incline, Dierks threw up Cookie's Post Toasties and half of Saigon city. The Mnong-Rhade shook their heads in sympathy.

In disgust I watched my sick partner. "I told you Saigon was a different war, rookie." Dierks did not acknowledge the remarks nor turn his watery eyes toward me.

On the second hill, Y Lull halted his warriors while I duplicated Doc's actions. It was there that the Rhade commander pronounced. "Saigon numbah ten."

As Hugo had predicted, Lieutenant Soy contributed to the command group when he could. His military bearing and apparent attachment to the highlanders was a novelty after Nugent. Unfortunately, the five-day operation ended without contact for the 7th Company, and marked the first time that Dierks and I had come back emptyhanded. At least the operation had nursed us back to health. But better times were a-coming.

CHAPTER 25

"**ROBIN MOORE** will visit Buon Mi Ga in the next few days," Captain Hugo said. "I would like for you to treat him as a guest and a friend. I don't know him personally, I only know what I've been told, and that's no big deal. I will tell you what I've heard about him, for whatever *that's* worth—he's a civilian author writing a novel called *The Green Berets*." Captain Hugo stopped so I could get my two cents' worth in.

"I hate civilians," I said.

Everyone grinned when I stated the obvious, but the team leader managed to continue. "Yes," said Hugo, "and the feeling is probably mutual. Let's get on with it! He's a civilian who was granted permission to go to jump school and Psychological Warfare School, and he comes to Vietnam with the government's blessings. Apparently he's here to write about Special Forces and our many missions. He's a Harvard graduate and is reportedly a friend of the Kennedys. And that could help one in an unusual situation such as this.

"He wants to go on an operation with the CIDG while he's here. Sergeant First Class Pronier and the Sixth Company will leave in two days for a five-day stint in the boonies. Mr. Moore, pen and camera in hand, will accompany Bob and his unit."

I grinned at Pronier. "I hadda put up with Nugent so I guess it's your time in the barrel, Bob."

Hugo immediately wiped the smile from my face. "He's going to put up with you, also, Sergeant. You'll be the second adviser with the Sixth Company. There must be two Americans on each operation—or none. I've got no one else to send, Bill; you're it."

It took a while for me to recover. "Moore's a damn American even if he is a Yankee bastard. Bob needs me like he needs a hole in the head."

"It's a regulation, Sergeant. Period. You wouldn't want Pronier out here with a stupid civilian, would you? The Sixth hasn't made contact yet anyway; it'll be a walk in the sun. Right, Bob?"

Pronier rankled at the statement. "We'll make contact, sir, that's what we're out there for. It's Craig's old hangout; we know they're there."

To make room for the visitor, Dierks moved into the dispensary. In less than eighteen months, Moore would make the Special Forces known throughout the world, and his words would affect Special Forces from that time unto eternity.

Shortly after, Robin Moore moved into the hootch and I met my new roommate. We had no time for long discussions as the operation briefing would occur in fifteen minutes. When the briefing was over, we were dismissed in time for Cookie's evening treats. Moore and Pronier sat together and discussed the nitty-gritty of the operation, but I didn't join them; I used the opportunity to harass Cookie.

That night, in the privacy of our quarters, the short, heavyset author watched me pack my rucksack. Going on an operation with seasoned SF combat veterans of two wars was a real challenge for a civilian who had, in six months or less, been transformed into an Airborne-guerrilla expert.

The Harvard grad balked when he noted that I stowed six packs of Lucky Strike cancer sticks in my ruck. "Christ, Bill, you ain't gonna die in combat, you're gonna die of lung cancer."

I didn't even crack a smile. "I hope so, Mr. Moore, at the very least that would give me a few more years."

Moore continued to pack but received more from the last

remark than I probably realized. He mulled it over in his mind while finishing his chore. "I guess many of the men, especially the NCOs, feel like that, that every day is probably their last. And that explains a lot of things, like their off-duty charades, their unconventional solutions to social and family problems, and Lord only knows what else. The way they shut out everyone except the people they serve with could be explained by that last statement, also."

When rucksacks were packed, canteens filled, grenades strapped, harnesses checked for aid kits, combat dressings, and a basic load of AR-15 ammunition, we sat on our bunks and relaxed. Pronier joined us and the preoperation bull session began.

Pronier and I had never been very close before or after premission training. Why? I could never explain it, but that situation was about to be resolved. Both of us were razor thin, but Pronier had the razor's edge. I had two inches in height on him, and we really contrasted with Robin Moore. We were positive that the Yards would comment on the fact. Pronier began the dialogue that would continue until lights out.

"We're going into your old stomping grounds, Bill. They wouldn't jump you or interfere with your last try. Tell us what you think is going on!"

I got very basic with my answers, because of the civilian, certainly not because of Ranger-qualified Pronier. "They're out there, Bob, and I believe they knew we were coming. A few of 'our' Yards apparently have mixed emotions about our presence and/or ideology."

"I've felt the same way, Bill, but damn if I know what to do about it."

"They don't have enough strength as yet to jump a 165-man company, and if we're successful, that day may never come. Sooo, if you want to make contact, I'd say take chances you normally wouldn't take. They may fall for it, but it could cost you your ass, Bob. You're in charge; it's your company, not mine. I'm just along to help when and if I can. What do you think, old soldier?"

"You've reinforced my thinking, Bill. Let me sleep on it. Thanks for the help and I'm glad to have you along with us, right, Robin?" Moore nodded.

The next morning, for some reason, Pronier had the 6th Company procrastinating about going out the gate. So it was after daylight before the unit cleared the home base. Captain Hugo was not happy about that; it was his policy the 6th Darlac Province Company had violated by exiting in broad daylight. I thought Pronier had deliberately delayed to insure that the Viet Cong would know we were coming and in what strength. Regardless, after we began to move, Moore followed Pronier, and I brought up the rear in the command party's single-file formation. Moore was having problems negotiating the terrain in a military manner, and it kept the Rhade entertained. After an uneventful march in the humid second growth and gnarled wait-a-minute vines, a night location was selected before 1700. A partially cleared knob overlooking a trail and an abandoned ville were secured for the command group.

Over a can of C rations Pronier announced his plans for the next day. "That village down there is where you made your first contact, Bill, so we're in the ballpark. Here's my plan. I welcome your suggestions, so make any comments you care to." I only nodded. Moore listened intently.

"I want to use this position as an FOB [forward operating base]. You stay with three platoons and I'll roam the AO with one platoon. Maybe this will give the Viet Cong the target they are waiting for. In other words, you'll be our reaction forces. Whatcha think, Bill?"

I glanced at the sweat-soaked Moore before committing myself. "I think it's the best idea since sliced bread, Bob. Your Ranger training is beginning to show. What's Robin gonna do?"

"I'm going where the action is, Bill, or where I hope it is. Okay, Bob?"

"We're going to start on that ridge across the valley, Robin. It's gonna be up and down and just plain ol' hard work. Are you sure you can keep up?"

"I'm not in the shape you guys are, but I'll make it. It's what I'm out here for. Okay?"

The next morning found Pronier and Moore ready to herd the first platoon across the valley to search the adjoining ridgeline. After a few handshakes and the exploring of details, the hunters were off, trying to become the hunted. They would not reach their objective until after lunch. The command party had shrunk to myself, the commander, an interpreter, an RTO, and a medic.

I had nothing better to do than join the CO as he checked security and the ambushes set up by the reaction forces. At 1400 hours, we were back in our temporary headquarters.

Pronier and I had agreed that there would be no commo until 1600 or first contact by either group. I took it upon myself to move the command post into the abandoned village. Naturally, the move aroused the commander's curiosity.

"Sir," I said, "we need to be closer to the action, if any. Also we can use that ville as an LZ for medevac helicopters in case of casualties. Have 'em ready to move in ten!"

We were crossing the small creek in order to enter the abandoned village when the fire fight began. Our party stopped and I opened the radio net. Pronier and Moore were obviously otherwise occupied, and I received no reply. We began to receive rounds from the action on the ridge, and one stray small-arms round went through my PRC-10 radio battery. The RTO changed the battery and we were back in business just as the firing on the ridgeline ceased.

The commander of the 6th Company notified the three platoons to establish a hasty perimeter while I notified base camp to stand by. "Darlac, we have one platoon in a world of excrement. Stand by. Over!"

I breathed a sigh of relief when Pronier broke in. "Darlac-five, this is Darlac-six. I'm busy but we're okay, be back in about five. Over!"

Five long minutes dragged on before Pronier again came up. "Darlac-five, Six, give me your location."

I answered promptly. "Darlac-six, we're securing the ville at LZ580546 at this time. Come back, over!"

"Roger your transmission, Five. We're moving to your location ASAP. Complete report at that time, but for your information we have negative casualties. Six, over and out!"

The commander completed the securing of the ville and to await the platoon's arrival the command group took cover under the only stilted shack.

In twenty-five minutes Pronier and Moore left their platoon on the perimeter and joined us under the hacienda. Only after notifying base camp he was alive and well did Pronier begin relaying the details of the firefight.

"We were walking the military crest of the ridge when about two platoons of VC jumped us. They were on the crest and firing down at us, that's why you took some of the fire. My platoon charged the ambush just like the immediate action drills teach you to do, and the Viet Cong broke and ran. We pursued only to the top and let 'em go. We have one North Vietnamese cadre as a prisoner and we counted eight bodies of dead VC in addition to capturing nine weapons. The troops were just great, Bill, and we didn't even receive one wounded-in-action."

"You were great, guys, and I'm proud of you. How did you like the action, Robin?" I asked.

"I was too busy taking pictures to really know, Bill, but like Bob said, the platoon didn't hesitate to charge. They were great."

"We need to operate on the NVA cadre prisoner, Bill," said Pronier. "He has a ricochet round in his arm. Think you can take it out?"

While Pronier was giving a situation report to base camp, a squad of Yards deposited a slender, tender, and tall prisoner of war. He and I sized each other up while an elated Pronier droned on to Hugo and base camp.

The POW was of Vietnamese extraction and dressed in black pajamas. Except for the bullet sticking from his shoulder, he was unharmed. Pronier signed off and joined Moore, me, and the POW.

"Give him a shot of morphine and use the medical tweezers, Bob. The round looks like it'll come out easy. It's just not my day for operating."

Pronier was so elated over his first contact that he called the Yard medic to give the POW a shot and had the round out in an instant. Rather than watch the minor operation, I rambled over to the enemy weapon cache and looked them over. An AK-47 got my attention immediately and I didn't have to be told who the previous owner was. It was the first AK I had seen since firing one at Fort Bragg.

I took Moore's picture holding the jewel, a shot that would soon be seen by people the world over. The picture became the cover for Robin Moore's bestseller, *The Green Berets*, which sold several million copies and was made into a movie as well. The book is still in print to this day. For my part, I hated making people filthy rich while working for starvation wages. Regardless, the uneventful night went into the history books.

After a light meal of coffee and pound cake, Pronier laid out his plans for the day.

The CO and I would stay in place with three platoons, and the Boss and Robin Moore would roam the perimeter and beyond for VC stragglers from yesterday's counterattack. Base camp had promised a helicopter to evacuate the POW and captured goodies but no evac time had been given. Again, we staybehinds were to use the village as a landing zone and would remain in place. Pronier seemed determined that I wouldn't have any fun on this excursion. Of course, his photographer would accompany him. Hell, we needed the publicity, I guess.

The Rhade CO and I had just returned from making minor adjustments in the perimeter when the PRC-10 radio sounded off. "Chopper your location, Darlac-six. Be ready to pop smoke and identify same at our request. Over and out!"

The NVA cadre, with his hands bound, was loaded on

the H-34 helicopter. Captain Hugo smiled and waved bye-bye, as the whirlybird turned up and out of the village confines. His wheels had not yet touched down back at Buon Mi Ga when an automatic weapon cranked out some death and destruction. No return fire was noted and in our defensive positions we could only wait for a Pronier-Moore situation report. To me, the rattle of the battle sounded like the ole faithful BAR and, to my knowledge, the Viet Cong had nary a one in their arsenal. In ten minutes, Pronier's radio transmission cleared everything up. "Contact at LZ280642. Two armed VC in black pajamas KIA by BAR fire, no friendly casualties, two weapons captured. Relay information to base camp. We'll be your location soonest. Darlac-six, over and out."

"I bet Moore took some good pictures," I mumbled.

Pronier returned in an hour with two more French-made MAS-36 rifles. After placing his warriors in our outer perimeter, we enjoyed C–ration refreshments and listened to war stories until darkness set in. I was secretly happy and proud for Pronier; a REMF he wasn't. Moore was so impressed with the contacts that he was beginning to believe some of the plots he had written for *The Green Berets*.

The 6th Company continued probing the VC sanctuary but the remainder of the ground operation was without incident. The six-day operation ended in Buon Mi Ga among the rice wine, buffalo steaks, and brass bracelets. After the celebration, Detachment A-132(-) prepared to turn over the camp and the Montagnard battalion to a fully implemented A detachment from the Hugh Hess Hay.

We were very proud of our accomplishments during that six-month stint: We had removed the bamboo fence and replaced it with double-apron and concertina barbed-wire fences; our recruiting and training programs had brought the battalion to a full complement of 640 well-trained, well-motivated soldiers; our combat operations had killed 132(!) Viet Cong—we had one Yard casualty, and he was treated and released to duty on the same day; we displaced over 200 civilians from VC sanctuaries and settled them into our area of operation, making sure they were clothed, fed, and gainfully employed.

The last part of May 1964, our detachment flew to Nha Trang and hooked up with the other half of A-132. Twelve very proud individuals landed at Kadena AFB in Okinawa on or about May 17, 1964.

Three months after detachment A-132 turned over Buon Mi Ga to Det A-121, the Montagnard revolt erupted. The revolt, centered around the Darlac Province capital of Ban Me Thuot, has been adequately reported in many books and periodicals. I do not care to rehash the disaster. *Green Berets at War* by historian Shelby Stanton describes the culmination of the Special Forces, Military Assistance and Advisory Command, and Vietnamese Special Forces (LLDB) dissension. I will only deal briefly with one aspect—the Buon Mi Ga situation.

At Buon Mi Ga by September 1964, the LLDB Detachment, under the tutelage of A-121, had grown to ten personnel. When the revolt against Republic of South Vietnam erupted, all of the ethnic Viets, including Nugent and Soy, were lined up and executed by some of the sharpshooters I had helped to train. The fate of Nugent's wife went unreported.

Personally, I had a hard time losing any sleep over the fate of the LLDB, but I had no problem blaming MACV and the ruling junta in the South. Regardless, the CIDG program and the Highlands of South Vietnam suffered a severe blow because of that fiasco. But, at that time I was having problems of my own in the tropical, coral-rock isle of Okinawa.

CHAPTER 26

WHEN THE C-130 cargo aircraft from Nha Trang, Republic of Vietnam, landed at Kadena Air Force Base, Okinawa, all the dependents of Detachment A-132 greeted their men—except for one. Hatsuko Craig was conspicuous by her absence. I was soon on my way to Kadena Circle and my unauthorized off-post residence.

I paid the cabbie and, gear and all, stopped at the locked front door of our apartment. The note was pinned to the screen door.

"Hatsuko and her son are in the hospital at Naha. Check with us soonest!" The note was signed by Staff Sergeant Frank and Suzie Fowler. Depositing my gear, I was quickly on my one-city-block trip to the house of Fowler and Okinawan bride Suzie. My knock was answered by Fowler's dog and his master as well.

"Come on in, Papasan!" I entered—it was eight o'clock on the night of May 17, 1964. My fatigues were damp because of the humid tropical night, but Fowler's wife managed to seat me on the small sofa and served me a cold beer before she began. Despite the fact that English was her third language, she was easily understood.

"You didn't know your wife was pregnant but obviously she was, in fact, she was seven-and-a-half months along when she delivered prematurely on May twelfth. She was refused admission at Camp Kue Armed Forces Hospital so I took her to the Seventh Day Adventist Hospital in Naha. Your son was born on that day and weighed in at four pounds and a half an ounce." Suzie paused and grinned at the look on my face before she continued.

"Hatsuko was released several days later, but your son is still in an incubator at the medical center."

"Suzie, I knew nothing about her being pregnant. Where's Hatsuko at now?"

"She's at the hospital right now and told me to tell you she'd be back as soon as she checked on the child."

"How's the kid doing, Sue, and what does he look like?"

"The boy's doing fine, and will be released once his weight is up to five pounds. He has round eyes and brown hair and he's a good-looking boy."

"What's his name?"

"He hasn't been named yet, but you're on the certificate as the father. Also, you'll owe a large hospital bill before it's over. I hope you've saved your money."

Her husband, Frank, who had been quiet up to this point, finally got in his two cents' worth. "Bill can pay the bill, Suzie! He just needs to go through the Army's red tape and become legally married. That would pay a ton of bills in the future. Welcome home, Bill. And good luck and congratulations on your first child."

Hatsuko returned home later that night from Naha and we wasted no time, our future plans being our first priority. It would be only one more night before I would see my son.

Thus my week off would be spent with administrative details that I had been completely ignorant of. Fortunately, thanks to Fowler, my '56 Ford convertible was running very well, and Hatsuko continued to fill me in on our problems as we drove thirty miles to Naha at thirty miles per hour, the island speed limit. Considering the frequent bumper-to-bumper conditions, even that speed was often too fast.

"Suzie and I decided on the Seventh Day Adventist Hospital because they have American doctors and facilities that the Okinawan hospitals don't have, Papasan. I stayed there five days and we were treated well. They weren't worried about the bill; they knew we would pay when you returned. One thing they didn't appreciate though was our son's not having a name. We need to correct that by the time we arrive. Have you any suggestions we can agree on?"

We used biblical names as a guide, and James Joseph Craig was properly named by the time we arrived at the very modern facility. The doctors and nurses were very gracious and commented on the resemblance of the son to his father. I was also pleased as I watched the youngster wiggle and squirm inside the apparatus. Whether I knew it or not, those moments were a-changing me. After I'd seen my son I questioned the escorting Okinawan nurse, who spoke passable English.

"He's at four pounds, three ounces this morning, Sergeant. You'll have just two weeks or less before you can take him home. He has to weigh five pounds before we can safely release him."

I reported back in to Company A and remained in a realigned A-132 while Captain Hugo went to group HQ in preparation for his majority. Other team members rotated back to the States. Our training was versatile enough to keep me interested and enabled us to shut out the usual boredom of garrison duty in the Army.

A three-day outing with the 1st SFG (Airborne) rigger detachment consisted of rigging equipment and weapons in preparation for air drops. The third day was spent in a packing demonstration of the T-10 parachute, followed by a practical exercise. That night we each jumped the chute we had packed that very day. The students must have paid attention—we had no major injuries.

I helped Sergeant First Class Perkins teach survival training to Marine and Air Force personnel. The courses, given at Matsuda range, consisted of familiarization with poisonous snakes; fire-building and cooking devices; edible plants; and preparation of fish and game. Perkins's instruction was not only entertaining, but informative as well.

After two long weeks, we brought our son home, but only after forking over four hundred dollars for his release.

Only then did our duel with the bureaucracy of the Army of the U.S.A. begin. It wasn't going to be easy. James J. Craig was apparently happy to be out of his incubator and on his way home in a seven-year-old Ford convertible. While Hatsuko was holding him like a seat belt, he managed to bring a grin to my face despite the bumper-to-bumper traffic. Arriving home, we placed Jim in a used baby bed given to us by an enlisted couple, and rehashed our unauthorized plans. I requested, and received, a thirty-day on-island leave. In defense of my unit, Company A, 1st SFG (Airborne), I received nothing but support and encouragement from them. Not so the higher headquarters or U.S. Army Ryukyu Islands (USARYIS) bureaucracy.

We moved into a larger home only a few blocks from our apartment and bought a German shepherd dog for protection and as an early-warning system against the thieving slicky boys who roamed the island. With some new furniture, we were ready for our assault on stupidity. We left the 1st Group S-1 (Personnel) with a handful of paperwork and were quickly moved to the office of the G-2 (Intelligence, more or less).

The twenty-seven-year-old captain only glanced at me—my being thirty-eight years old—and my twenty-eight-year-old bride, before handing us the paperwork for a background investigation of a foreign national. Despite not being geniuses, we knew at a glance that after weeks of research to locate her relatives, it would still take hours to fill out the paperwork correctly. I couldn't resist commenting on the U.S. government's main stumbling block to marrying a foreign national.

"What does this investigation attempt to prove that the U.S. bureaucracy doesn't already know, sir?"

"Many, many things, Sergeant," the officer said defensively. "Is the applicant a Communist? Does she have kinfolk behind the bamboo curtain? Is she a known prostitute?" The last question even embarrassed the young, dumb captain.

Hatsuko and I also colored a tad at the last remark, but

I responded. "She would have a tough time being a whore, being as how she's been working for the U.S. government lo these many years. I don't appreciate your remark, sir!"

"Just doing my job, Sergeant. You're dismissed, unless you have any other questions."

"Yes, I do, sir," I said. "How much time does this investigation take, for Christ's sake?"

"At least three months or so. Anything else?"

When we departed the Sukiran Puzzle Palace, we were determined to cut down that time, if possible.

Our next appointment was a counseling session with the group chaplain. The path to legitimacy was becoming rocky and kinda kinky. A week later we entered that major's office and waited on the advice for the married of a person who was sworn to celibacy. Things couldn't get worse! Could they?

The chaplain, sensing some hostility from his flock, went so far as to comment on the ridiculous situation and fixed us with a brown-eyed stare before he spoke. "I know this type of thing, due to your ages and experiences, is embarrassing to you. I also know you have a son and really need to resolve your situation. My congratulations on the birth of your son. How is he doing, Sergeant?"

"He's fine, sir, and growing every day. In fact, for a youngster that the U.S. refuses to recognize, he's doing very well. Let's get on with the counseling, sir!"

The session took a turn for the better. "Let's don't and say we did, Sarge! Let's talk about the future of Special Forces and the brushfire war in Vietnam. I know you're up on it much more than I am."

To my surprise and Hatsuko's consternation, we did just that. It was not lost on me that the chaplain was glancing at the clock on the wall from time to time. At the appointed time—apparently—the bantering ceased. The Army's Catholic priest signed our clearance form and we were dismissed.

The only obstacle remaining in our path was my wife's background investigation, one that should have been conducted twenty years ago before the government hired her. Regardless, months dragged by, months filled with resentment at my family's predicament, months filled with appointments for my dependents at the civilian medical center in ·Naha.

The situation was finally brought to a head in a mild form of blackmail by a B detachment commander in August 1964. Major Fixit (not his real name of course) called me into his small office at Camp Kue one day and laid it on me. I entered the quonset hut and was escorted to the major's office by a Sergeant Major Avery. I saluted the O, and was asked to be seated by the heavyset leader.

"I need people with experience for my Vietnam-bound B detachment. I've been told that you have that experience and I'm asking you to consent to go with us as an assistant operations sergeant. You've been back three months—hell, that's about par for the course. Whatcha say, young man?"

"Sir, I've got problems that you're more than likely unaware of and if I can help it, I'm not going any place until they're concluded to my satisfaction. You can put me on orders and I'll not quit; I'll go but I damn sure won't like it. It's up to you, I reckon."

"Sergeant Craig, I don't want anyone who doesn't want to be there, so tell me your troubles. I may be able to help."

For ten minutes, I filled the room with my matrimonial problems before concluding my saga: "So, I'll not leave her and my son here until it's settled."

To my surprise, Fixit said, "It's not a major obstacle, best I can tell, Bill. We don't leave for war-torn until the fifteenth of September, giving me enough time to grease the skids for the paperwork that's hung up in some office to be completed. I'll give you time off to hand-carry it from place to place and it'll be over quickly."

I doubted him but fell for the well-laid trap in a New York minute. "If you can, sir, you've got an operations sergeant for your trip to Can Tho, Republic of Vietnam."

"You've got a deal, Sergeant Craig. Now get outta here,

so I can use this telephone. But be back at 0800 tomorrow morning to begin the processing. Bye!"

Nine days later on September 8, 1964, Hatsuko and I were at the United States consulate in Naha. We repeated the nuptial vows in three different languages before signing two hundred sheets of paper. At 1700, we relieved an Okinawan lass of her baby-sitting duties and breathed a sigh of relief. A major had done in nine days what the Army couldn't accomplish in three months.

Hatsuko graciously allowed me to change Jim's diaper but watched closely. When I had finished the unpleasant chore, she asked, "What's our son gonna be when he grows up, Daddy?"

"It's hard to tell, hon, but I do know what he's not gonna be," I replied.

"What's that, Sergeant?"

"A goddamn lifer in the U.S. Army!"

INDEX